Preparing natural foods quickly and efficiently—without sacrificing quality—is what this book is all about. When it comes to natural foods, quality is synonymous with taste.

Those aware of the connection between diet and health are already familiar with the whole grains, beans, tofu, and other high-protein soy foods which form the basis of many of these recipes. Fresh farm and garden vegetables and fruits, along with natural seasonings such as miso and tamari, enhance both the taste and nutritional value of these dishes.

An incredible variety of tastes and textures can be created from the natural ingredients recommended in this book. With just a little creativity and imagination, healthful eating can be exciting and delicious.

"The [macrobiotic] diet is consistent with the recently released dietary guidelines of the National Academy of Sciences and the American Cancer Society in regard to possible reduction of cancer risks."
>> —Congressional Subcommittee on Health and Long-Term Care

"To master the art of cooking—to choose the right kinds of foods and to combine them properly—is to master the art of life, for the greatness and destiny of all people reflects and is limited by the quality of their daily food."
>> —Michio Kushi
>> Founder, The Kushi Institute for One Peaceful World
>> Founder, Erewhon Foods

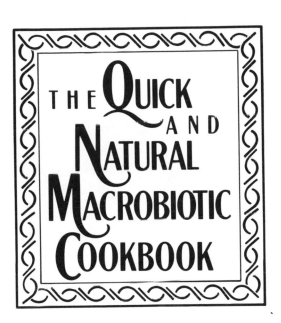

THE QUICK AND NATURAL MACROBIOTIC COOKBOOK

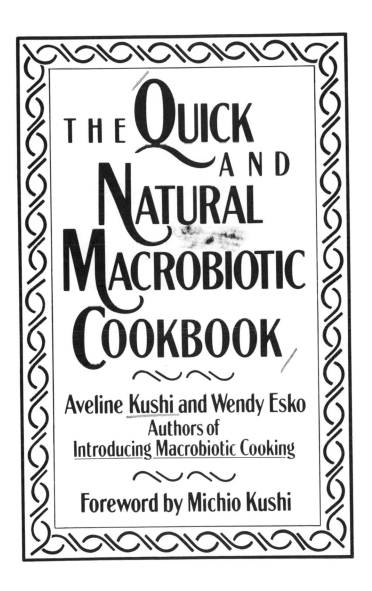

THE QUICK AND NATURAL MACROBIOTIC COOKBOOK

Aveline Kushi and Wendy Esko
Authors of
Introducing Macrobiotic Cooking

Foreword by Michio Kushi

CB
CONTEMPORARY
BOOKS
CHICAGO · NEW YORK

Library of Congress Cataloging-in-Publication Data

Kushi, Aveline.
   The quick and natural macrobiotic cookbook / Aveline Kushi
and Wendy Esko : foreword by Michio Kushi.
       p.   cm.
   Bibliography: p
   Includes index.
   ISBN 0-8092-4436-5 : $10.95
   1. Macrobiotic diet—Recipes.   I. Esko, Wendy.   II. Title.
RM235.K865   1989
641.5′637—dc19   89-30689
                                                 CIP

Published by Contemporary Books, Inc.
180 North Michigan Avenue, Chicago, Illinois 60601
Manufactured in the United States of America
International Standard Book Number: 0-8092-4436-5

Published simultaneously in Canada by Beaverbooks, Ltd.
195 Allstate Parkway, Valleywood Business Park
Markham, Ontario L3R 4T8 Canada

CONTENTS

Foreword by Michio Kushi ix

PART I Macrobiotics: The Way To Good Health 1
  1 Introduction 3
  2 Your Diet, Your Health 9
  3 Macrobiotic Principles 23
  4 Yin and Yang Made Simple 35
  5 Adopting The Macrobiotic Lifestyle 49

PART II The Macrobiotic Kitchen 63
  6 Foods In The Standard
    Macrobiotic Diet 65
  7 Shopping For Natural Foods 101
  8 The Quick and Natural Kitchen 117
  9 Food Preparation 131

PART III Quick and Natural Meals 145
  Staples To Make Ahead 153
  Day One 165
  Day Two 175
  Day Three 193
  Day Four 207
  Day Five 223
  Day Six 239
  Day Seven 255
  Day Eight 273

  Glossary 281
  Macrobiotic Resources 287
  About the Authors 295
  Index 297

FOREWORD

All things in nature—human events included—move in expanding and contracting spirals. As we enter the final decade of the 20th century, the spiral of social change is accelerating rapidly.

Compared with the past, people today seem more pressed for time. For many, the daily appointment calendar has become the present-day equivalent of the Bible. The modern world is governed more by the clock and less by the rhythms of nature. However, if we are not careful, the stressful pace of modern living can cause us to lose sight of the most important things in life. Nowhere is this more apparent than in the realm of food and cooking. All too often many of us seem willing to sacrifice the quality of our food—and ultimately our health—for the sake of speed and convenience.

In this book my wife, Aveline, explains how to select and prepare the highest-quality foods for health and well-being, based on nearly 40 years of experience in cooking for her family and many friends. She is assisted in this effort by Wendy Esko, a well-known author and teacher of macrobiotic cooking. The recipes in this book reflect the macrobiotic understanding of the vital role of daily food in creating health and happiness.

The recipes have also been designed to help everyone save time in the kitchen, without compromising the quality of daily meals. Aveline and Wendy are eminently qualified to write this book. Aveline has raised five children, started numerous enterprises, authored a variety of books, and taught cooking to thousands of students in over a dozen countries. Wendy is the mother of seven active children. She has coauthored more than half a dozen books and gives regular cooking classes. Even while juggling very busy schedules, both cook for their families on a regular basis. Those who are busy outside the home, including people who often eat in restaurants, may find this basic guidebook very useful. Quick macrobiotic cooking is also helpful during travel, when there is little time to prepare elaborate meals.

Aveline and Wendy have selected these dishes to reflect optimum nutritional balance. The combinations of foods presented here can help everyone meet daily nutritional requirements for personal needs and activity. Macrobiotic cooking is also economical. Although certain items may seem expensive, on the whole a macrobiotic diet costs 30 to 50 percent less than the average modern diet.

Today the importance of macrobiotics in securing human health and restoring ecological harmony to the planet is recognized throughout the world. Thanks to macrobiotic education, the natural foods movement has grown from a small grass-roots effort into a major industry. The wide availability of whole natural foods in supermarkets, co-ops, and natural foods stores across the country makes healthful eating more convenient than it was a decade ago.

It is my hope that this new cookbook will introduce many people to the benefits of macrobiotic eating and living and contribute to the health and well-being of society as a whole.

I would like to thank Aveline and Wendy for writing this wonderful new book and Contemporary Books for producing this edition. I also appreciate the continuing effort of our friends at the Kushi Institute, the Kushi Foundation, and related macrobiotic centers to bring awareness of better diet to people in all corners of the globe. I also thank our friends in the natural foods and ecology movements, including organic farmers, natural foods distributors, and the producers of traditional foods, for their untiring dedication to human health and well-being. I also extend thanks to doctors, nutritionists, and others in the health professions who have furthered awareness of the relationship between diet and health, including government and public health organizations that have issued dietary guidelines for the prevention of cancer, heart disease, and other chronic illnesses. Finally, I thank our millions of macrobiotic friends throughout the world for pioneering a natural approach to life and health.

Michio Kushi
Brookline, Massachusetts

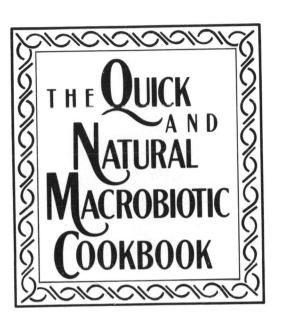

THE QUICK
AND
NATURAL
MACROBIOTIC
COOKBOOK

PART I
MACROBIOTICS: THE
WAY TO GOOD HEALTH

1
INTRODUCTION

From the beginning, macrobiotic education has stressed the role of daily food in creating and maintaining health. Our message has been simple: the key to health and happiness lies in our ability to manage daily food and drink. The experiences that hundreds of thousands of people all over the world have had in securing health through macrobiotics confirm this basic truth. Since each of us exercises control over the foods we eat and how we prepare them, the key to health is in our hands.

Today most people would agree that a naturally balanced diet is essential to a healthy life. In America alarms over the potential hazards of the modern diet are now being sounded with increasing regularity. Happily millions of people have made health-conscious dietary changes in the last 10 years, and macrobiotics has been at the forefront of this growing movement for better nutrition.

In our cooking classes students often ask: "Is the macrobiotic diet nutritious?" "Do the foods taste good?" "Are they quick and easy to prepare?" As you will discover in this book, the answer to these questions is yes.

Nutritionally the wide range of foods included in the macrobiotic diet can help everyone satisfy basic daily requirements according to age, sex, and level of activity. Moreover, macrobiotics offers low-fat, high-fiber meals that contain no additives, preservatives, or refined sugar. Complex carbohydrates, which are highly nutritious, are featured at every meal. Tastewise, whole natural foods are the real thing. The rich flavors and appetizing textures of well-prepared natural foods simply can't be duplicated in the laboratory. In the interest of taste and nutrition, the macrobiotic diet, including our recipes, uses only genuine foods rather than artificial ingredients.

When it comes to convenience, we need to ask ourselves a few basic questions. Do we want convenience at any price, or are we willing to let other considerations—namely, our health—guide our dietary choices? Do we view cooking as an unnecessary chore that technology can render obsolete, or do we think of it as vital for our health and destiny? Moreover, do we look at food as something that comes ready-made, prepackaged, in uniform rows on a shelf or as something that comes from the Earth? How we answer these questions could determine how much time and energy we are willing to devote to improving our diets.

Given the rapid pace of modern life, speed and convenience are often prized over quality. A recent article in *Parade* magazine about the way Americans eat listed speed of preparation as the most important factor influencing food choices, followed by taste and nutrition. The article summarized current priorities about food and cooking: "We want our food fast—even when we cook. The ideal cooking time for men is 15 minutes or less; for women, 30 minutes or less." When carried to an extreme, however, the preoccupation with speed can become counterproductive. Too many of us are willing to sacrifice the quality of our food for the sake of convenience.

Health and the quality of life depend on the quality of daily food. Therefore, when it comes to selecting daily food for ourselves and our families, *quality* should be our most important consideration.

Certain things can't be rushed without spoiling their quality. Miso, the dark puree made from soybeans, unrefined sea salt, and fermented barley or rice, is a good example. Natural miso contains living enzymes that facilitate digestion, strengthen the quality of the blood, and provide a nutritious balance of complex carbohydrates, essential oils, protein, vitamins, and minerals. Sweet and delicious to the taste, subtle in flavor, and available in various hues of brown, orange, red, and yellow, miso is traditionally prepared by allowing the ingredients to ferment slowly in wooden kegs. This healthful and nourishing food is used both in macrobiotic and traditional cooking as a base for a wide variety of soups and as a seasoning in other dishes. However, today most miso in the Far East is made quickly in artificial temperature-controlled environments with chemically treated ingredients. Fortunately most of the miso in natural foods stores is made the long, slow way with all natural ingredients.

Although the art of preparing tasteful and nourishing meals can take a lifetime to master, basic macrobiotic dishes can be learned fairly quickly. Most are simple and easy to prepare. As your familiarity with natural foods increases, and your cooking skills improve, you will discover that healthful eating doesn't require spending the whole day in the kitchen.

Preparing natural foods quickly and efficiently—without a sacrifice of quality—is what this book is all about. We believe that emphasizing speed at the expense of quality undercuts the foundation of our life and health. Therefore, in this book we recommend only the highest-quality natural ingredients and the most peaceful, natural methods of cooking.

When it comes to natural foods, quality is synonymous with taste. As every good cook knows, fresh, whole foods are vibrant and delicious in comparison to their canned, frozen, or processed counterparts. An incredible variety of tastes and textures can be created from the natural ingredients recommended in this book. With just a little creativity and imagination, healthful eating can be exciting and delicious.

We count among our friends some of the most dynamic people in society today. Corporate executives, artists, working mothers and fathers, doctors, lawyers, and other professional people, writers, and well-known celebrities have all managed to balance eating well with successful careers. As you will discover in these pages, a macrobiotic diet need not interfere with an active lifestyle, and vice versa.

Both of us have cooked for our families for many years. During this time we have not had to spend money for medical care (except for natural childbirth), as no one in either of our families has had any serious illness. And since the macrobiotic way of life is so economical in the long run, we don't mind occasionally purchasing a few high-quality food items that cost a little more.

Over the years we have authored many books, each of which presents a different aspect of macrobiotic cooking. The recipes in this book are only a small sampling of the thousands of dishes used by macrobiotic cooks around the world. Hundreds of variations are possible with each of these dishes. Ultimately your cooking and sense of timing will become intuitive. Nowadays, when students ask how long to cook brown rice or carrots, Aveline sometimes replies, "Ask the carrots and rice. If you know their personalities, you will be able to make wonderful dishes."

We have arranged the recipes in this book a little differently from those in our previous books. First, they are presented as part of complete menus rather than listed individually by food category. Meal planning is vital in creating a balanced diet, and the menus presented here illustrate how to translate the dietary guidelines of macrobiotics into complete meals. Second, the recipes are formatted in a new way so that even though they are longer and more detailed than those in the other cookbooks, they are designed to help you cook more quickly and easily.

One new feature is the listing of utensils as well as ingredients with each recipe. This eliminates the need to read through the directions in order to find out exactly what you'll need to prepare the dish. Another new feature is the presentation of directions in numbered steps rather than in paragraph form. This makes it easier to proceed step by step through each recipe from beginning to end. A third new feature is the inclusion of the approximate time it takes to prepare the dish, together with the time it takes to complete the whole meal. We also distinguish between the amount of time needed for washing, cutting, mixing, and other preliminary steps and the time it takes for the foods to cook by themselves on the stove. We hope our new format will make it easier for beginning cooks to plan ahead and budget their time for maximum efficiency.

Actually the *Quick and Natural Macrobiotic Cookbook* is more than just a collection of wholesome recipes. It is an all-in-one, step-by-step guide to changing diet for the better. We include background on the relationship between diet and health, including up-to-date findings that point to a low-fat, high-fiber diet—based on complex carbohydrates—as essential in preventing chronic illness. We also introduce the principles of the macrobiotic diet, including an explanation of yin and yang balance. Suggestions for making a smooth transition to the macrobiotic way of life complete the introductory section.

In Part II we address the practical aspects of macrobiotics, beginning with an explanation of the foods in the Standard Macrobiotic Diet. There we present a practical guide to selecting the highest-quality foods, along with the nutritional and health benefits of selected items. Part II also enumerates all the preliminary steps in setting up a macrobiotic kitchen: shopping for high-quality foods, equipping your kitchen with the right utensils, and arranging your cooking space for speed and efficiency. We then discuss how to prepare foods for cooking, from washing them to cutting them properly.

Part III, which contains a full week's menus and recipes, starts with an explanation of how our recipes are structured and how the menus are set up so that one evening's dinner provides time-saving leftovers for the next day's breakfast and/or lunch. The recipes begin with condiments and beverages that can be prepared in advance. In the menu section we offer advice on putting individual dishes together for the whole week to make complete meals and suggestions on preparing for the meals that follow. By outlining each preliminary step in such detail, we hope to help you save time when you actually start to cook.

This book is intended to help dispel the notion that macrobiotic cooking takes too much time for a busy modern lifestyle. As you will discover in these pages, you don't have to return to the 19th century in order to eat natural foods. However, healthful cooking does involve the investment of a certain amount of time each day. The approach presented in this book is in between the idealized Old World practice of spending the day in the kitchen lovingly preparing a meal from homemade ingredients (although this is sometimes nice, especially on holidays or special occasions) and the modern practice of taking a ready-made dinner out of the freezer and popping it into the microwave (in macrobiotic thinking, it is questionable whether or not this qualifies as "cooking") or the more extreme practice of eating out constantly, without ever cooking at home. Needless to say, we believe the price for such "convenience" today could be tremendous "inconvenience" tomorrow, especially if one's dietary habits spoil one's health. We define *quick cooking* as saving time with the various preliminaries, while not rushing the actual cooking of the foods or trying to get by with less than complete meals.

Flexibility is at the heart of macrobiotic living, so feel free to adapt these guidelines to your personal needs. Vary your cooking as the seasons change and as you change. Become aware of nature and learn to cook in response to its changes. In this way your creations will become like original works of art. We hope the basic guidelines in this book will help you create delicious and healthful meals for yourself and your family.

We would like to thank everyone who contributed to this book. We thank Michio Kushi for writing the foreword and for guiding many people toward health and peace through his traveling, lectures, and writing. We thank Edward Esko for encouraging us to write the book and for patiently guiding it to completion. We express appreciation to Bernard Shir-Cliff, Chris Benton, and the staff of Contemporary Books for guidance in producing this volume, and thank Cindy Briscoe, a teacher of macrobiotic cooking in Kansas City, for the wonderful illustrations.

2
YOUR DIET, YOUR HEALTH

"Your choice of diet can influence your long-term health prospects more than any other action you might take."
— *1988 Surgeon General's Report on Nutrition and Health*

Health is our most precious resource and is the wellspring of an active life. When we have it, practically anything is possible. Without it, life becomes difficult. Increasingly we are coming to realize that a well-balanced diet is essential if we wish to remain healthy.

Concern over the relationship between diet and health is not a passing fad. People from all walks of life have discovered the benefits of healthful eating. In an article entitled "Negotiating Nutrition" in the May 1988 issue of *USAIR* magazine, Karen Collins describes how business executives have discovered that eating better helps them perform more consistently at peak levels:

> What are the goals of eating right? First, limited fat consumption. Mental processes tend to slow down after a high fat meal, and a high fat diet is linked to heart disease and certain forms of cancer. Second, caloric intake at the level that is right for you. A healthy weight is good for both you and your executive image. Finally, a diet that provides adequate amounts of the nutrients and dietary fiber that you need, but not too much sodium. Nothing can replace good health for looking and functioning at your best. Enough fiber seems to reduce the risk of colon cancer and certain intestinal disorders, and it also helps in the short term to avoid that bloated, uncomfortable feeling that many people experience after a few days away from home.

In the days of the executive martini-and-steak lunch, such advice would have been considered ludicrous. The fact that Collins's "power meals" follow the general nutritional guidelines set forth by not only the U.S. government and organizations such as the American Heart Association but also macrobiotics shows how far we have come in recognizing the importance of diet. There is also compelling evidence that during the last 20 years we have substantially improved our way of eating. Heart disease is down by about 20 percent in the United States, primarily as a result of a drop in meat and dairy food consumption and an increase in the consumption of whole grains and fresh vegetables.

Even with these improvements, however, we still have a long way to go. For example, in the summer of 1988 the U.S. surgeon general issued a 712-page summary of the evidence linking diet and health. Based on over 2,000 studies, the *Surgeon General's Report on Nutrition and Health* concluded that diet helped account for more than two-thirds of the 2.1 million deaths in the United States in 1987. The report strongly implicated the modern diet in coronary heart disease, stroke, atherosclerosis, diabetes, and some cancers, noting that fat, which increases the risk of heart disease, cancer, and obesity, now accounts for 37 percent of the calories in the American diet. Like earlier reports, the *Surgeon General's Report* recommended cutting back on cholesterol and saturated fat, mainly from meat and dairy products, and increasing consumption of whole grains, vegetables, fish, and fruits. "The depth of the science underlying this report's findings," concluded the surgeon general, "is even more impressive than that for tobacco and health in 1964."

Macrobiotic principles are actually quite simple. The word *macrobiotics* comes from the Greek *macro*, meaning "large or great," and *bios*, which means "life." It has been used throughout history to describe a way of eating and living in harmony with nature for the purpose of achieving health, happiness, and longevity.

During the 1960s, macrobiotic educators introduced the term *natural foods* to distinguish things like whole grains, fresh produce, soybean products like miso and tamari soy sauce, and other whole foods from the wheat germ, vitamins, and supplements that were referred to as *health foods.* Today the term *natural foods* is familiar to everyone, and the natural foods industry has become one of the leading growth industries in the United States. The growing popularity of natural foods has been encouraged by the dietary guidelines issued by leading public health agencies in the United States and abroad over the last 15 years, including the following:

1. The United States Congress Senate Select Committee on Nutrition and Human Needs report, *Dietary Goals for the United States* (1976–1977)
2. The U.S. Surgeon General's report, *Healthy People: Health Promotion and Disease Prevention* (1979)
3. Dietary guidelines issued by the American Heart Association, the American Diabetes Association, The American Society for Clinical Nutrition, and the U.S. Department of Agriculture
4. A 1981 report by a panel of the American Association for the Advancement of Science
5. Interim dietary guidelines for preventing cancer issued by the National Academy of Sciences in the 1982 publication *Diet, Nutrition and Cancer*
6. Dietary guidelines issued by the National Cancer Institute and the American Cancer Society
7. Dietary guidelines in *The Surgeon General's Report on Nutrition and Health* (1988)

Such reports have convinced millions of people to change their diets in a more healthful direction by eating whole grains and fresh vegetables and cutting back on or avoiding saturated fat, cholesterol, and refined sugar. As many have discovered, eating well increases vitality, endurance, and energy levels, which means more energy for doing what they want to do. Simply stated, balanced natural diet enhances our ability to live life to the fullest.

For several decades macrobiotics has been at the forefront of nutrition awareness in this country and abroad. More than 30 years ago Michio Kushi and other macrobiotic educators started recommending a high-fiber, low-fat diet to improve health and reduce the risk of chronic illness.

What we intend to show in this chapter is that macrobiotic dietary recommendations parallel many of the nutritional guidelines recently put forward by public health organizations and that adopting the macrobiotic diet *can* help us live life to the fullest.

DIETARY GOALS FOR THE UNITED STATES

During the 1970s the U.S. Senate Select Committee on Nutrition and Human Needs conducted hearings on the link between the modern diet and chronic illness. According to committee staff member Nicholas Mottern, "Our first attempt at studying limits of consumption involved calories and amounts of food, but this approach seemed of only limited value. Next, we began to investigate healthful limits to fat, carbohydrate, and protein consumption as a percent of calories, and this seemed much more useful. This approach was reinforced by an article describing work done in Sweden and other Scandinavian countries as early as 1968 in establishing healthful limits to food consumption." (East West Foundation, *Cancer and Diet*, 1980.)

The result was evidence linking the modern diet—high in saturated fat, cholesterol, and refined sugar—to 6 of the 10 leading causes of death in the United States, including heart disease, cancer, and diabetes. After reviewing the evidence, the Senate committee, chaired by Senators George McGovern and Robert Dole, issued a series of dietary recommendations aimed at lowering the risk of heart disease, cancer, and other degenerative diseases. *Dietary Goals for the United States*, released in 1977, produced a quantum leap in nutrition awareness.

SUMMARY OF DIETARY GOALS FOR
THE UNITED STATES
(Excerpted from the Second Edition, 1977)

"The purpose of this report is to point out that the eating patterns of this century represent as critical a public health concern as any now before us. If we as a government want to reduce health costs and maximize the quality of life for all Americans, we have an obligation to provide practical guidelines to the individual consumer as well as to set national dietary guidelines for the country as a whole."

—Senator George McGovern

1. To avoid overweight, consume only as much energy (calories) as is expended; if overweight, decrease energy intake and increase energy expenditure.
2. Increase the consumption of complex carbohydrates and "naturally occurring" sugars from about 28 percent of energy intake to about 48 percent of energy intake.
3. Reduce the consumption of refined and processed sugars by about 45 percent to account for about 10 percent of total energy intake.
4. Reduce overall fat consumption from approximately 40 percent to about 30 percent of energy intake.
5. Reduce saturated fat consumption to account for about 10 percent of total energy intake and balance that with polyunsaturated and monounsaturated fats, which should account for about 10 percent of energy intake each.
6. Reduce cholesterol consumption to about 300 mg a day.
7. Limit the intake of sodium by reducing intake of salt to about 5 g a day.

The goals suggest the following changes in food selection and preparation:

1. Increase consumption of fruits and vegetables and whole grains.

2. Decrease consumption of refined and other processed sugars and foods high in such sugars.
3. Decrease consumption of foods high in total fat and
   partially replace saturated fats, whether obtained
   from animal or vegetable sources, with polyunsaturated fats.
4. Decrease consumption of animal fat and choose
   meats, poultry, and fish that will reduce saturated
   fat intake.
5. Except for young children, substitute low-fat and
   nonfat milk for whole milk and low-fat dairy products for high-fat dairy products.
6. Decrease consumption of butterfat, eggs, and other
   high-cholesterol sources.
7. Decrease consumption of salt and foods high in salt
   content.

Macrobiotic Dietary Recommendations

1. Increase the intake of complex carbohydrates and reduce
   the use of simple sugars.
2. Rely more on vegetable-quality protein and less on protein from animal sources.
3. Reduce the overall consumption of fat and use more
   unsaturated fats and oils and less saturated fat.
4. Give adequate consideration to the ideal balance among
   vitamins, minerals, and other nutrients.
5. Use more organically grown and natural-quality foods
   and fewer chemically sprayed or fertilized items.
6. Use more traditionally processed foods and fewer artificially and chemically processed foods.
7. Increase intake of foods in their whole form and reduce
   intake of refined and partial foods.
8. Increase consumption of foods rich in natural fiber in
   place of foods that have been devitalized.

As you can see, the central thesis of *Dietary Goals*—the suggestion to increase intake of complex carbohydrates, such as those in whole grains and vegetables, and decrease consumption of saturated fat, cholesterol, and refined sugar—dovetails remarkably with the nutritional recommendations of macrobiotics. The macrobiotic diet both anticipated and, in many respects, went beyond the *Dietary Goals* in recommending a disease-preventive way of eating.

The *Dietary Goals* also support—though perhaps only by implication—the macrobiotic principle of eating a traditional diet based on foods that are indigenous to where you live.

The Senate committee evidence seemed to suggest that as people changed from the more traditional dietary pattern centered around whole cereal grains and fresh local vegetables, the rates of degenerative disease began to increase.

According to surveys conducted by the U.S. Department of Agriculture, for example, the American diet has changed radically in this century. Consumption of traditional staples, such as grains and their products, beans, and fresh vegetables and fruit, plummeted, while the intake of meat, poultry, sugar, cheese, soft drinks, and processed foods skyrocketed. USDA surveys show that from 1910 to 1976 per-capita intake of grains fell 51 percent, with corn, the traditional staple of North and South America, falling 85 percent and other traditional staples such as rye falling 78 percent, wheat 48 percent, barley 66 percent, and buckwheat 98 percent. The intake of beans fell 46 percent, fresh vegetables 23 percent, and fresh fruit 33 percent. During the same period the intake of beef rose 72 percent, cheese 322 percent, poultry 194 percent, canned vegetables 320 percent, frozen vegetables 1,650 percent, processed fruit 556 percent, yogurt 300 percent, ice cream 852 percent, corn syrup 761 percent, sugar 29 percent, saccharine 300 percent, and soft drinks 2,638 percent. The per-capita intake of artificial food colors added to the diet rose 995 percent since 1940, the first year that consumption of chemical additives and preservatives was recorded.

DIET, NUTRITION AND CANCER

If the 1970s were the decade in which awareness of diet and heart disease came to the fore, the eighties are the diet and cancer decade. In 1982 the National Academy of Sciences issued a 472-page report, *Diet, Nutrition and Cancer*, calling on the general public to reduce substantially consumption of foods high in saturated and unsaturated fat and increase daily intake of whole grains and vegetables. The panel reviewed hundreds of medical studies associating long-term eating patterns with the development of most common cancers, including those of the colon, stomach, breast, lung, esophagus, ovary, and prostate. The 13-member scientific committee suggested that diet could be responsible for 30 to 40 percent of cancers in men and 60 percent in women. "Most common cancers are potentially preventable, for they appear to be determined more by habit, diet, and custom than by genetic differences," the scientific panel concluded. Dr. Clifford Grobstein, chairman of the panel, told a press conference following release of the report, "The evidence is increasingly impressive that what we eat does affect our chances of getting cancer." He suggested that the dietary recommendations in the report be implemented without delay, "given the long time frame over which most cancers develop."

For many years, epidemiological studies have associated dietary patterns with the incidence of cancer. For example, a decline in cancer incidence occurred in Holland and other European countries following food shortages during the Second World War. Between 1942 and 1946 the incidence of cancer in Holland dropped 35 to 60 percent, depending on what part of the country was studied. Dr. F. de Waard, a Dutch epidemiologist, correlated this decline with the changes in diet that occurred when foods such as cheese, butter, milk, eggs, and meat became scarce and people had to live on simpler fare such as homegrown vegetables and whole-grain bread and porridge. With the return of normal conditions after the war, cancer rates jumped back to their prewar levels.

Despite the spread of refined and synthetic foods around the world, cooked whole grains, beans, and vegetables are still eaten as main foods in many cultures today. For example, corn tortillas and black beans are the staple foods in Central America, rice and soybean products are eaten throughout Southeast Asia, and whole and cracked wheat and chick-peas are daily fare in the Middle East. These regions have the lowest rates of cancer in the world. For instance, recent international surveys comparing the rate of cancer mortality in males in 44 countries found the least cancer in countries where traditional dietary patterns still prevail, such as El Salvador, Thailand, and Egypt. In comparison, European nations registered the highest incidence, and the United States, Canada, and Australia were also found to be in the upper range. In these parts of the world the modern diet has all but replaced traditional ways of eating.

THE BEST SOLUTION: THE MACROBIOTIC DIET

The macrobiotic diet is based on traditional dietary practices from around the world. It meets and in many cases exceeds the preventive dietary guidelines of the Senate Select Committee, the National Academy of Sciences, the American Heart Association, and other public health organizations. Recent studies by scientists, medical doctors, and public health officials have found that macrobiotic eating is completely sound and meets all the nutritional standards of the Recommended Dietary Allowances (RDA) published by the National Academy of Sciences and the international guidelines put forth by the Food and Agricultural Organization and the World Health Organization (FAO/WHO). For example, a study published in the *Journal of the American Dietetic Association* in 1980 found that macrobiotic subjects received acceptable amounts of iron, vitamin C, vitamin A, thiamine, riboflavin, vitamin B_{12}, and folate. The study also noted that macrobiotic people tended to weigh less than other people. While tables of recommended weights have fallen consistently in recent years, macrobiotic people still weigh about 10 to 20 pounds less than the recommended amounts. Though lean to modern observers, these weights are perfectly normal for people in traditional societies and are often preferable for reducing the risk of chronic illness.

Prevention of Cardiovascular Disease

As early as 1972–74, a series of studies was conducted on the macrobiotic community by researchers at Harvard Medical School and the Framingham Heart Study. Drs. Edward Kass, Frank Sacks, and associates led a series of cardiovascular studies in cooperation with Michio Kushi and the East West Foundation. The experiments were designed to investigate the possible role of macrobiotic dietary practice in reducing blood pressure and blood cholesterol levels, two of the known leading risk factors in degenerative heart disorders.

The results were startling: diet not only seemed to be a key factor but also appeared to outweigh many other factors previously thought to be primary. A brief summary of the two experiments follows:

The first study, "Blood Pressure in Vegetarians" (first appearing in the *American Journal of Epidemiology*, Vol. 100, No. 5), took place during 1972 and 1973. The investigators visited 210 macrobiotic individuals living in 17 households in the Boston area, measured their blood pressure levels (BP), and questioned them on dietary history and other possibly relevant background factors. Their results included the following:

- Mean BP for age group 16–29 was 106/60mm Hg, significantly lower than that normally found in Western populations.
- Advancing age in this group had significantly less effect on BP than in usual populations.
- Various other nondietary considerations (marital status, occupation, physical stress, meditation practice, national or ethnic background, etc.) were not found to be significant when compared with dietary factors.

- Of the various dietary factors, only declared percentage in the individuals' diets of *animal food consumption* appeared to significantly alter both systolic and diastolic pressures. ("Animal food" was given to include all foods of animal origin, including fish, eggs, dairy foods, etc.)
- Half of the participants shifted to a macrobiotic diet within the previous two years, indicating that dietary effects on BP are established fairly rapidly.
- Furthermore, the BP of subjects with under two months of macrobiotic eating were not significantly different from those of the whole.

These conclusions were presented together with references to 6 "prospective studies" and 24 epidemiological surveys, which further indicated that diet and particularly animal food intake may be a primary causative factor in hypertension, or elevated BP, and that dietary change may be a practical, fairly rapid means to reduce elevated blood pressure, regardless of the patient's background, environment, or other variations in lifestyle.

The second study, "Plasma Lipids and Lipoproteins in Vegetarians and Controls" (first appearing in the *New England Journal of Medicine*, May 29, 1975), compared a group of 116 macrobiotic individuals with a randomly selected control group consuming the usual American diet and matched with the study group by age and sex. The results are summarized as follows:

- Cholesterol levels in the macrobiotic group were found to be strikingly lower than in the controls or than usual U.S. levels.
- These low levels were found in all age groups, and the rise of cholesterol with age, usually significantly steep, was very slight.
- The macrobiotic subjects were also found to weigh less than average. Obesity is a known key risk factor in cardiovascular disease as well as cancer, diabetes, liver disease, and others.
- However, comparison of subjects and controls with identi-

cal weight still yielded a pronounced difference in blood lipid levels. In other words, lower weight could not by itself account for the unusually low cholesterol levels.

- Animal food consumption appeared to be the prime correlating factor in the different cholesterol levels.
- Consumption of fish did not appear to be significant; consumption of dairy products and eggs seemed to have the most direct influence on elevated cholesterol level.
- The longer the individual had been following the macrobiotic diet, the lower his or her cholesterol level had dropped below the usual levels.

The researchers also cited various epidemiological studies of nonindustrialized populations and noted that, with regard to blood cholesterol level, these peoples closely resembled the macrobiotic group studied here, despite the generally middle-class background, relatively short time on the new diet, varied occupational stresses, and highly industrialized urban/suburban environment of the latter group.

In summary, the two reports strongly suggest that factors such as age, background, stress, personal habits, environment, and others play at most a minimal role in the causation of high blood pressure or cholesterol levels and therefore of cardiovascular disease as a whole; that dietary factors, and particulary animal food consumption, play a primary role; that the adoption of a macrobiotic dietary pattern may significantly reduce these two risk factors within a relatively short time; and that this approach would be equally effective for members of all age groups and backgrounds.

General Health and Disease Prevention

In 1984 the Congressional Subcommittee on Health and Long Term Care investigated the dietary practices of several groups and concluded:

> The current macrobiotic diet is essentially an almost pure vegetarian diet as compared to the predominantly lacto-ovo-vegetarian diet primarily practiced by Seventh Day Adventists. The macrobiotic diet appears to be

nutritionally adequate if the mix of foods proposed in the dietary recommendations are followed carefully. There is no apparent evidence of any nutritional deficiencies among current macrobiotic practices .... The diet would also be consistent with the recently released dietary guidelines of the National Academy of Sciences and the American Cancer Society in regard to possible reduction of cancer risks.

The American Medical Association also lent its general support to macrobiotics, in the 1987 edition of *The American Medical Association Family Medical Guide.* In a section on special diets, the AMA reference guide states:

> In the macrobiotic diet foods fall into two main groups, known as yin and yang (based on an Eastern principle of opposites), depending on where they have been grown, their texture, color, and composition. The general principle behind the diet is that foods biologically furthest away from us are better for us. Cereals therefore form the basis of the diet and fish is preferred to meat. Although fresh foods free of additives are preferred, no food is actually prohibited, in the belief that a craving for any food may reflect a genuine bodily need. In general, the macrobiotic diet is a healthful way of eating.

In its own revised dietary guidelines, the AMA recommended:

1. Eat meat no more than once a day and choose fish or poultry over red meat.
2. Bake or broil food rather than frying it and use polyunsaturated oils rather than butter, lard, or margarine.
3. Cut down on salt, MSG, and other flavorings high in sodium.
4. Eat more fiber including whole-grain cereals, leafy green vegetables, and fruit.
5. Eat no more than four eggs a week.
6. For dessert or a snack choose fresh fruit rather than cookies, cakes, or puddings.

Modern nutritional studies, such as those cited in *Dietary Goals for the United States; Diet, Nutrition and Cancer,* and *The Surgeon General's Report on Nutrition and Health,* have lent credence to the principles underlying the practice of macrobiotics. It is increasingly clear that to secure health and well-being we need to eat a naturally balanced diet in accord with our universal dietary heritage. In the next chapter, we will look more closely at traditional macrobiotic principles, which approach the issue of diet and health from a different direction yet produce remarkably similar conclusions.

3
MACROBIOTIC PRINCIPLES

"For 15,000 years, the epoch of grain has been one with the epoch of man."

—H. E. Jacob, 6,000 Years of Bread

Below we describe the principles behind the macrobiotic diet. As you will see, they help orient diet in the direction of closer cooperation with nature. And as we point out, they lead to a way of eating similar to that recommended by leading public health agencies for the prevention of cancer, heart disease, and other chronic illnesses.

BALANCING HUMAN NEEDS

Every species on this wonderful planet of ours is part of the delicately balanced web of life. Each has its own niche and appropriate diet. Human beings have the widest scope of eating possibilities in the animal kingdom, which means that we can and often do eat practically anything. However, in order to be healthy, we need to select our foods wisely, in accord with our genuine biological needs.

What is the ideal pattern of nourishment for human beings? The answer could very well lie in the structure of the teeth and digestive system. We have 32 adult teeth, 20 of which are molars and premolars, 8 of which are incisors, and 4 of which are more sharply pointed canines. The molars and premolars, which comprise the majority of our teeth, are ideally suited for crushing and grinding tough plant fibers such as those in cereal grains, beans, seeds, and other foods (the word *molar* comes from the Latin for "millstone"). The front incisors are ideally suited for cutting vegetables; hence the name *incisor*, which means "to cut." The canines are specialized cutting teeth that, when necessary, can be used for tearing animal food. However, some people don't have sharply pointed canines, an indication that animal food may not be necessary for everyone.

Human tooth structure differs markedly from that of lions, tigers, and other meat-eating animals. The pattern of the teeth reveals that a diet based on animal protein and fat is not well suited to our needs. The evidence linking saturated fat and cholesterol contained in animal foods to heart disease and cancer is beginning to confirm this.

If we use the ratio of the teeth as a guide to diet, ideally five parts of the diet would be composed of grains, beans, seeds, and other tough plant fibers; two parts, vegetables; and depending on climate and need, up to one part animal food. The ideal ratio of plant to animal food would be about seven to one. The structure and function of the digestive system also indicates that plant fibers are ideal foods. Unlike meat-eating tigers and lions, the human digestive tract, especially the large intestine, is long and convoluted. If we eat plenty of animal food, the long transit time through the human intestine allows plenty of time for animal proteins to decompose into toxic bacteria and compounds like ammonia. With shorter digestive tracts, carnivores are able to rapidly discharge these toxins, with less possibility of toxic buildup in the body.

With the rise of the Darwinian theory of the survival of the fittest, there developed a modern notion that primitive human societies lived primarily on animal-quality food killed in the hunt. However, the popular image of early man as a hunter-gatherer may be closer to myth than reality. Recent studies of Paleolithic cultures, as well as dietary investigation of the hunter-gatherer tribes remaining on the planet today, have shown that they consumed primarily vegetable-quality food, including undomesticated grains, wild plants and grasses, tubers, berries, and roots. Fish and animal life, comprising about 5 to 25 percent of food intake, was taken only when necessary and consumed in small amounts. Summarizing the new view of the early diet, the *New York Times* reported in its science section:

> Recent investigations into the dietary habits of prehistoric peoples and their primate predecessors suggest that heavy meat-eating by modern affluent societies may be exceeding the biological capacities evolution built into the human body. The result may be a host of diet-related health problems, such as diabetes, obesity, high blood pressure, coronary heart disease, and some cancers.
>
> The studies challenge the notion that human beings evolved as aggressive hunting animals who depended primarily upon meat for survival. The new view—coming from findings in such fields as archaeology, anthropology, primatology, and comparative anatomy—instead portrays early humans and their forebears more as herbivores than carnivores. According to these studies, the prehistoric table for at least the last million and a half years was probably set with three times more plant than animal foods, the reverse of what the average American currently eats.

EATING TRADITIONALLY

For countless generations, since before the dawn of recorded history, the majority of humanity ate a natural, ecologically balanced diet. Our ancestors in all parts of the world nourished themselves with the products of their regional agriculture: whole cereal grains, fresh local vegetables, beans and their products, seasonal fruits, and occasional animal products, usually in much smaller amounts than at present. Of course each region or culture developed its own unique tradition of farming, food processing, and cooking based on climatic and environmental differences, but all were united in their respect for whole cereal grains and fresh local vegetables as principal foods. The central place accorded to whole grains, for example, is built into the language: in English the word *meal*, or ground grain, is used to describe eating itself; while in Japanese, a meal is referred to as *gohan*, which means "rice." There is also a saying in

Japanese: "A meal without rice (or grain) is no meal."

In a fascinating 1973 article in *National Geographic* entitled "Every Day Is a Gift When You Are Over 100," Dr. Alexander Leaf of the Massachusetts General Hospital investigated the lifestyle and diets of the Hunza in Kashmir, the Vilcabambans in Ecuador, and other long-lived peoples noted for their extraordinary health and freedom from degenerative disease. Dr. Leaf reported that the average man in Hunza consumed about 1,923 calories a day, with about 50 grams of protein, 36 grams of fat, and 354 grams of carbohydrate. Fats of animal origin were scarce, as the lack of pastureland made it difficult to raise meat and dairy animals. The Hunzas use primarily oil from apricot seeds in cooking, rather than butter or other animal fats, and base their diets around whole cereal grains, often in the form of whole-wheat chapatis, beans and bean products, and fresh seasonal vegetables and fruits.

A nutritional study of the long-lived people in the Andean village of Vilcabamba revealed that the average daily diet was composed of 1,200 calories, with 35 to 38 grams of protein, 12 to 19 grams of fat, and 200 to 260 grams of carbohydrate. As in Hunza, protein and fat were largely of vegetable origin. Again, whole grains, beans, and local vegetables were eaten as principal foods.

Commenting on the extraordinary health of these people, Dr. Leaf stated, "Needless to say, one sees no obesity among the elderly in either Vilcabamba or Hunza; neither were there signs of undernutrition. The weight of current medical opinion would concur that a diet such as that described for Hunza and Vilcabamba would delay development of atherosclerosis—that is fatty deterioration of the arteries of the heart."

A large-scale shift away from these traditional staples began with the Industrial Revolution and coincided with the rise of modern degenerative illnesses. In his article, Dr. Leaf compared the modern diet with that of the long-lived peoples he studied: "In the United States, though, nearly everyone consumes more. A U.S. Department of Agriculture Study lists average daily intake for Americans of all ages at 3,300 calories, with 100 grams of protein, 157 grams of fat, and 380 grams of carbohydrate." Unlike the Hunza and other traditional people who rely on vegetable-quality protein, most of the protein in the modern diet comes from meat, eggs, poultry, dairy products, and other animal sources. Most of the fat is saturated animal fat rather than polyunsaturated vegetable oil, and, whereas in the past people based their diets on unrefined complex carbohydrates—such as whole grains, beans, and vegetables—people today consume carbohydrates primarily in the form of refined grains and simple sugars.

ECOLOGICAL EATING

For thousands of years people ate the foods produced in their local environment. People in temperate zones ate the foods of temperate zones: whole grains, beans, fresh seasonal vegetables and fruits, and other products of their regional agriculture. This traditional practice underscores an important principle of macrobiotic eating: to eat foods that come from the climate in which we live.

Eating foods from the same climate makes it easier to make balance with our immediate environment. Traditionally, for example, the Eskimo and other people in the far north based their diets around fish and other animal foods found in the Arctic region. Vegetable foods were scarce, and a diet high in animal products helped them make balance with their harsh climate, since animal foods generate plenty of heat in the body. Following this principle, people in tropical regions lived on the unique plant and animal species found there. In India, for example, people intuitively adopted a vegetarian or semivegetarian way of eating because minimizing the intake of animal food makes it easier to adapt to a hot climate.

Not only did foods vary from one climate to the other, but so did traditional methods of cooking and food processing. For people in colder regions, food is an important source of internal warmth. People in northern latitudes naturally cook their dishes thoroughly and include a higher percentage of salt, animal protein, and fat in their diets. In warmer regions, where lighter cooking is appropriate, people eat a larger volume of fresh foods and lightly cooked dishes and include less animal food and salt in their diets.

The varieties of brown rice—the staple grain in most macrobiotic households—in use throughout the world illustrate how climate naturally influences food choices. The three main varieties of rice—short-, medium-, and long-grain—were traditionally used in different climatic regions. Short-grain rice is the most compact and glutenous and contains a higher proportion of minerals than the other two varieties. It is cultivated in northern latitudes and is the mainstay in Japan, Korea, China, and other temperate Asian countries. It was traditionally prepared by boiling it under pressure in cast-iron pots with heavy wooden lids (modern pressure cooking is roughly equivalent to this ancient method). This method of cooking rice is very appropriate in cold or temperate regions, as it concentrates energy and nutrients in the grains. Medium- and long-grain rices are lighter, fluffier, and less glutenous and are used in warm or tropical regions, such as India and Southeast Asia. They are usually boiled without pressure to produce less concentrated dishes that help balance a warmer climate. Similar patterns developed in the use of other grains, so that hardier, more concentrated grains such as winter wheat, rye, and buckwheat were used more in cold northern regions, such as Russia and northern Europe, while corn, a lighter grain, was used more in warm, sunny regions.

A comparison of cooking methods used traditionally in East and West also illustrates how climate and environment influence diet. In Japan and other Far Eastern countries with bright sunny climates, there was, until recently, no tradition of baking. The first loaves of bread were brought to Japan by European traders and missionaries; however, baking did not really catch on until after World War II. In the Far East, grains were used mostly in their whole form—for example, whole rice and millet. When flour was used, it was made into noodles or dumplings that, rather than being baked, were boiled to make them softer.

It was in regions with cold, damp climates—such as northern Europe—that the art of baking flourished. These are the regions where harder, more fibrous grains such as wheat and rye predominate. Unlike rice, millet, and barley, these grains are difficult to eat in their whole form and are usually crushed into flour or cracked or partially milled to create foods such as bulgur or couscous. These products are boiled to make soft, moist dishes and are traditional in Middle Eastern countries, where the climate is hot and dry.

Baking is a concentrated form of cooking that helps balance a cold, damp climate. When grains are baked, they are first crushed into flour. This fragments and disperses their energy. Then water is added to make dough, along with some type of fermenting agent (natural sourdough starter in the case of macrobiotic baking), further adding to the expansive quality of the flour. However, the dough is then placed in an enclosed oven and baked at high temperatures until it rises and hardens. Concentrated heat causes the flour to become hard and dry, and so overconsumption of bread, muffins, cookies, crackers, and other baked flour products can cause one to crave liquid.

The shift to the modern diet blurred distinctions that for centuries had been rooted in the unique climate and environment of each region. In North America, for example, people dramatically increased their intake of meat and other forms of animal food, which from an environmental standpoint are suited to cold polar regions. As a result they were inevitably attracted to the opposite extremes, fruits, vegetables, spices, refined sugar, chocolate, and other products from the tropics.

With a high intake of extremes like meat and sugar, people tend to bypass the traditional staples of their region, such as whole grains and beans. Today, rather than being eaten directly, these foods are fed to livestock and then eaten in the form of animal food. This highly inefficient practice not only depletes our human resources—in the form of increasing degenerative illness—but also depletes the Earth's natural resources.

In *Diet for a New America*, John Robbins describes the inefficiency of the modern food system: "The livestock population of the United States today consumes enough grain and soybeans to feed over five times the entire human population of the country. We feed these animals over 80 percent of the corn we grow, and over 95 percent of the oats . . . . By cycling our grain through livestock, we end up with only 10 percent as many calories available if we ate the grain directly."

Macrobiotics advocates a return to a climatically based, ecologically balanced diet, both to enhance personal health and to preserve the integrity of the planet.

CHANGING WITH THE SEASONS

Our selection of foods and cooking methods needs to reflect changes in climate and weather that occur throughout the year. During the winter, for example, we naturally seek hearty, warming foods, while in summer, quick, lightly cooked dishes are appealing. Also, cold weather tends to increase our appetite, while hot weather diminishes it. To a certain extent we intuitively change our diet from season to season, but if we understand how to adjust our cooking and selection of foods, the transition can be much smoother. This is especially important today, since modern foods are often monotonously standardized throughout the year.

Below are some basic suggestions for varying your cooking and selection of food to balance the changing seasons (all of the foods mentioned below are used often in macrobiotic cooking and are available in natural foods stores):

Spring
As spring approaches, include more fresh greens in your diet, especially those that are lightly steamed or quickly boiled. You can also serve more quick-cooked vegetables and slightly reduce the amount of salt, oil, and salty seasonings used in cooking.

Grains that have matured over the winter and were harvested in the spring—such as winter barley and wheat—can be included often, along with other whole grains. Wholewheat products such as noodles, seitan (wheat gluten), and fu (dried and puffed wheat gluten) can be used for this purpose.

Lightly fermented foods, such as amasake (rice milk), natto (fermented whole soybeans), light pickles, pressed salads, umeboshi plums and vinegar, sauerkraut, and tempeh (soy meat) can be included often in meals. As the weather turns warmer, serve plenty of light, quickly cooked dishes, and fewer dishes cooked for a long time.

Summer

During the summer, gardens and markets overflow with an irresistible variety of fresh vegetables and seasonal fruits. Summer foods are generally watery and expansive in comparison to the foods of other seasons. Summer squashes, melons, sweet corn, cucumbers, lettuce, juicy fruits, and fresh greens are abundant in summer and can be included in the diet. The transition to summer cooking can be gradual and steady. Lighter methods of cooking, such as quick boiling, steaming, and light sautéing, can be used often. Crispy blanched vegetables and occasional raw salads are especially nice in summer, as are grain, noodle, pasta, bean, tofu, and sea vegetable salads. Lightly cooked vegetable dishes and raw salads help us to stay cool and relaxed. Homemade sushi (brown rice rolled in toasted nori sea vegetable) is also nice as a quick, light snack in the summer.

Until modern times people were often wary of consuming icy cold foods and drinks, even in hot weather. Writing in his *Regimen*, for example, Hippocrates said of this practice, "It is dangerous to heat, cool, or make a commotion all of a sudden in the body, because everything that is excessive is an enemy of nature. Why should anyone run the hazard in the heat of summer of drinking iced waters, which are excessively cold, and suddenly throwing the body into a different state from the one it was in before, producing thereby many ill effects?" We agree with Hippocrates that overintake of icy cold foods and beverages can weaken one's condition, and we recommend using them in moderation if at all. However, slightly chilled foods or drinks can be enjoyed from time to time in hot weather.

Somen, udon, or other whole-grain noodles may be served with refreshing cool broths, while kanten, a natural gelatin dessert made from agar-agar sea vegetable, can also be served chilled. Cool tofu dishes and vegetable aspics also help balance the heat. Fresh fruit salads, melon, and cucumber are refreshing and can be eaten chilled when needed. Lightly seasoned soups and broths can be served cool or at room temperature from time to time.

Autumn

As autumn approaches, gradually change your cooking to include more rich, hearty dishes. In general, a little more salt and oil can be used in cool weather cooking. Fall squashes, cabbage, carrots, onions, parsnips, and other vegetables with naturally sweet flavors are abundant at this time of year and can be included regularly. Since autumn vegetables come in a variety of colors, your dishes can be naturally colorful and attractive. Well-cooked dishes that warm the body are appropriate in the autumn, and it is natural to reduce the intake of raw salads, fresh fruit, and other chilled dishes. Many of the foods harvested in autumn store easily and can be used throughout the winter.

Hearty grain, bean, and vegetable stews warm the body on chilly fall days. Among the grains, rice and millet are especially delicious at this time of year. Deep-fried vegetables (tempura) or fish can be prepared on occasion, while sweet brown rice and mochi (pounded sweet brown rice dumplings) are especially warming because of their higher protein and fat content. Pureed squash and carrot soups— served piping hot—are also delicious in cool weather.

In the fall, vegetables are often more appealing when cut into larger sizes such as rounds and chunks. Large, solid cuts lend themselves to long, slow cooking over a low flame, which makes them soft and sweet. Sea vegetable side dishes can be seasoned with a little more salt and oil. Cooked fruit and other naturally sweetened desserts can be used in place of the cool, juicy melons and fresh fruits of summer. Noodles served in hot broth can be included frequently in the fall, and fried rice or noodles can be eaten occasionally.

Winter

During the cold winter months it is important to prepare foods that help the body stay warm. Raw salads or chilled dishes make it more difficult to be comfortable in the cold. Leafy green vegetables are often not as plentiful in winter, especially in northern latitudes, but it is still important to serve them daily. Root and ground vegetables can also be served regularly.

A little more salt and oil can generally be used in winter, but these changes are best kept subtle. Deep-fried vegetables (tempura), slowly sautéed dishes (with or without oil), and hearty grain, bean, and vegetable soups and stews are very warming in winter. Keep in mind that although rich, hearty dishes are preferred, it is still important to prepare greens and other lightly cooked vegetables regularly in order to avoid one-sided eating.

YIN AND YANG

No doubt you're aware that the principle of yin and yang plays a significant role in macrobiotics. So that you can expand your macrobiotic repertoire beyond the recipes and foods in this book, the next chapter provides a basic explanation of yin and yang. Once you understand the principle, you will be able to choose foods, devise your own recipes, and plan meals that are centrally balanced, in keeping with the precept of orienting your diet to the climate you live in.

4
YIN AND YANG MADE SIMPLE

Our discussion of macrobiotics would not be complete without an explanation of yin and yang. Actually, yin and yang are not mysterious at all, although the words may sound foreign to some readers. They are as close to us as day and night, summer and winter, man and woman, left and right. In macrobiotic cooking we employ the understanding of these primary energies to create balance in our daily meals and, since we are what we eat, in our body and mind as well.

We can begin with basic definitions. The term *yin* describes the primary force of expansion in the universe. Centrifugal force, which is defined by *Webster's* as "the force that tends to impel a thing or parts of a thing outward from a center of rotation," qualifies as an example of yin. The term *yang* describes the primary force of contraction in the universe. Centripetal force, defined as "the force that is necessary to keep an object moving in a circular path and that is directed inward toward the center of rotation," qualifies as an example of yang. These are the most basic forces in the universe, and together they create everything, including food, the human body, stars, and planets.

In life everything has its opposite (which actually complements or makes it more complete). Day exists with night, male with female, fire with water, activity with rest, time with space, and animal with vegetable. Moreover, within any particular object or thing, numerous complementary aspects can always be discerned. So, for example, everything has an inside and outside, a front and back, a downward and upward section, and a left and right side. This means that

35

yin and yang, or complementary/antagonistic aspects, exist within everything as well as in the relationship that things have to other things.

When we compare these complementary attributes, we see that in some the force of contraction is more predominant. These aspects are classified as being more yang. Others have an opposite nature, so that the force of expansion is stronger, and these are defined as more yin. However, yin and yang always exist in combination in any particular thing, so nothing is absolutely one or the other. That is why we say that something is "more yin" or "more yang" in relation to something else or that certain parts are more yin or yang than others. In other words, these terms are relative and are a matter of comparison or degree.

So, the first step in using yin and yang to create health and harmony is to begin seeing them in ourselves and in the world around us. In the chart opposite, we classify a variety of things into two categories. You can refer to this chart when you are trying to figure out whether something is more yin or more yang.

The second step in using yin and yang is to see how they interact. As everyone knows, life is a process of change. Day changes into night, summer into winter, youth into old age. Life occurs in cycles, like the rising and falling of the tides and the waxing and waning of the moon. The rhythms of the human body are examples, as are the patterns of daily life. We breathe in, making our lungs expand, then we breathe out, making them contract. The heartbeat is also an alternating rhythm of expanding and contracting movement. In the morning we get up and are active, then we rest and sleep at night. Every movement in nature, from the motion of planets around the sun to the spinning of electrons around the nucleus of the atom, is the result of the interplay of these two primary forces.

All changes in life take place in accord with three simple laws: (1) yin attracts yang and yang attracts yin (2) yin repels yin and yang repels yang, and (3) yin changes into yang and yang changes into yin. Examples of the first law

Attribute	Yin/Centrifugal (▽)	Yang/Centripetal (△)
Tendency	Expansion	Contraction
Function	Dispersion, decomposition	Assimilation, organization
Movement	More inactive, slower	More active, faster
Vibration	Shorter waves, high frequency	Longer waves, low frequency
Direction	Vertical; ascending	Horizontal; descending
Position	More outward and peripheral	More inward and central
Weight	Lighter	Heavier
Temperature	Colder	Hotter
Light	Darker	Lighter
Humidity	More wet	More dry
Density	Thinner	Thicker
Size	Larger	Smaller
Shape	More expanded, fragile	More contracted, harder
Length	Longer	Shorter
Texture	Softer	Harder
Atomic particle	Electron	Proton
Elements	N, O, K, P, Ca	H, C, Na, As, Mg
Environment	Vibration—Air—Water	Earth
Climate	Tropical	Arctic
Biological	Vegetable	Animal
Sex	Female	Male
Organ structure	Hollow, expansive	Compact, condensed
Nerves	Orthosympathetic	Parasympathetic
Attitude	Gentle, negative	Active, positive
Work	Psychological & mental	Physical & social
Consciousness	More universal	More specific
Mental function	Dealing with the future	Dealing with the past
Culture	Spiritually oriented	Materially oriented
Color	Purple—Blue-Green—Yellow—Brown—Orange—Red	
Season	Winter	Summer
Dimension	Space	Time
Taste	Hot—sour—sweet—Salty—Bitter	
Vitamins	C	K, D
Catalyst	Water	Fire

are the attraction between man and woman, plus and minus charges, and electrons and protons. Examples of the second are what happens when we mix oil and water (both of which are more yin) or try to combine two positive or two negative electrical charges. The changing of the seasons and the other life cycles described above are examples of things changing into their opposites.

Things that are very yang are naturally attracted to things that are very yin and vice versa. Two things with very strong yang natures repel more forcefully than two mildly yang things, and the same applies to things with more yin natures.

Someone who spends several days in the hot sun, for example, is more strongly attracted to water than someone who has been relaxing in an air-conditioned hotel. As another example, people who have experienced the harsh reality of war are often more firmly committed to peace than people who have not. In the same way, when the weather turns cold, we turn on the heat rather than the air conditioner. Or in the heat of summer, we don't start the furnace; we try to cool off. These adaptations occur spontaneously and are a matter of common sense. We all balance yin and yang intuitively day by day. Furthermore, these principles explain how and why we seek certain foods—we will get back to them later.

IN THE KITCHEN

Now, let's return to our classification of things into yin and yang in order to see how they influence our daily foods. In our planetary environment, out of which our foods are created, yin and yang appear as two complementary energies that originate in the universe itself. One includes various forms of light, energy, and radiation generated by celestial bodies and appears as a comprehensive force that pushes or holds everything on the surface of the planet. This comprehensive force is more yang or centripetal. At the same time, the earth is constantly rotating, and as a result, it gives off an upward, expanding, centrifugal force that we classify as more yin. (We can also refer to these complementary forces as gravity and antigravity.) All things on Earth, including plant and animal life, are created by the interaction of these two dynamic forces.

Simply looking at the foods we eat can help us discover how yin and yang appear in them. Although any foods will do, we can begin by observing the shape, size, and other features of common vegetables. As examples we can use several daikon radishes, a burdock root, a hard fall squash, several onions, and Chinese cabbage.

Begin by placing a daikon root on your table or cutting board. Compare the upper part with the tip. Which part has stronger contracting energy? As we can see, the upper portion is wider and more expanded, and the tip is narrower and more contracted. Downward or contracting energy is stronger in the tip of the radish, which is the part that grows deeper in the soil, while upward, or expanding energy is stronger in the upper part.

If the greens are still attached, notice how they grow in a direction that is opposite to the root. The root grows in a downward direction and is more dense or solid than the stems and leaves that branch upward. These sections complement and make balance with one another.

Looking more closely at the greens, notice how the stems are tighter and more contracted, while the leaves are larger and more expanded. Although the greens are on the whole more expanded than the root, within their structure certain regions have more expanding energy and others more contracting energy.

Place another radish on the table. Notice how each vegetable has a different shape and size. One will be longer, the other shorter; one thicker, the other thinner; one straighter, the other more curved or irregularly shaped. Place one of the radishes in your left hand and the other in your right. You may notice that one is heavier than the other. Here we see that although they are generally alike, no two vegetables have exactly the same proportion of expanding and contracting, or yin and yang, energies.

Then place the burdock root alongside the radishes. Notice how it has a tougher and more fibrous skin. Moreover, burdock root normally grows deeper in the soil than daikon radishes. If you slice each vegetable in half, you will notice that the burdock is drier and less juicy inside. These qualities indicate that, compared to daikon, burdock has stronger contracting energy. Also, when you cook these vegetables, daikon becomes sweet while burdock has a mildly bitter flavor.

Next, place the squash and onions on the table with the root vegetables. Think about how these vegetables grow. Burdock and daikon grow farther below the soil under the influence of stronger contracting energy. However, the expanding energy in round vegetables is not as strong as that in daikon greens, which grow in a more upward direction. The rounded shape of these vegetables means that neither upward nor downward force is overly predominant. Both are somewhat balanced. From these considerations we can see that squash and onions are more yin than root vegetables and more yang than leafy greens.

Take the Chinese cabbage and place it on the table with the other vegetables. First compare its size, shape, and structure to the daikon greens. Notice how the daikon leaves have a more differentiated leaf structure. Each leaf is smaller in comparison to the broader Chinese cabbage leaves. Smaller, more finely differentiated leaves have more contracting energy than broader, more expanded ones. On the whole, leafy greens are more expanded than root or round-shaped vegetables, but among them some varieties have more expanding and more contracting energy.

THE FOOD SPECTRUM

From these basic examples we can now begin to judge the qualities of other foods and classify them according to yin and yang. Just as light can be broken down into a range of colors—from red and orange (more yang) through to blue and purple (more yin)—we can arrange foods along a continual spectrum of yin and yang based on a variety of factors.

Aside from the things we can see, including the size, shape, moisture content, and density of a particular food, a number of other factors are also important. These include where and in what season the food was grown, its chemical composition, especially the proportion of more yang minerals such as sodium to more yin ones such as potassium, the speed at which it grows, and whether it was grown naturally or with artificial fertilizers and chemicals. The factors that help determine the degree of yinness or yangness of foods can be summarized as follows:

Yin Energy Creates	Yang Energy Creates
Growth in a hot climate	Growth in a cold climate
More rapid growth	Slower growth
Foods containing more water	Drier foods
Fruits and leaves, which are nurtured more by expanding energies	Stems, roots, and seeds, which are nurtured more by contracting energies
Growth upward high above the ground	Growth downward below the ground
Sour, bitter, sharply sweet, hot, and aromatic foods	Salty, plainly sweet, and pungent foods

When classifying foods, we need to see which of these factors are most predominant, since as we saw above, all foods have both expanding and contracting energies. One of the most accurate methods of classification is to observe how the cycle of the seasons influences the growth of the particular plant. During the winter the climate is colder. At this time of year energy in the atmosphere becomes more contracting. In plants, leaves wither and die as the sap descends to the roots and the vitality of the plant becomes more condensed. As the earth becomes hard and frozen, branches of trees and other plants become bare and the grass dries up and turns yellow or brown. Plants used for food and grown in late autumn and winter are drier and more concentrated. They can be kept for a longer time without spoiling. Examples of these plants are carrots, turnips, and cabbages.

During the spring and early summer nature erupts with new life. As the weather becomes hotter, the energy in plants and in the atmosphere ascends and green replaces brown as the predominant color in the vegetable world. Spring and summer plants are more yin in nature. They are more watery, perish more quickly, and provide a cooling effect, which is needed in warm months. In late summer the energy in plants reaches its zenith as many fruits become ripe. They are very watery and sweet and develop higher above the ground.

The yearly cycle shows how the energies of expansion and contraction alternate as the seasons change. Cooler, or more yin, weather produces more contracting energy; warmer, or more yang, weather produces more expansive energy. The same cycle can be applied to the part of the world in which a food originates. Foods that find their origin in hot tropical climates, where the vegetation is lush and abundant, are more expanded, while foods originating in northern or colder climates are more contracted.

We can also generally classify plants according to color, although there are often exceptions, from the more yin colors—violet, indigo, green, and white—through the more yang colors of yellow, brown, and red. And, as mentioned above, we should also consider the ratio of chemical components such as sodium, which is contractive, to potassium, which is expansive, in determining the quality of a particular food.

So far we have been discussing the different qualities of plant foods. Now let us consider the differences between plants and animals. For the most part animal foods are classified as having more contracting energy. Why are plants more yin than animals? Well, for one, vegetables are generally immobile while animals move around actively. Plants also have a more expanded structure; their major portion branches upward and differentiates above the ground, while animals are more compact units with less external differentiation. Further, animals often have high body temperatures, while plants are cool. Plants are also

General Yin (▽) and Yang (△) Categorization of Food

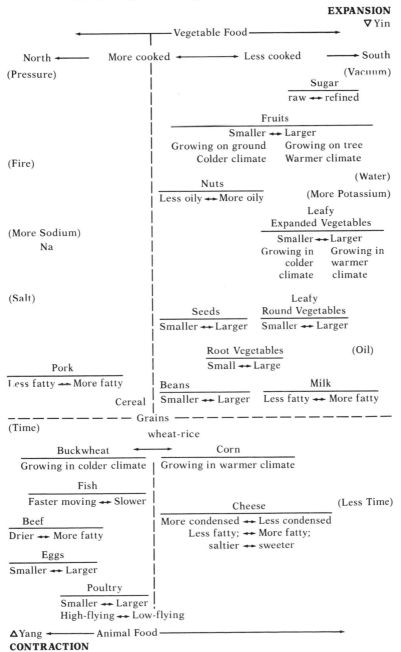

EXPANSION
▽ Yin

Vegetable Food

North ← More cooked ←→ Less cooked → South
(Pressure)   (Vacuum)

Sugar
raw ←→ refined

Fruits
Smaller ←→ Larger
Growing on ground   Growing on tree
(Fire)   Colder climate   Warmer climate

(Water)

Nuts
Less oily ←→ More oily   (More Potassium)

Leafy
Expanded Vegetables
Smaller ←→ Larger

(More Sodium)   Growing in   Growing in
Na   colder   warmer
climate   climate

(Salt)   Leafy
Seeds   Round Vegetables
Smaller ←→ Larger   Smaller ←→ Larger

Root Vegetables   (Oil)
Small ←→ Large

Pork   Milk
Less fatty ←→ More fatty   Beans   Less fatty ←→ More fatty
Smaller ←→ Larger

Cereal

Grains

wheat-rice

(Time)

Buckwheat ←→ Corn
Growing in colder climate   Growing in warmer climate

Fish
Faster moving ←→ Slower

Cheese   (Less Time)
Beef   More condensed ←→ Less condensed
Drier ←→ More fatty   Less fatty; ←→ More fatty;
saltier ←→ sweeter

Eggs
Smaller ←→ Larger

Poultry
Smaller ←→ Larger
High-flying ←→ Low-flying

△ Yang ← Animal Food
CONTRACTION

represented by the color green, chlorophyll, while animals are manifested in the color red, hemoglobin. Plant foods have a more cooling and relaxing effect on the body, while animal foods have a more warming or constricting effect.

In the diagram on the preceding page, foods are arranged according to yin and yang. The foods at the lower left generally have a greater degree of contracting force. Those appearing closer to the center of the diagram (represented by two intersecting lines of balance) have a more even balance of both forces, and those toward the upper right have a predominance of more expanding energy.

There is a tremendous range of variation within each category of food. Animal foods are generally more condensed than grains or vegetables, but among the many varieties of animal food some are more contracting and others less so. Eggs, meat, and poultry, for example, have more extreme contracting energy than fish and other types of seafood. Among fish, those with red meat and blue skin are more extreme than white-meat varieties. Although dairy products come from an animal source, certain varieties— such as hard, salty cheeses—are more contracting, while others, such as yogurt, butter, ice cream, and cottage cheese, have a more expansive quality.

The quality of energy in cereal grains is generally more centrally balanced, and this is reflected nutritionally in the average proportion of minerals to protein to carbohydrate they contain. However, a wide range of energies can be found among grains. Varieties such as buckwheat, millet, and winter wheat have a more contracting effect, while summer wheat, barley, and corn are more expansive. Brown rice is generally in between, but again this depends on the variety being considered. Short-grain rice, which is the most suitable variety for temperate climates, is generally the most balanced, followed by medium- and long-grain varieties, which are used more frequently in warmer areas.

Beans are generally more expanded than grains, but as with other categories of food, a wide range of variation exists among them. For example, certain varieties—includ-

Strong Yang Foods
Refined salt
Eggs
Meat
Hard cheese
Chicken and poultry
Lobster, crab, and other shellfish
Red-meat and blue-skinned fish

More Balanced Foods
Unrefined white sea salt, miso, tamari soy sauce, and other naturally
    salty seasonings
Tekka, gomashio, umeboshi, and other naturally processed salty
    condiments
Low-fat white-meat fish
Sea vegetables
Whole cereal grains
Beans and bean products
Root, round, and leafy green vegetables (from temperate climates)
Seeds and nuts (from temperate climates)
Temperate-climate fruit
Nonaromatic, nonstimulant beverages
Spring or well water
Naturally processed vegetable oils
Brown rice syrup, barley malt, and other natural grain-based
    sweeteners (when used moderately)

Strong Yin Foods
White rice, white flour
Frozen and canned foods
Tropical fruits and vegetables (including those originating in the
    tropics, such as tomato and potato)
Milk, cream, yogurt, and ice cream
Refined oils
Spices (pepper, curry, nutmeg, etc.)
Aromatic and stimulant beverages (coffee, black tea, mint tea, etc.)
Honey, sugar, and other refined sweeteners
Alcohol
Foods containing chemicals, preservatives, dyes, and pesticides
Artificial sweeteners
Drugs (marijuana, cocaine, etc., with some exceptions)
Medications (tranquilizers, antibiotics, etc., with some exceptions)

ing azuki beans, chick-peas, and lentils—are smaller and lower in fat. They have more balanced energy than beans that are relatively larger or higher in fat—such as pinto, kidney, and lima beans.

Sea vegetables generally have more concentrated energy than most land varieties, and this is reflected in their high mineral content. Those that grow closer to the shore or in warmer water are lighter and more expansive; those that grow in deeper, colder waters are more concentrated, as are those with a higher mineral content.

Vegetables generally have more expanding energy than grains or beans. As we saw in our comparison of foods, leafy green vegetables have more upward or rising energy; round-shaped vegetables—such as cabbage, onion, and squash—are more evenly balanced; and root vegetables are more contracted. However, aside from shape, size, and direction of growth, where a vegetable originates is a key factor in creating its energy quality. Vegetables such as tomatoes, potatoes, yams, avocados, eggplant, and peppers originated in South America or other tropical areas before being imported into Europe and North America. Compared to temperate varieties, like cabbage or kale, they have more extreme expanding energy, and for this reason it is better for people in temperate zones to avoid using them.

In general fruits have stronger expanding energy than vegetables. They are softer, sweeter, juicier, and composed of more simple sugar. The place of origin also plays a decisive role in creating the quality of energy in each variety of fruit. Tropical or semitropical fruits—including pineapple, banana, kiwi, and citrus—have more extreme expanding energy than apples, pears, peaches, melons, and others that grow in the temperate zones. As with vegetables that originate in the tropics, these more extreme varieties of fruit are also best avoided by those who live in temperate zones.

A variety of foods have even more extreme energy. Concentrated sweeteners such as honey, maple syrup, and molasses are all very expansive, as are refined sugar and artificial sweeteners. Simple sugars are more fragmented or expansive than complex carbohydrates such as those in whole grains, beans, and local vegetables. Other products that originate in the tropics—such as spices, coffee, and chocolate—are also included in the more extreme yin category, as is alcohol. But many medications, including aspirin and antibiotics, and drugs such as marijuana and cocaine, are even further out on the energy spectrum. These products all have extremely expansive effects.

MAKING BALANCE

An optimum diet is one that is well balanced in terms of yin and yang. As we saw earlier, yin and yang attract one another just as man and woman or the opposite poles of a magnet do. As consumption of foods with strong contracting energy increases, so does the desire for foods with strong expanding energy. Today people consume a large volume of sugar, tropical fruits, soft drinks, ice cream, chocolate, and other extremely yin foods in order to balance a high intake of animal products. The craving for sugar, chocolate, and other concentrated sweeteners, which many people now experience, is fueled by the overintake of foods with extremely contracting energy. These cravings are simply the result of opposites attracting.

We people in the temperate zones describe this modern diet as a "polar-tropical" diet. Too many of us have replaced the whole grains, beans, fresh local vegetables, and other foods appropriate to our region with meat, eggs, cheese, poultry, and other foods more suited to cold polar climates and with sugar, chocolate, spices, coffee, tropical fruits and vegetables, and other items more suited to equatorial zones.

What exactly *should* we eat? We've laid it all out for you in Part II. But first we'll give you some tips for making a smooth transition to macrobiotics.

5
ADOPTING THE
MACROBIOTIC LIFESTYLE

Changing your way of life may seem formidable, but the macrobiotic lifestyle is really quite simple and flexible. In this chapter we offer suggestions for making a smooth transition to macrobiotics.

The Standard Macrobiotic Diet presented in Chapter 6 is generally appropriate for persons living in temperate, or four-season, climates, such as most of North America, Europe, and the Far East. These guidelines require modification if you live in a tropical or semitropical climate, or a polar or semipolar region. However, the percentages indicated below are generally valid in all but the most extreme polar climates. Whole grains, beans, fresh local vegetables, and sea vegetables are the ideal principal foods in the tropics as well as in northern climates. The main difference between temperate and tropical diets lies in the varieties of these foods we select and the methods we use to cook them. These and other personal adjustments underscore the importance of adapting these principles flexibly, according to our personal needs. In this sense macrobiotics is not a fixed "diet" that can be followed rigidly without considering individual circumstances.

The Standard Macrobiotic Diet can be modified to suit an endless variety of circumstances. Every day hundreds of thousands of people of all ages and backgrounds and in all corners of the globe enjoy the foods listed in this book. Macrobiotic people range in age from toddlers to senior citizens and can be found from Kyoto to Kansas.

BALANCING PERSONAL NEEDS

Everyone has different dietary needs, and our way of eating needs to reflect this. Babies and children, for example, have different needs from adults. Someone who builds houses needs to eat differently from someone who works in an office. A nursing mother has different nutritional requirements from a grandmother. Factors such as age, activity, dietary background, and state of health need to be taken into account when designing an appropriate diet. Further, everyone has certain food preferences, eating habits, and likes and dislikes, and these need to be considered as well.

Even with these differences, however, most of us in the modern world come from the background of the modern diet. Although individual differences are endless, the overall pattern of modern eating is generally the same, with items such as meat, eggs, cheese, refined sugar, soft drinks, processed foods, tropical vegetables and fruits, and artificial foods comprising the mainstay of modern diets. The trend toward standardization, mass production, and global marketing of food has tended to erase many unique ethnic and regional differences in diet that developed over thousands of years.

When transitioning from the Standard American Diet (SAD) to macrobiotics, which is sometimes referred to as the Great Life American Diet (GLAD), it may be helpful to proceed gradually and not try to make the change all at once. Meat and poultry are relatively easy to give up, and most people discover they have little or no desire to consume them after a few weeks. However, if cravings occur, low-fat white-meat fish, seitan (wheat meat), or tempeh (soy meat) can be included more often. Wheat or soy meat can be made to look and taste like roast beef and hamburger, and many people cannot tell the difference.

Although complex carbohydrates like whole grains, beans, and sweet vegetables have a subtle, naturally sweet flavor, sugar and concentrated sweeteners are sometimes difficult to give up. A gradual transition to more natural sweeteners can be made to allow the body to adjust itself to new sources of blood sugar. Over a period of several weeks to several months, rice syrup, barley malt, or other grain-based sweeteners, amasake, and cooked local fruits can be used to provide extra sweetness. Meanwhile, naturally sweet vegetables—fall squashes, carrots, onions, parsnips, and cabbage—can be served often. When full health is restored, a single mouthful of food containing sugar, honey, maple syrup, or artificial sweetener can trigger a headache or an upset stomach as the body reacts to the ingestion of highly imbalanced food. Many people, however, have eaten so much sugar and sweets over the years that their bodies have lost this natural reactivity.

For psychological reasons the third category of foods, dairy products, is sometimes the most difficult to give up. In many cases dairy food was the original food of infants and children for several generations of mothers who avoided breast-feeding. Many of us have strong emotional ties to the food on which we were initially raised. In the case of cow's milk and other dairy products, it often takes a long time for modern people, including otherwise nutritionally aware individuals, to overcome this unconscious dependency. Soy foods and other bean products, which have little saturated fat and no cholesterol, provide an excellent alternative to dairy products, as does amasake, a naturally fermented sweet rice milk. In the natural foods kitchen a wide variety of foods that have a taste and texture similiar to dairy products can be prepared for those in transition, including amasake, soy milk, amasake pudding, soy yogurt, tofu cheese, and tofu cheesecake.

In order to make a successful change in your way of eating, proper cooking is essential. Everyone is strongly encouraged to learn how to cook from qualified macrobiotic instructors. Until you have actually tasted the full range of macrobiotically prepared foods and seen how they are made, you may not fully appreciate the depth and scope of the diet or have a standard against which to measure your own cooking. Besides, people with years of experience can offer you many valuable time-saving hints and can help you locate high-quality natural foods. Cooking is an art, and you will save time in the long run by receiving the proper guidance and instruction, especially at the beginning. Once you have mastered the fundamentals you can improvise and experiment on your own and ultimately learn to cook with only your intuitive sense of balance as your guide.

Macrobiotic cooking classes and educational programs, such as *The Macrobiotic Way of Life Seminar* presented by the Kushi Foundation in Boston, can be invaluable in learning to adapt macrobiotic principles to your individual needs. Educational programs offer individual dietary guidance and hands-on training, both of which can be essential in helping you create the most appropriate diet under any circumstances.

Cooking classes are presented at hundreds of macrobiotic educational centers around the world. To find out if they are taking place near you, please contact the Kushi Foundation in Boston for a copy of the *Worldwide Macrobiotic Directory*, which lists international educational centers and friends.

SUGGESTIONS FOR HEALTHY LIVING

Macrobiotics is more than just a diet. It encompasses the various aspects of daily living commonly referred to as "lifestyle." Practices such as staying physically active and using natural cooking utensils, fabrics, and materials in the home are recommended as part of a naturally healthy life. In the past, people lived closer to nature and ate a balanced, natural diet. With each generation we have gotten further and further from our roots in nature and have experienced a corresponding increase in chronic illnesses. The suggestions presented below complement a balanced natural diet and can help everyone enjoy satisfying and harmonious living.

- Live each day happily, without being worried about your health. Be active mentally as well as physically. Sing every day and encourage others to join you.
- Greet everyone and everything with gratitude, in particu-

lar offering thanks before and after each meal. Encourage others to give thanks for their food and their natural environment.

- Try to get to bed before midnight and get up early in the morning.
- Try not to wear synthetic clothing or woolen articles directly against your skin. Wear cotton instead. Keep jewelry and accessories simple, natural, and graceful.
- If you are able, go outdoors in simple clothing every day. When the weather permits, walk barefoot on grass, soil, or beach. Go on regular outings, especially to beautiful natural areas.
- Keep your home clean and orderly. Make your kitchen, bathroom, bedrooms, and living rooms shiny clean. Keep the atmosphere of your home bright and cheerful.
- Maintain an active correspondence. Express love and appreciation to your parents, husband or wife, children, brothers, sisters, relatives, friends, and associates.
- Try not to take long hot baths or showers unless you have been consuming too much salt or animal food.
- Every morning or every night, scrub your whole body with a hot, moist towel until your circulation becomes active. When a complete body scrub is not convenient, do at least your hands, feet, fingers, and toes.
- Use natural cosmetics, soaps, shampoos, and body care products. Brush your teeth with natural preparations or sea salt.
- Stay as physically active as you can. Daily activities such as cooking, scrubbing floors, cleaning windows, washing clothes, and others are excellent forms of exercise. You may also try systematic exercises such as yoga, martial arts, aerobics, and sports.
- Try to minimize time spent in front of the television. Color TV especially emits unnatural radiation that can be physically draining. Turn the TV off during mealtimes. Balance television with more productive activities.
- Heating pads, electric blankets, portable radios with earphones, and other electric devices can disrupt the body's

natural flow of energy. They are not recommended for regular use.

- Put many green plants in your living room, bedroom, and throughout the house to freshen and enrich the air.

EATING HABITS

The way in which we eat can be just as important as the choice of foods. Regular meals are better, and the amount of food eaten depends on each person's needs. Snacking is best in moderation so that it doesn't replace meals, while tea and other beverages can be enjoyed throughout the day as desired.

Chewing is also very important; try to chew each mouthful of food until it becomes liquid. Thorough chewing allows for the efficient digestion and absorption of foods. Chewing also mixes food with saliva, a natural substance that helps protect the body from illness.

You can eat whenever you feel hungry, but try to avoid eating before bedtime, preferably for three hours, except in unusual circumstances. Finally, learn to appreciate your foods and their health-giving properties. Let your gratitude overflow to include nature, the universe, other people, and all forms of life on this wonderful planet we call home.

THE PEACEFUL COOK

The attitude of the cook has a profound influence on the food he or she prepares and on the health and well-being of those who eat the meal. That is one reason why home-cooked meals prepared with love and care are better than restaurant meals prepared with indifference by strangers.

Ideally you should have a calm and peaceful mind when cooking. It also helps to visualize the people who will eat the meal and convey the positive energy of health to them through each dish prepared. Cooking with a positive, happy, and peaceful mind enhances your creativity. The best cooking is always inspired by the image of health and peace.

A variety of factors can get in the way of a peaceful state

of mind when you enter the kitchen. Two of the more common forms of interference are stress and fatigue.

Stress

In some cases people enter the kitchen after a stressful day at work followed by a long, tiring commute home. A certain amount of stress is inescapable in the modern world. However, it is better to leave your stress and tension at the kitchen door when you start to cook. The key to coping with stress is to keep your internal condition calm and relaxed, and the key to this is diet.

Foods such as meat, eggs, cheese, chicken, and other animal products produce tightness in the body. They also reduce flexibility and the capacity to respond creatively. In this condition we become more sensitive to external stress and feel that we are always under pressure. On the other hand, too much sugar, soft drinks, spices, tropical fruits, ice cream, chocolate, and similar foods creates hyperactive energy that contributes to the feeling that things are "out of control." A moderately balanced diet of whole grains and vegetables produces a calming and centering effect on the body and mind and relaxes feelings of tension or pressure. We become more relaxed, centered, and in control.

Eating well is the long-term answer to stress. Of course the other aspects of your lifestyle, whether or not you exercise, how you interact with others, and the goals you set for yourself either contribute to or lessen stress. In addition to eating well, the following practices are recommended to calm and center your energy. They can be done anytime or, if necessary, before you start cooking.

Body Scrubbing Scrubbing your body with a moist, hot towel is wonderfully relaxing and invigorating. It melts and relaxes stress and tension and takes only about 10 minutes.

Body scrubbing can be done before or after a bath or shower or anytime. All that is needed is a sink with hot water and a medium-sized cotton towel. Turn on the hot water. Hold the towel at either end and place the center part under the stream of hot water. Wring out the towel and, while it is still hot and steamy, begin to scrub with it. Do a section of the body at a time, for example beginning with the hands and fingers and working your way up the arms to the shoulders, neck and face, and then downward to the chest, upper back, abdomen, lower back, buttocks, legs, feet, and toes. Scrub until the skin turns slightly red or until each part becomes warm. Reheat the towel by running it under the hot water after scrubbing each area or as soon as it starts to cool.

Quiet Meditation   If you feel tense or mentally distracted, sitting quietly can help center your energy. Find a quiet space, sit with a straight but relaxed posture, close your eyes, and relax your breathing. Allow any unnecessary or distracting thoughts to leave your mind. Let yourself become peaceful and quiet. This simple practice harmonizes your energy and quiets the mind. It allows your intuition to flow smoothly without interference. After sitting quietly for five minutes or so you are ready to begin cooking or any other activity.

Being rushed or feeling the pressure of time is another form of stress. However, cooking is an art, and no great artist can create when rushed. Like a child playing or an artist in the midst of creation, we should detach ourselves from past and future and place ourselves firmly in the moment when we cook. Ideally cooking should be a form of creative play that fully absorbs our energies.

Fatigue

Cooking demands a certain amount of vitality, endurance, and patience. It is a kind of meditation in action that challenges us to remain calm and centered in the midst of focused activity. We need to maintain a relaxed yet alert state of mind when we cook.

Chronic fatigue or lack of energy interferes with our ability to cook and do other things in life. Lack of vitality is the reverse side of stress. Both arise when the body is forced to cope with an extreme diet on a daily basis.

Hypoglycemia, or low blood sugar, underlies many cases of fatigue. It is caused primarily by overintake of foods such as chicken, cheese, eggs, shellfish, and others that cause hard fats to accumulate in the pancreas. Fat interferes with the pancreas's ability to secrete glucagon—or antiinsulin—the hormone that normally raises the level of glucose, or sugar, in the blood to within the normal range. Insulin, which is complementary to glucagon, lowers the blood sugar level.

The symptoms of hypoglycemia include tiredness and chronic fatigue, depression, and cravings for sweets. These symptoms are especially acute in the late afternoon or early evening, when the sun begins to set. As the level of blood sugar dips below normal, the hypoglycemic person will reach for chocolate, soft drinks, or a cup of coffee with plenty of sugar in it in an attempt to raise it. However, since simple sugars are absorbed rapidly into the bloodstream and burn quickly, the level of sugar soon dips below normal and the person again experiences the symptoms of hypoglycemia. This repeating cycle results in chronic fatigue and depletion of energy.

The solution to hypoglycemia, and to the fatigue and other symptoms it produces, is to provide the body with a slow, steadily burning source of energy. Complex carbohydrates, especially in whole grains, beans, and sweet-tasting vegetables, provide the best source of this energy. Unlike simple sugars, complex carbohydrates do not produce extreme fluctuations in blood sugar levels, and they help restore the pancreas to normal functioning. It is also important to avoid the foods above and others that contribute to the buildup of fat in the pancreas. Sugar, chocolate, honey, and other extreme simple sugars are also best avoided. Below are special drinks and recommendations that can help accelerate recovery from hypoglycemia and chronic fatigue:

Sweet Vegetable Drink To prepare this special drink, cut equal amounts of carrots, onions, orange squash, and green cabbage into very fine pieces (refer to Part II for instructions on cutting). Place the cut vegetables in a pot with 4 times as much water, cover, and bring to a boil. Reduce the flame to low and simmer for 10–15 minutes. Remove from the stove and strain the liquid through a fine-meshed strainer into a large glass jar. The strained liquid—"sweet vegetable drink"—can be stored in the refrigerator for several days. One or two cups can be taken daily or several times per week, depending on the severity of the condition. Sweet vegetable drink may be continued indefinitely until the symptoms of hypoglycemia begin to diminish. To serve, heat in a saucepan until warm or allow it to sit for several minutes until it reaches room temperature. Sweet vegetable drink also helps relieve the craving for sugar and other sweets.

Ume-Sho-Kuzu   This drink, made from umeboshi plum, tamari soy sauce (known in Japanese as *shoyu*), and kuzu root powder, helps restore vitality and energy. Kuzu (or kudzu as it is known in the southern United States, where it is found in abundance) grows in the mountains of Japan and has very deep roots. It is traditionally harvested and processed by hand into a white chalklike substance. It is often used in macrobiotic cooking as a thickener in sauces, stews, and desserts. Along with promoting vitality, it strengthens the digestive organs. Umeboshi plums and tamari soy sauce, both known for their mild alkalizing effects in the body, also help restore vitality.

   To prepare ume-sho-kuzu, dilute a heaping teaspoon of kuzu powder in 2 teaspoons water. Add another cup of water and mix well. Then separate the meat of an umeboshi plum from the seed and add the meat. Bring the water to a boil, stirring constantly to prevent lumping. Reduce the flame to medium-low and simmer until thick and translucent. Near the end, add ½–1 teaspoon tamari soy sauce and simmer for several seconds more. For a lighter preparation, add a small amount of grated ginger at the end. Pour into a bowl or cup and drink hot. Take a bowl or cup three or four times per week for several weeks to help relieve chronic fatigue.

Ginger Body Scrub   Body scrubbing, which stimulates circulation, is also good for restoring vitality. A special body scrub, done with hot ginger water, is especially effective. To prepare a ginger body scrub, you will need a piece of fresh gingerroot about the size of your fist (available at most natural foods or Oriental markets), a flat metal grater, some cheesecloth, a medium-sized cotton towel, and a medium to large pot with a lid.

Grate the gingerroot on the metal grater and place a clump the size of a golf ball in a double layer of cheesecloth. Tie the cheesecloth at the top to form a sack. Then place a gallon of water in the pot and bring it up to but not over the boiling point. Just before the water starts to boil, turn the flame down to low.

Next, hold the sack over the pot and squeeze as much of the ginger juice as you can into the water. Then drop the sack into the pot. Make sure the water doesn't boil as this will weaken the effect of the ginger scrub. Place the lid on the pot and let the ginger sack simmer in the water for about five minutes. Then fold your towel several times lengthwise so that it becomes long and thin. Hold it from both ends and dip the center into the hot ginger water. Wring it out tightly, and if it is too hot to place on the skin, shake it slightly. Then begin scrubbing your body as described earlier. Many people find plain hot water body scrubbing more convenient during the week and use the ginger body scrub on the weekends when they have more time. One pot of hot ginger water can be used for two days of body scrubs. Simply reheat the water before using (don't bring it to a boil). The ginger body scrub is wonderfully refreshing and invigorating.

Exercise   Together with these simple practices, a regular program of exercise helps restore vitality and energy levels. Choose a form of exercise to suit your needs and make it a part of your daily lifestyle. Walking is also a very convenient form of nonstrenuous exercise. We recommend taking a half-hour walk every day, regardless of the weather.

Singing is also a wonderful form of exercise that lifts the spirit. We recommend singing a happy song every day. When the person in the kitchen is singing happily, we know that the meal is being prepared with joy.

Also, have confidence in what you are doing. Don't worry if your dishes don't turn out well every time you prepare them. If you make a mistake, try again. With time and patience your cooking will become graceful and effortless. Even as your cooking improves, however, remember that there is always much more to learn. Be creative and go beyond what you have done before. This spirit of challenge and adventure is an attribute shared by all good cooks.

PART II
THE MACROBIOTIC
KITCHEN

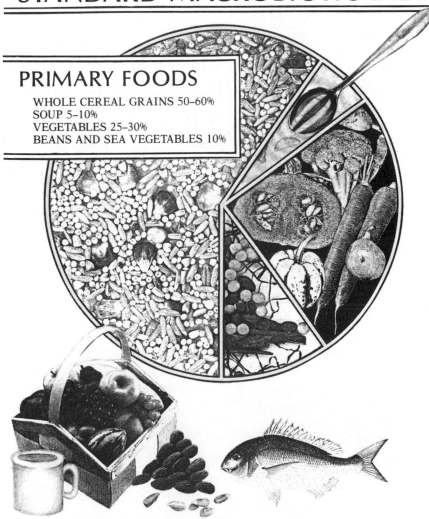

STANDARD MACROBIOTIC DIET

PRIMARY FOODS

WHOLE CEREAL GRAINS 50–60%
SOUP 5–10%
VEGETABLES 25–30%
BEANS AND SEA VEGETABLES 10%

SUPPLEMENTARY FOODS

SEASONINGS • CONDIMENTS • FISH • FRUITS • SNACKS •
SEEDS • NUTS • BEVERAGES • PICKLED VEGETABLES

6
FOODS IN THE STANDARD MACROBIOTIC DIET

In this chapter we introduce the Standard Macrobiotic Diet. Based on macrobiotic principles, the guidelines presented are broad and flexible and really quite simple to follow.

Similar dietary practices were observed by many of the world's cultures for thousands of years. Even before the dawn of recorded history, whole grains, beans, and fresh seasonal vegetables were considered the "staff of life." Today, as we have seen, the health benefits of these foods are increasingly being recognized by nutritionists and public health agencies around the world.

The foods in the Standard Macrobiotic Diet can be divided into primary and supplementary categories. The primary category consists of the macrobiotic "four food groups"—those foods eaten daily—while supplementary foods are those eaten either several times a week or daily but in very small amounts.

The percentages in the Standard Macrobiotic Diet come from an understanding of food as it relates to human development and evolution, as well as consideration of traditional dietary practices throughout the world. As we pointed out in Part I, human tooth structure shows that, ideally, about five parts of the diet are composed of whole grains, beans, seeds, and other fibrous plant foods, corresponding to the number of molars and premolars found in adults. The vast majority of this amount should be made up of whole grains—humanity's traditional staple food—with beans, seeds, and nuts eaten in much smaller amounts as supplementary foods. Half of this amount—roughly two parts of the diet—corresponds to the front incisors and is ideally made up of vegetables from land and sea, with land vegetables comprising the majority. The proportion of animal food, which corresponds to the canine teeth, can be up to one part of the diet. The overall ratio of plant to animal food, based on human tooth structure, is about seven to one.

These proportions are ideal in a temperate climate. People in the far northern or Arctic regions need a larger volume of animal food, while those in the equatorial zones can eat less. We also need to adjust the proportion and way of cooking foods when designing a diet for babies or children. (Guidelines for babies and children are presented in the book *Macrobiotic Child Care and Family Health,* by Michio and Aveline Kushi, Japan Publications.)

The percentages of foods in the Standard Macrobiotic Diet are based on the overall amount of food—calculated by approximate volume and not by weight—consumed each day. Therefore, it isn't necessary to include foods from each major category every time you eat, though we do recommend eating whole grains at each meal. Breakfast, for example, can be as simple as a bowl of whole-grain porridge with bancha tea or cereal grain coffee or can include lightly steamed vegetables, miso soup, whole-grain bread, and other side dishes. The number and variety of side dishes you prepare to complement your grain dishes depends on your appetite, preferences, and time available for cooking.

The menus and recipes in Part III are designed to reflect these general proportions. Grains are featured at every meal, and side dishes from each of the four food groups are included in the menus for each day. Preparing the meals as they are presented will make it easier for you to follow the guidelines of the Standard Macrobiotic Diet. However, how well you fulfill these percentages depends on how much of each food you actually eat, so care needs to be taken when serving each meal. After preparing the menus and dishes in this book, your sense of how to balance meals in accord with macrobiotic principles will become second nature.

The Standard Macrobiotic Diet *is* broad and flexible, so

don't be surprised by the wide variety of foods included in this chapter. Nor should you feel intimidated or overwhelmed. The foods discussed here are intended to show you how many choices you have; it isn't necessary to buy or use them all at once, especially when getting started. In the next chapter you'll find a shopping list for all of the items you'll need when preparing the recipes.

Most of the whole grains, beans, vegetables, and fruits listed below are familiar to everyone and require no explanation. Other foods in the Standard Macrobiotic Diet may be new and unfamiliar. Less familiar foods are explained briefly in this chapter as well as in the glossary at the back of the book. Actually, all of these foods have been part of traditional diets for centuries. Like tofu, another traditional "health food," items such as miso, sea vegetables, tempeh, and umeboshi plums are rapidly gaining acceptance on dinner tables throughout the world. We have found that the best way to familiarize yourself with these foods is to begin cooking with them.

On the following pages we list the foods that fall into the primary and supplementary categories in the Standard Macrobiotic Diet, along with information on their nutritional values. Expanding on the information in Part I, we also discuss research showing that many of these foods have specific value in preventing cancer, heart disease, and other chronic illnesses. In addition, we offer general suggestions on selecting the highest-quality foods (more specific tips on shopping for certain ingredients can be found in Chapter 7).

THE MACROBIOTIC FOUR FOOD GROUPS

Primary foods are divided into these groups:

1. Whole cereal grains and their products: 50 to 60 percent daily
2. Soups: 5 to 10 percent or approximately one or two small bowls daily
3. Fresh local vegetables: 25 to 30 percent daily
4. Beans, bean products, and sea vegetables: 10 percent daily

Whole Cereal Grains

Whole grains ideally should comprise up to 50 to 60 percent of daily intake. They are the most centrally balanced foods in terms of expanding and contracting, or yin and yang, energies and can be included as principal foods at each meal. It is much easier to create balance in your meals if they are based around whole grains.

Whole grains can be cooked by themselves, combined with other grains (for example, brown rice with barley, millet, or whole wheat berries), or combined with beans, bean products such as tofu and tempeh, or vegetables or sea vegetables. They can be pressure-cooked, boiled, fried, or crushed into flour to make products such as bread, muffins, pancakes, and cookies. They can also be used as the base for desserts, and sweeteners derived from grains such as brown rice or barley can be used in a number of ways. Whole-grain dishes are the centerpiece of the recipes and menus in this book: the hub of the wheel around which other side dishes revolve.

The complex carbohydrates, or polysaccharides, in whole grains exist together with an ideal balance of minerals, proteins, fats, and vitamins. These complex sugars are gradually and smoothly assimilated through the digestive organs, providing a slow and steady source of energy to the body. In the mouth, an enzyme in saliva initiates predigestive activity and is the main reason why all foods, and especially whole grains, need to be chewed well.

In contrast to the gradual burning of complex carbohydrates in grains, the predominantly simple carbohydrates, or sugars, in fruits, milk and other dairy food, sugar, honey, and other highly refined sweeteners burn faster, contributing to rapid and uneven digestion and erratic fluctuations in the body's metabolism. Refined sugar produces an immediate burst of energy—a sugar "high"—and the rapid depletion of energy in the inevitable "low" that comes afterward.

Whole grains are also high in niacin and other B vitamins, vitamin E, and vitamin A. The B group, in particular, along with complex carbohydrates, contributes to mental clarity. Because whole grains contain an ideal balance of protein, carbohydrates, fat, and vitamins and minerals, they are, nutritionally speaking, very well suited as principal foods.

Whole Grains for Use in Temperate Climates Below are the varieties of whole grains and grain products for regular use:

Brown Rice
Brown rice—short-, medium-, and long-grain
Genuine brown rice cream (the liquid squeezed from cooked brown rice)
Puffed brown rice
Brown rice flakes

Sweet Brown Rice
Sweet brown rice grain (a more glutinous variety of brown rice)
Mochi (pounded sweet rice)
Sweet brown rice flour products

Barley
Barley grain
Pearl barley (a special variety of barley known in Japanese as *hato mugi*)
Pearled barley
Puffed barley
Barley flour products

Oats
Whole oats
Steel-cut oats
Rolled oats
Oatmeal
Oat flakes
Oat flour products

Whole Wheat
Whole wheat berries
Whole-wheat flakes
Whole-wheat flour
Couscous
Bulgur
Fu (baked puffed wheat gluten)
Seitan (wheat gluten)
Whole-wheat bread
Whole-wheat chapati (and other unyeasted whole-wheat Near Eastern breads)
Whole-wheat noodles and pastas
Other whole-wheat flour products such as crackers, matzos, muffins, etc.

Corn
Corn on the cob
Corn grits
Corn flour
Cornmeal
Puffed corn
Popped corn
Arepas (traditional South American cakes made from whole corn)
Corn flour products such as bread, muffins, etc.

Millet
Millet grain
Millet flour products
Puffed millet

Buckwheat
Buckwheat groats (kasha)
Buckwheat noodles (soba)
  and pastas
Buckwheat pancakes

Rye
Rye grain
Rye flakes
Other rye flour products
Rye bread

When you begin to design your own menus, we recommend using brown rice as a principal grain (it can be eaten every day) with other grains used as supplements. Brown rice contains the most ideal balance of nutrients, as found in its ratio of minerals to protein to carbohydrate. It is also the easiest and most delicious to cook and eat in its whole form, without having to crush it into flour as is usually done with whole wheat. In order to ensure variety in your grain dishes, we suggest changing your grain recipes often. Brown rice, for example, is delicious when cooked by itself or when combined with barley, millet, or wheat berries (it is also delicious when combined with azuki or other beans). When preparing these combination dishes, use about 80 percent brown rice and about 20 percent other grain or bean. Other grains can be used in addition to brown rice up to three or four times per week.

Whole grains are one of the most versatile foods. When cooked with 1.5 or 2 times as much water, they make wonderful main dishes for use at any meal. At breakfast a wonderful whole-grain porridge can be made by cooking leftover grains from the night before with additional water. Although any of the grains can be used throughout the year, certain varieties can be emphasized as the seasons change. Wheat, barley, and rye are especially good as secondary grains in the spring, while corn (particularly in the form of corn on the cob) is very nice in the summer. Millet is especially flavorful in the early autumn, and brown rice (although fine as a staple year-round) is particularly good in the autumn. Buckwheat, the heartiest of the cereal plants and their relatives, is especially nourishing during the cold winter months.

High-Quality Grains   Cooked whole grains are easier to digest than flour products or cracked or rolled grains and are preferred for regular use. In general, it is better to keep intake of flour products or cracked or rolled grains to less than 15 to 20 percent of your daily intake of grains.

While it is growing, a grain such as brown rice is surrounded by a hard shell or husk, which is normally removed after harvest. The outer layer, or skin, of the grain contains proteins, enzymes, vitamins, and minerals. The inside portion is made up of complex carbohydrate. When rice is polished, or "refined," the outside skin is removed and white rice is left. In brown rice the outer skin is left intact, and each grain retains its essential nutrients.

The outermost layer of brown rice—the cellophanelike, transparent skin—is very resistant to chemicals but is very weak when it comes to physical attack. Brown rice grains are easily chipped, and once this has happened, oxidation occurs and the color and quality of the rice begin changing. The vitality and nutritional value of the grains are diminished.

In general, naturally grown, organic grains found in natural foods stores are fine for regular use. They can be purchased prepackaged or in bulk. The important point is to avoid using refined, polished, or chemically treated varieties.

Although the whole grains available in most natural foods stores are adequate for regular use, the highest-quality grains are grown organically, without pesticides or chemical fertilizers, and are hulled just before use. Unhulled rice must be ordered directly from the growers.

The highest-quality natural rice available today is called *paddy rice* and is purchased unhulled. The husk is removed in a home rice-hulling machine just before use. Among all grains, freshly hulled rice has the most perfect balance of energy and nutrients and the sweetest, most delicious flavor.

Information on home rice-hulling machines is available from the Kushi Foundation in Boston (see "Macrobiotic Resources" at the back of the book).

Soups

Soups should comprise 5 to 10 percent of each person's daily intake. For most people, that averages out to about one or two cups or small bowls of soup per day, depending on their needs and desires. Soups can include vegetables, grains, beans, sea vegetables, noodles or other grain products, bean products like tofu, tempeh, and others (the foods in the other three groups), or occasionally fish or seafood. Soups are actually not a separate category of food as much as a way of cooking and combining foods from the other categories. They are especially easy to digest. Digestion itself is the process of breaking down foods in a liquid medium (provided by saliva and other digestive juices), and by allowing foods to cook in plenty of water we accelerate this process. The notion that soups are easier to digest is a part of folk tradition around the world: for example, soup is often one of the first foods served to someone who is ill. Soup is often served at the beginning of the meal to ease the stomach and digestive organs into functioning, although it is not necessary to finish it before beginning to eat your other dishes. Although we don't usually think of soup as a breakfast food, miso soup has been used at breakfast for centuries in the Far East. It is especially delicious in the morning when served with grains and other simple side dishes. Soup can be enjoyed at any of your meals.

Soups are delicious when moderately seasoned with either miso, tamari soy sauce, sea salt, umeboshi plum or paste, or occasionally ginger. Spices and other highly expansive seasonings are best avoided in temperate climates.

Soups can be thick and rich or simple clear broths. The texture of soups can vary with seasonal change and personal desire. Vegetable, grain, or bean stews can also be enjoyed, while a variety of garnishes, such as scallions, parsley, nori sea vegetable, and croutons may be used to enhance the appearance and flavor of soups.

Miso Soup A second bowl or cup of another kind of soup may also be enjoyed, preferably mildly seasoned with tamari soy sauce or sea salt. Light miso soup, with vegetables and sea vegetables, is recommended daily.

As we saw in Part I, natural miso contains living enzymes that aid digestion. This highly nutritious food strengthens the quality of the blood and provides a wonderful balance of complex carbohydrates, essential oils, protein, vitamins, and minerals.

Natural miso, used for centuries in traditional diets, is now gaining recognition as an essential ingredient in a healthful way of eating. In 1981 the National Cancer Center of Japan, after completing a 10-year study on diet and cancer, reported that people who ate miso soup daily were 33 percent less likely to develop stomach cancer than those who never ate it. The study also found that miso was effective in preventing heart and liver disease.

Other Soups

- Bean and vegetable soups
- Grain (e.g., brown rice, millet, barley, pearl barley, etc.) and vegetable soups
- Pureed squash and other vegetable soups

High-Quality Miso The best miso is naturally aged for several summers or longer and is made from whole, round soybeans—without chemically treated ingredients or artificial aging procedures. It has a deep, rich flavor. Mugi (barley) miso is normally the best for regular use, followed by soybean (hatcho) miso.

Mugi miso is the most balanced among misos aged for the necessary length of time. Hatcho miso is stronger-flavored and can be used on occasion. Other misos, most of which are aged for less time than these varieties, can also be used on occasion. Often short-term misos are saltier than the mild-tasting, properly aged mugi miso.

Vegetables

Roughly one-quarter to one-third (25 to 30 percent) of

each person's daily intake should consist of vegetables. Nature provides an incredible variety of fresh seasonal vegetables to choose from. For those in temperate climates, centrally balanced vegetables from the same climate are recommended. Vegetables that originated in the tropics, such as tomatoes, potatoes, and eggplant, are too extreme for optimum health. Also, cooked vegetables are preferred to raw; although raw salads may be eaten several times a week by those in good health.

Vegetables can be served in soups or with grains, beans, or sea vegetables. They can also be used in rice rolls (homemade sushi), served with noodles or pasta, cooked with fish, or served alone. The methods for cooking vegetables introduced in this book include boiling, steaming, pressing, sautéing (both with water and with oil), and pickling. A variety of natural seasonings, including miso, tamari soy sauce, sea salt, and brown rice or umeboshi vinegar, are recommended to add taste and nutrients to vegetable dishes.

Grandmother's admonition to eat fresh vegetables is gaining support among many scientific and medical associations. Their importance in preventing and relieving degenerative diseases is now just beginning to command official attention. In its report *Diet, Nutrition and Cancer*, the National Academy of Sciences recommended daily consumption of yellow and orange vegetables such as carrots and winter squashes high in beta-carotene (a precursor to vitamin A) and green leafy vegetables, especially cabbage, broccoli, cauliflower, and brussels sprouts, as part of a prudent diet to help prevent cancer. The American Heart Association, the American Diabetes Association, and many other organizations have issued guidelines on vegetable consumption that are similar in direction to macrobiotic diet recommendations.

Fresh vegetables are high in complex carbohydrates, fiber, vitamins, and minerals. As part of a balanced whole foods diet, they help provide all of the nutrients essential for optimal health and vitality. The following are examples of nutrients found in particular vegetables:

- Winter squash, broad beans, burdock, dandelion greens, gingerroot, green peas, lotus root, shiitake mushrooms, onions, parsley, and parsnips are especially high in complex carbohydrates.
- Broad beans, broccoli, brussels sprouts, burdock, carrots, cauliflower, collard greens, daikon leaves, dandelion greens, gingerroot, green peas, kale, lotus root, mustard greens, parsley, parsnips, pumpkin, scallions, and winter squash are rich in fiber.
- Broccoli, carrots, daikon, dandelion greens, kale, mustard greens, and winter squash are high in vitamin A.
- Broccoli, brussels sprouts, cabbage leaves, cauliflower, chives, collard greens, watercress, kale, mustard greens, and turnip greens are good daily sources of vitamin C.
- Broccoli, collard greens, daikon leaves, dried daikon, dandelion greens, kale, mustard greens, parsley, turnip greens, and watercress contain substantial amounts of calcium.

Vegetables for Use in Temperate Climates   As we saw in Part I, whole grains have the most ideal balance of yin and yang energy. Beans are more yin than grains, and vegetables are more yin than beans. Because vegetables are as a category more yin, it is important to avoid those that are extremely yin. In the following table are a variety of factors that can be used when determining whether a vegetable has a more yin or yang quality. More extreme varieties are those with a warmer or tropical origin, a higher water content, a more rapid speed of growth, a strong spicy or sour taste, a higher fat content (such as avocado), and a high ratio of potassium to sodium. As you continue to cook and eat macrobiotically, your ability to judge the yin and yang quality of vegetables and other foods will become intuitive.

Acorn squash
Bok choy
Broccoli
Buttercup squash

Burdock root (a long brown root that grows uncultivated throughout North America)

Butternut squash
Cabbage
Celery
Celery root
Carrots
Carrot tops
Cauliflower
Chinese cabbage
Chives
Collard greens
Cucumbers
Daikon (long white radish)
Daikon greens
Dandelion greens
Dandelion root
Endive
Escarole
Green beans
Green peas
Hubbard squash
Hokkaido pumpkin (a
    variety of winter squash
    originally grown in
    northern Japan)
Iceberg lettuce
Jinenjo (Japanese mountain
    potato)
Jerusalem artichoke
Kale
Kohlrabi
Leeks
Lotus root (the edible root
    of the lotus flower)
Mushrooms
Mustard greens
Onions
Pak choy
Parsley
Parsnips
Pumpkin
Patty pan squash
Radishes
Red cabbage
Romaine lettuce
Scallions
Shiitake mushrooms (fresh
    or dried Japanese
    mushrooms)
Snap beans
Summer squash
Turnips
Turnip greens
Watercress
Wax beans

High-Quality Vegetables As much as possible, try to use vegetables that are organic and natural. Canned, frozen, and (in temperate zones) vegetables of tropical origin are best avoided. Scientific tests show that organic produce contains up to three times more minerals and trace elements than inorganic vegetables. In one study, supermarket vegetables were found to have as little as 25 percent of the mineral content of organic vegetables. If you are unable to start a backyard organic garden, look for high-quality vegetables at natural foods stores, co-ops, or farmer's markets.

Yin and Yang in the Vegetable Kingdom

	Yin (▽) Centrifugal	Yang (△) Centripetal
Environment:	Warmer, more tropical	Colder, more polar
Season:	Grows more in spring and summer	Grows more in autumn and winter
Soil:	More watery and sedimentary	More dry and volcanic
Growing direction:	Vertically growing upward; expanding horizontally underground	Vertically growing downward; expanding horizontally above the ground
Growing speed:	Growing faster	Growing slower
Size:	Larger, more expanded	Smaller, more compacted
Height:	Taller	Shorter
Texture:	Softer	Harder
Water content:	More juicy and watery	More dry
Color:	Purple—blue—green—yellow—brown—orange—red	
Odor:	Stronger smell	Less smell
Taste:	Spicy—sour—sweet—salty—bitter	
Chemical components:	More K and other yin elements	Less K and other yin elements
	Less Na and other yang elements	More Na and other yang elements
Nutritional components:	Fat—protein—carbohydrate—mineral	
Cooking time:	Faster cooking	Slower cooking

Beans and Sea Vegetables

Nutritionally beans and sea vegetables complement each other well. Beans are rich in fat and protein, and these nutritional factors are well balanced by the minerals present in sea vegetables. As you will notice in the recipes, beans are usually cooked with kombu, a nutrient-rich sea vegetable, in order to help balance their protein and fat content and make them more digestible and easier to cook.

Beans and Bean Products   About 5 percent of daily meals should include beans or bean products. Beans that are smaller in size—such as azuki, chick-peas, and lentils—usually contain less fat and more protein and are more like grains in terms of energy and nutrients (and are therefore more centrally balanced), so they are preferred for regular use.

A variety of other nutrients are found in beans. They are very high in calcium, phosphorus, iron, thiamine, niacin, and vitamin E. Although they contain only modest amounts of vitamin A, beans contain phosphatides that increase the absorption of beta-carotene, the precursor to vitamin A found in carrots and other yellow and orange vegetables. Fermented soy foods, especially tempeh and miso, all contain vitamin B_{12}, an important nutrient otherwise found primarily in animal foods, and eating these foods regularly ensures an adequate supply.

For centuries, beans have formed a central part in the cuisine of all traditional cultures, and their nutritional superiority to animal foods is beginning to be recognized by modern scientists. Beans and bean products contain about twice as much protein as a comparable amount of meat or dairy food, their fat is unsaturated in quality, and they are entirely free of cholesterol. Beans and bean products are also very high in calcium. Tofu, for example, contains more calcium by weight than dairy milk.

Beans and bean products are digested more easily when cooked with a small volume of seasonings such as sea salt, miso, or kombu sea vegetable. They may also be prepared with vegetables, chestnuts, dried apples, or raisins or occasionally sweetened with grain sweeteners like barley malt and rice honey. Beans and bean products may be served in soups and side dishes or cooked with grains or sea vegetables. You may select from any of the following:

Beans
Azuki beans
Black-eyed peas
Black turtle beans
Black soybeans
Chick-peas (garbanzo beans)
Great northern beans
Kidney beans
Lentils (green and red)
Lima beans
Mung beans
Navy beans
Pinto beans
Soybeans
Split peas
Whole dried peas
Bean sprouts

Bean Products
Dried tofu (soybean curd that has been naturally dried)
Fresh tofu
Okara (pulp or residue left from making tofu)
Natto (fermented soybeans)
Yuba (dried soy milk)
Tempeh (fermented soybeans or combination of soybeans and grains)

High-Quality Beans and Bean Products

True organically grown beans are grown in soil that has not been subjected to chemical fertilizers or pesticides for at least several years. In terms of growing procedures this produces a higher-quality bean. After harvest, beans are cleaned and bagged. About 10 to 15 percent are lost in the process to damage or cracking. At the natural foods store or market, beans should be well formed, uniform in size, smooth-skinned, and generally full and shiny in color. Spots, flecks, streaks, wrinkles, and pits show that the beans have lost their vitality. Beans that are open at the seams are called *fish-eyes*. These show oxidation from drying too quickly. Good-quality beans should have only 1 to 2 percent broken skins and surface chips.

In purchasing tofu, several considerations of quality need

to be kept in mind. Traditionally, tofu is solidified from soy milk with a mineral-rich substance called *nigari* in a way that is somewhat similar to the curding of dairy cheese with rennet. Nigari is the concentrated residue, rich in magnesium and other mineral compounds, remaining from sea salt that has been extracted from sea water. Another good-quality natural solidifier is unrefined calcium sulfate, which is obtained in the mountains from gypsum. Today most of the tofu available in the Far East and Oriental foods stores is made with vinegar, alum, refined calcium sulfate, or other low-quality ingredients. Good-quality tofu should be made with organic soybeans and real nigari or natural calcium sulfate. If these are unavailable, lemon juice is the best substitute.

Sea Vegetables   Sea vegetables may be used daily in cooking, making up about 5 percent of daily food. Side dishes can be made with arame or hijiki and included several times per week. Wakame and kombu can be used daily in miso and other soups, in vegetable and bean dishes, or as condiments. Toasted nori is also recommended for daily or regular use, while agar-agar can be used from time to time in making a natural gelled dessert known as kanten (agar-agar also has natural laxative properties).

Sea vegetables are among the most nutritious foods and have long been valued for their health-giving properties. Dried sea vegetables are high in complex carbohydrates, fiber, protein, vitamins, and minerals and low in fat. Polysaccharides account for about 50 to 60 percent of their weight, protein up to 7 percent, and minerals and vitamins up to 30 percent. The remaining 10 to 20 percent is water, plus only about 1 to 2 percent fat.

Sea vegetables contain proportionally more minerals than any other type of food. Nori, for instance, has from 2 to 4 times more vitamin A than carrots and 10 times more than spinach. Hijiki, wakame, and arame have from 11 to 14 times more calcium than milk. Kombu, wakame, arame, hijiki, and nori have from 3 to 8 times more iron than beef.

In the Far East, sea vegetables are the main source of

iodine in the diet, so refined, chemically iodized salt is not necessary. Sea vegetables are also proportionately higher in vitamin A, thiamine, riboflavin, vitamin B_6, vitamin B_{12}, and niacin than most land vegetables and fruits. Nori is also rich in vitamin C and protein.

Recent scientific studies have upheld many of the traditional beliefs associating sea vegetables with a variety of health benefits. In 1984 medical researchers at Harvard University reported that a diet containing 5 percent kombu significantly delayed the inducement of breast cancer in experimental animals. Extrapolating these results to human subjects, the investigators concluded, "Seaweed may be an important factor in explaining the low rates of certain cancers in Japan." Japanese women, whose diet normally includes about 3 to 5 percent sea vegetables, have from three to nine times less breast cancer incidence than American women, for whom sea vegetables are not a part of the usual diet.

Sea Vegetables for Use in Temperate Climates Below is a list of the sea vegetables for use in macrobiotic cooking:

Arame	Kombu
Agar-agar	Nori
Dulse	Sea palm
Hijiki	Wakame
Irish moss	

High-Quality Sea Vegetables

Sea vegetables are generally among the least processed and safest natural foods. Unlike mushrooms and other wild plants, there are no toxic varieties of sea vegetables. Some species are noxious-smelling, tough, and bad-tasting, but they are not harmful. For foragers today, the primary concern is chemical pollution, which can affect the quality of life growing below the water as well as above. A clean shore away from industrial areas and possible toxic material that has seeped into the water is best.

In addition to these considerations, the quality of sea vegetables depends on a variety of environmental factors. Water temperature, ocean currents, the cycle of the tides, intensity of the sunlight striking the water, and the relative roughness or calmness of the sea will also affect the natural properties of the plants as well as their taste, flavor, and texture when cooked. Growing season is also very important. Sea vegetables that have aged too long are tough, lose color, and have less taste. Traditionally the time and season of harvesting were carefully observed in order to obtain the freshest and most delicious young fronds.

As with other natural foods, sea vegetables are ideally consumed in whole form as much as possible rather than processed. Dulse, kelp, and nori are often manufactured into flakes, powders, and in some cases capsules and pills. Some of these products are naturally processed and may be used occasionally. However, they should not be the primary regular form in which sea vegetables are consumed. Moreover, like making flour from wheat berries at home, making sea vegetable condiments from whole sea vegetables by grinding in a suribachi or bowl and roasting gives a fresher quality and retains more of the energy and nutrients of the original than store-bought products.

Supplementary Foods

Supplementary foods are those that are eaten periodically, usually several times per week, or daily in very small amounts.

Foods eaten periodically include:

1. Low-fat white-meat fish: an average of once or twice per week
2. Seasonal fruits: about three or four times per week
3. Seeds and nuts: several times per week on average

Other supplementary foods, some of which are eaten daily, include:

1. Sea salt, miso, tamari soy sauce, and other natural seasonings
2. Umeboshi plums and other condiments
3. Pickled vegetables
4. Garnishes

5. Desserts using sugar-free, grain-based sweeteners
6. Snacks
7. Natural, caffeine-free beverages

Fish and Shellfish

Fish and shellfish can be eaten on occasion to supplement the primary foods. Amounts eaten can vary, depending on each person's needs and desires, but generally seafood can be eaten once or twice a week as a part of a balanced meal. White-meat varieties, which are lower in saturated fat and more easily digested than blue-skinned and red-meat types, are recommended for regular use.

Garnishes are especially important in balancing fish and seafood. In general, garnishes provide nice yin balance to certain dishes. Soba or buckwheat noodles offer an example. By themselves, soba, which are more yang or contractive, are a little one-sided. Freshly chopped scallions or parsley adds a touch of yin that makes a bowl of noodles more complete. Other garnishes can also be used to help dissolve or counteract the effects of fat or oil, such as that in fish and fried foods. Recommended garnishes include chopped scallions or parsley, grated raw daikon, ginger, radish or horseradish, green mustard paste (wasabi), and raw salad.

Fish is generally served as a side dish at the main meal, along with whole grains, vegetables, soup, and other foods. Also, since fish has a more yang or contracting quality, cooked fruit or other natural desserts are often included in meals that include fish.

Fish and shellfish are high in protein, contain unsaturated rather than saturated fat, and have plenty of B vitamins. In northern regions where the growing season is short and whole grains and vegetables are less plentiful, seafood is an important supplementary source of these nutrients.

Traditional societies that consumed high volumes of fish and seafood, such as the Inuit (Eskimo), remained relatively healthy and active. Medical studies have shown that such cultures showed no signs of heart disease, cancer, or other degenerative disease until modern civilization brought them into contact with white sugar, white flour, and other processed foods.

In the industrialized nations, nutritionists and scientists have recommended that meat and dairy foods be substantially reduced and replaced in the diet by fish and shellfish that are low in fat and cholesterol. Researchers have recently identified a fatty acid found in fish, in some marine oils, and in sea vegetables and other plant foods that is protective against thrombosis, the formation or presence of a blood clot inside a blood vessel or the heart itself. The substance in the fish, EPA or eicosapentaenoic acid (also known as omega-3), was shown to lower serum cholesterol up to 17 percent in healthy persons and 20 percent or more in heart patients. EPA has also been shown to lower triglycerides (fats that circulate in the blood) and to reduce inflammatory arthritis. EPA has been found in sea vegetables as well as in soybeans and soy foods such as tofu.

Seafood Choices for Temperate Climates

Regular Use

Carp	Scrod
Cod	Smelt
Small dried fish (iriko)	Snapper
Flounder	Sole
Haddock	Trout
Halibut	Other white-meat fish
Herring	

Occasional Use

Cherrystone clams	Lobster
Littleneck clams	Oyster
Crab	Shrimp

Infrequent Use

Bluefish	Tuna
Salmon	Other blue-skinned and
Sardines	red-meat fish
Swordfish	

High-Quality Seafood Until recently, fish was one of the least contaminated and least processed foods. However, in modern times its quality has been greatly affected by pollution, and seafood has been subjected to many potentially harmful industrial processing techniques. Finding a reliable source of truly fresh and uncontaminated fish is very important for people who wish to include this supplementary food in their diet. As a general rule, saltwater species are less polluted than freshwater varieties. Among deep-water species, moreover, white-meat fish are less fatty and oily than red-meat and blue-skinned varieties. Store-bought fish and shellfish should be obtained fresh as often as possible rather than frozen, smoked, canned, prestuffed, prebreaded, concentrated, or otherwise commercially processed. However, fish or shellfish that has been dried, pickled, or naturally processed without artificial preservatives may be used occasionally.

Fruit

In the macrobiotic diet, fruits are regarded as supplemental foods and eaten mainly for variety and enjoyment. Compared to whole grains, beans, and vegetables from land and sea, fruits contain much smaller amounts of complex carbohydrates, fiber, protein, unsaturated fat, and essential vitamins and minerals. They are largely made up of water. Fructose, the primary carbohydrate in fruit, is a simple sugar and enters the bloodstream more rapidly than the complex carbohydrates found in grains and vegetables. Moreover, the energy fruits give is very light and expansive and needs to be balanced by the strong centering energy of the other foods recommended in macrobiotics to maintain health and vitality.

In most cases fruit can be enjoyed three or four times per week. Locally grown or temperate-climate fruits are preferable, while tropical fruits—which are extremely expansive—are not recommended for regular use in temperate zones. Cooked or dried fruits are preferable; raw fruit in season is fine for occasional use by those in good health.

Fruits Suitable for Consumption in Temperate Climates

Apples	Plums
Apricots	Raisins
Blackberries	Raspberries
Cantaloupe	Strawberries
Grapes	Tangerines
Honeydew melon	Watermelon
Lemons	Wild berries (loganberries,
Mulberries	boysenberries,
Persimmons	dewberries, huckleberries,
Peaches	cranberries)

In general citrus fruit is not recommended for regular consumption by persons living in the temperate zones. However, small amounts can be used as special garnishes (for example to balance fish) or in special salads during the summer. Lemons, because of their smaller size and sour taste, are less expansive than sweet, juicy oranges and can therefore be used more often. Tangerines are also less expansive than oranges and can also be used on occasion.

High-Quality Fruit   Obtaining good-quality fruit is essential because of the poor quality of most commercially available varieties. Whenever possible, try to obtain organically grown fruit. Organic or more naturally grown fruit will generally be slightly smaller in size and duller in appearance and will contain more blemishes and evidence of nibbling by small insects than commercially grown fruit. However, it will generally have a more symmetrical shape, fresher aroma, and sweeter taste than the other kind.

Pickles

Pickles can be eaten frequently as a supplement to main dishes. They stimulate appetite and help digestion. Some varieties—such as pickled daikon, or takuan—can be bought prepackaged in natural foods stores. Other quick pickles can be prepared at home. Certain varieties take just a few hours to prepare, while others require more time.

A wide variety of pickles are fine for regular use, including salt, salt brine, bran, miso, tamari, umeboshi vinegar, and others. Sauerkraut may also be used in small volume on a regular basis.

Good Pickle Choices
Natural sauerkraut
Umeboshi pickles (see index for recipe)
Tamari soy sauce pickles (see index for recipe)
Brine pickles (see index for recipe)
Takuan pickles
Ginger pickles

High-Quality Pickles   The best pickles are made from natural ingredients, such as fresh organic vegetables, high-quality natural sea salt, and naturally fermented miso, tamari soy sauce, umeboshi, and vinegars. Pickles processed with strong spices, sugar, artificial vinegar, or chemicals are best avoided for maximum health. Spicy pickles, for example, are often eaten to balance the consumption of meat and other animal foods. However, in temperate climates the intake of strong spices or artificial vinegar creates imbalance with the surrounding environment and can weaken health.

Seeds and Nuts
Seeds and nuts can be eaten from time to time as snacks and garnishes: up to 1½ cups of lightly roasted seeds may be eaten per week; ½ to 1 cup of lightly roasted nuts. They can be roasted with or without sea salt, sweetened with barley or rice malt, or seasoned with tamari soy sauce. Seeds and nuts can be ground into butter, shaved and served as a topping or garnish, or used as an ingredient in desserts and other dishes. Below are varieties that can be used.

Seeds and nuts contain many essential nutrients. Compared to meat and dairy products, they are a much better source of protein, and their fat and oil are either neutral or unsaturated. However, their composition is not as balanced as that of whole grains. Seeds and nuts are much higher in fat, higher in protein, and much lower in complex carbohydrates. Chestnuts, which are more like grains, are an exception. They contain up to 50 times less fat than other common nuts, less protein, and from two to four times as much complex carbohydrates.

Seeds and nuts are also very high in fiber, iron, calcium, vitamins A, B, and E, and other minerals and vitamins. Sesame seeds and pumpkin seeds are especially rich in iron, containing about five times more than meat and more than any other plant foods except sea vegetables. Sesame seeds are also a major source of calcium, containing about 10 times that of a comparable amount of dairy milk. In medical studies, cancer researchers have recently identified an ingredient in seeds called a *protease inhibitor* that helps protect against tumor development.

Seeds and Nuts for Use in Temperate Climates
Nuts (More Regular Use)

Almonds	Pecans
Chestnuts	Pine nuts
Filberts	Spanish peanuts
Peanuts	Walnuts

Nuts (Infrequent Use)

Brazil nuts	Macadamia nuts
Cashews	Others

Seeds

Alfalfa seeds	Squash seeds
Poppy seeds	Sunflower seeds
Pumpkin seeds	Umeboshi plum seeds
Sesame seeds, black and white	Others

High-Quality Seeds and Nuts   Whenever possible, try to find seeds and nuts that are grown organically and unprocessed.

Snacks
Snacks can be eaten whenever someone is hungry (preferably not before going to bed or as "midnight snacks" during the night). They can be enjoyed in between meals, at home or at work. As long as the quality is high and people chew

them well, snacking is fine within the practice of macrobiotics.

A variety of natural snacks may be enjoyed from time to time, including those made from whole grains, like cookies, bread, puffed cereals, mochi (pounded sweet brown rice), rice cakes, rice balls, and homemade sushi. Nuts and seeds may also be used as snacks, for example by roasting them with sea salt or tamari soy sauce or sweetening them with grain-based sweeteners.

High-Quality Snacks For optimal health, it is best to select the highest-quality natural snacks and avoid items made with refined sweeteners, honey, carob, tropical fruits, or poor-quality oils. Snacks made from foods within the Standard Macrobiotic Diet are preferred and can often be made simply at home. Those that are easiest to digest, such as rice balls, homemade sushi, mochi, noodles, and steamed whole-grain bread, are preferred for regular use. Hard, baked flour products, such as crackers, cookies, and muffins, can interfere with digestion when eaten in excess.

Condiments

Condiments and garnishes, which are both added to dishes after they are cooked, offer a good example of yin and yang. Most of the condiments used in macrobiotic cooking add taste and nutrients, especially minerals, to dishes. Their quality is generally more yang. Garnishes usually consist of uncooked or lightly cooked scallions, parsley, and other vegetables, and have a lighter, more yin quality. Condiments concentrate the energy and nutrients in dishes, while garnishes lighten it. Both help to adjust the energy and nutrient balance in your dishes. Seasonings are different in the sense that they are added to dishes during cooking and not afterward.

Small amounts of a variety of condiments can be sprinkled on foods to adjust taste and nutritional value and to stimulate appetite. They can be used on grains, soups, vegetables, beans, and sometimes desserts. Some condiments may be used daily and others occasionally.

Daily Use
Gomashio (roasted sesame seeds and sea salt)
Sea vegetable powders (with or without roasted sesame
   seeds)
Tekka (a special condiment made with soybean miso,
   sesame oil, burdock, lotus root, carrots, and ginger)
Umeboshi (pickled salt) plums

Occasional Use
Roasted sesame seeds
Roasted and chopped shiso (pickled beefsteak plant) leaves
Shio kombu (kombu cooked with tamari and water)
Green nori flakes
Cooked nori condiment
Cooked miso with scallions or onions
Umeboshi or brown rice vinegar

Sea vegetable powders are an excellent way to introduce mineral-rich sea vegetables into the meal and are tasty on whole grains, noodles, salads, soups, and other dishes. Those made with nori and dulse are the lightest-tasting and are rich in iron. Kombu and kelp powders are the heaviest-tasting, and wakame powders have a saltier flavor. Sea vegetable powders are prepared by roasting the sea vegetable for about 10 to 15 minutes, until dark and crisp, and crushing and grinding in a suribachi until it becomes a fine powder. They may be combined with roasted sesame seeds for variation. Sea vegetable powders can also be purchased in natural foods stores.

On average these condiments can be used two or three times per week. Since the condiments tend to have a salty taste, using too many of them is not recommended. Only small amounts are enough to add nutrients and make balance within dishes.

Among these condiments, gomashio, or sesame salt, is especially nutritious. It is rich in calcium, iron, and other nutrients and is an excellent source of polyunsaturated vegetable oil in whole form. Also, because they are roasted, the sesame seeds in gomashio are easier to digest. The roasted salt with which they are combined provides a harmonious balance to the oil in the seeds. A small amount of gomashio can be used daily; it is especially delicious on brown rice and other whole grains.

Tekka, a traditional condiment made of burdock, carrots, lotus root, hatcho miso, and ginger that have been cooked down into a concentrated black powder, is also recommended for regular use. Since it provides very strong, concentrated energy, tekka is best used in small amounts sprinkled on grains, noodles, and other dishes.

It takes about 16 hours to prepare tekka at home, but the ready-made tekka available at natural foods stores is generally of perfectly acceptable quality.

Umeboshi plums, which are available ready to eat at most natural foods stores, are also recommended for regular use. They grow in the warmer southern and middle regions of Japan and are related to the apricot. Traditionally fermented with sea salt and pickled with shiso leaves, umeboshi plums combine a sour and salty taste. They are a very balanced food, give a strong centering energy, and have a wide range of uses.

High-Quality Condiments The proportion of sesame seeds to sea salt can vary from about 10 to 1 to 18 to 1, depending on activity level and climate. For children, who need much less salt than adults, a ratio of 20 to 25 to 1 can be used. The best-quality sesame seeds for use in gomashio are natural black sesame seeds. It is important to be careful when choosing seeds, however, because some black seeds are dyed. To distinguish dyed seeds from natural black seeds, put them in water. If the seeds have been dyed, the artificial coloring in them will gradually dissolve and the water will turn black.

Seasonings

A variety of seasonings can be used in macrobiotic cooking, but as a rule it is best to avoid strongly expansive seasonings such as curry, hot pepper, and other spices and use those that are naturally processed from vegetable products or natural sea salt. These traditional seasonings have more centrally balanced energy, though even these should be used in small amounts.

High-Quality Seasonings   Salt is essential to life. The discovery of fire and salt enabled our ancestors to adapt to practically any environment on the earth and signaled the beginning of civilization. Throughout the world, salt is probably the most common seasoning, and overuse of poor-quality refined table salt is one of the major factors in the rise of chronic illness in modern society. The modern diet usually contains about three to four times the amount of sodium in the macrobiotic diet. In addition to the large amount of refined salt used in frozen, canned, and convenience foods and salt added to foods at the table, sodium is consumed in large volume in animal foods, including eggs, meat, poultry, and dairy products. Excessive sodium from these sources as well as refined salt is a major factor in some forms of cardiovascular disease and other degenerative conditions.

Recommended Seasonings
Unrefined sea salt
Tamari soy sauce (fermented soybean and grain sauce)
Miso (fermented soybean and grain paste; e.g., rice, barley,
    soybean, sesame, and other misos)
Brown rice and umeboshi vinegar
Barley malt and rice syrup
Grated daikon, radish, and ginger
Umeboshi plum and paste
Lemon, tangerine, and orange juice
Green and yellow mustard paste
Sesame, corn, safflower, mustard seed, and olive oil
Mirin (fermented sweet brown rice sweetener)
Amasake (fermented sweet brown rice beverage)

Good-quality vinegar provides a pleasant sour flavor to dishes and is used in macrobiotic food preparation. The best-quality vinegars are naturally processed brown rice and sweet brown rice vinegar. Another type of vinegar regularly used in the macrobiotic kitchen is umeboshi vinegar, also marketed as ume-su. Good-quality apple cider vinegar is much more acidic than grain-based vinegars and is used very occasionally for variety or enjoyment. Wine vinegars and commercial vinegars containing herbs, spices, and additives are avoided in macrobiotic food preparation.

Brown rice vinegar and sweet rice vinegar give a wonderful sour taste and make excellent sauces and dressings. They are not ordinarily used in cooking or soups, but a touch may be added occasionally to soften burdock or sea vegetables, especially if the latter are hard and salty. Umeboshi vinegar also makes flavorful dressings and sauces. It is occasionally added from the beginning of cooking to cabbage, cauliflower, and red radishes. Umeboshi vinegar is also sometimes added to noodles, salads, and steamed greens and is used in making a variety of quick pickles.

Mirin, a liquid natural sweetener made from fermented sweet rice, and sake, the traditional rice wine of Japan, are traditionally used in small volume for holiday cooking or other special occasions. Mirin or sake may be added from time to time to sweeten whole grains, beans, sea vegetables, and vegetables. Mirin in particular mellows the flavor of excessively salty or overly spicy foods. A touch of mirin added to noodle broths, dressings, sauces, or marinades gives a unique, subtle taste.

Amasake is made from fermented sweet rice and a grain starter called koji. It is creamy, thick, and delicious. White or beige in color, amasake may be used as a sweetener for pies, cakes, puddings, and other desserts in addition to being served warm or chilled as a porridge or beverage. When combined with other ingredients and cooked, amasake gives a thick texture and refreshing, delicious taste. It may be made at home or purchased at selected macrobiotic natural foods stores.

Barley malt is made by fermenting barley and cooking down the resulting liquid. It has a rich, toasted flavor, a dark opaque color, and thick consistency. It is used in pies, cakes, puddings, and other desserts. It is important to obtain the

100 percent variety rather than barley malt that has been mixed with refined corn syrup. A very delicious malt concentrate made from pearl barley and one that tastes like butterscotch is imported from Japan under the name Hato Mugi Malt.

Rice syrup is white, transparent, or amber in color and has a much milder flavor and delicate texture than barley malt. It is usually made with a small amount of barley malt. The subtle flavor and light taste of rice syrup are enjoyed on pancakes and waffles, with cooked fruit, in cookies, pies, and baked goods, and in teas and beverages. Rice syrup is also known as *rice malt, rice honey,* or *ame.* It is also sold under the trade name Yinnie Syrup.

In temperate climates natural sweeteners of tropical origin such as raw sugarcane, date sugar, chocolate, carob, and sorghum molasses are generally avoided. These products are high in fructose, glucose, or sucrose and can cause elevated blood sugar levels. Most chocolate and carob products, moreover, are usually prepared with refined sugar, dairy milk, hydrogenated oil, or other poor-quality ingredients.

The quality of salt, the amount consumed, and the way salt is used in cooking are paramount issues in the life of an individual, family, community, and culture. In proper volume, high-quality unrefined natural sea salt, containing trace minerals and elements, contributes to smooth metabolism, steady energy and vitality, and a clear, focused mind. Unrefined sea salt (usually available only in natural foods stores or through natural foods mail order companies) made in the largely traditional manner contains compounds of several minerals such as magnesium as well as trace amounts of about 60 other elements naturally found in the sea. The proportion of trace minerals varies according to the way in which the salt is processed, usually from a high of about 3 percent to a low of 0.5 percent.

There are various types of sea salt, ranging in color from white to off-white to gray. White sea salt is the best for daily cooking. Gray or off-white salt is not recommended for cooking but can be used when making pickles that require a long time for aging, such as whole pickled root vegetables.

Regular table salt is a highly industrialized product containing about 99.5 percent sodium chloride. While it is made from either sea salt or rock salt, most of the natural trace elements have been removed in processing, and magnesium carbonate, sodium carbonate, and potassium iodide have been substituted. Furthermore, dextrose, a highly refined industrial sugar, is customarily added to table salt to stabilize the iodine.

Natural soy sauce, known in macrobiotics as *tamari*, should also be the highest quality. Soy sauce is traditionally made from organically grown soybeans and wheat, good-quality water, and unrefined sea salt that have fermented naturally for several years in well-aged cedar vats. Modern commercial soy sauces are a far different product. They are made with defatted soybean meal, chemically grown grains, and refined salt and usually contain monosodium glutamate, caramel, sugar, or other additives or preservatives. Moreover, commercial varieties are aged artificially in temperature-controlled stainless-steel or epoxy-coated vats to reduce their aging to several months. Their taste is harsh and flat in comparison to natural tamari soy sauce.

Garnishes

A variety of garnishes can be used to create balance within a dish and facilitate digestion.

Recommended Garnishes

Grated daikon (for fish, mochi, noodles, and other dishes)
Grated radish (used like grated daikon)
Grated horseradish (used mostly for fish and shellfish)
Chopped scallions (for noodles, fish and shellfish, etc.)
Parsley
Lemon, tangerine, and orange slices (mainly for fish and
    shellfish)

Desserts

The sweet flavor in macrobiotic cooking comes primarily from the complex carbohydrates in whole grains, beans, and fresh vegetables. Carbohydrates are generally known as sugars, but in speaking of sugar it is important to specify the variety. Single sugars, or monosaccharides, are found in fruit and honey and include glucose and fructose. Double sugars or disaccharides are found in cane sugar and milk and include sucrose and lactose. Complex sugars or polysaccharides are found in grains, beans, and vegetables. In the normal digestive process, complex sugars are decomposed gradually and at a nearly even rate by various enzymes in the mouth, stomach, pancreas, and intestines. Complex sugars enter the bloodstream slowly after being broken down into smaller saccharide units. During the process, the pH of the blood maintains a normally healthy slightly alkaline quality.

By contrast, simple (single and double) sugars are metabolized quickly, causing the blood to become overacidic. To compensate, our chemical metabolism uses stored minerals, including calcium, for buffer reactions that are necessary to maintain blood alkalinity. This process produces excessive carbon dioxide and water that are normally eliminated through breathing and urination. Moreover, the intake of refined sugar causes the pancreas to secrete insulin, which allows excess sugar in the blood to be removed and enter the cells of the body. This produces a burst of energy as the glucose (the end product of all sugar metabolism) is oxidized and carbon dioxide and water are given off as waste products.

Much of the sugar that enters the bloodstream is originally stored in the liver in the form of glycogen until needed, when it is again changed into glucose. When the amount of glycogen exceeds the liver's storage capacity of about 50 grams, it is released into the bloodstream in the form of fatty acid. This fatty acid is stored first in the more inactive places of the body, such as the buttocks, thighs, and midsection. Then, if cane sugar, fruit sugar, dairy sugar, and other simple sugars are eaten excessively, fatty acid continuously becomes attracted to organs such as the heart, liver, and kidneys, which gradually become filled with fatty mucus.

As these accumulations penetrate the inner tissues, the normal functioning of the organs begins to weaken. In some cases, blockage—as in atherosclerosis—can occur. The buildup of fat can also lead to the formation of cysts, tumors, and eventually cancer. Still another form of degeneration may occur when the body's internal supply of minerals is mobilized to offset the effects of simple sugar consumption. For example, calcium in the teeth and bones may be depleted to balance the excessive intake of candy, soft drinks, and sugary desserts.

In order to prevent these degenerative effects, it is important to minimize consumption of refined carbohydrates, especially simple sugar, as well as naturally occurring lactose and fructose in dairy foods and fruits, and to derive the sweetness of complex carbohydrates primarily in the form of grains, beans, bean products, and fresh vegetables.

Macrobiotic Sweets   A variety of natural desserts may be eaten three or four times a week, usually at the end of the main meal. They can be made from the following foods:
Azuki beans (sweetened with grain syrup, chestnuts,
    squash, and raisins)
Cooked or dried fruit
Agar-agar (natural sea vegetable gelatin)
Grains (e.g., rice pudding, couscous cake, Indian pudding)
Flour products (e.g., cookies, cakes, pies, muffins, etc.,
    prepared with fruit or grain sweeteners)

Beverages

The quality, volume, and frequency of the liquids we drink are very important factors in our everyday health and vitality. Modern people tend to overconsume beverages of all kinds as well as drink too much milk, soft drinks, fruit juices, and other extreme or highly concentrated fare because of overeating in general, especially the overconsumption of foods rich in animal-quality protein, fat, and minerals, together with foods with large amounts of simple sugars. Stimulant beverages, such as coffee, black tea, and cola drinks, are particularly harmful and have been linked with a wide range of physical and mental disorders. The frequency and amount of beverage intake vary according to each person's condition and needs as well as the climate, season, and other environmental factors. Generally it is advisable to drink comfortably when thirsty and to avoid icy cold drinks.

A variety of beverages may be consumed, some daily and others occasionally. Amounts should be dictated by each person's needs and the weather conditions. Soft drinks, frozen orange juice, coffee, commercial tea, and other drinks with more extreme expanding energy are best avoided. The beverages listed below can be used to satisfy comfortably the desire for liquid.

Macrobiotic Beverages
Bancha twig and stem tea
Roasted brown rice or barley tea
Cereal grain coffee
Spring or well water
Amasake
Dandelion tea
Soybean milk (prepared with kombu)
Kombu tea
Lotus root tea
Mu tea
Other nonstimulant and nonaromatic natural herbal
   beverages
Sake (fermented rice wine, without chemicals or sugar)
Beer (without additives)
Apple, grape, and apricot juice
Apple cider
Carrot, celery, and other vegetable juices
Sweet vegetable drink (see Part I)

High-Quality Beverages   A source of good-quality water is essential for daily cooking and drinking. Natural spring or well water that is moving and alive (charged with natural energy from the earth) is best. City tap water often contains chlorine, as well as pesticide residues, detergents, nitrates, and heavy metals such as lead. Several mechanical methods are used to filter tap water of impurities, but it is still preferable to drink natural spring water that comes up from the earth or clear well water from an underground vein. However, it is important to have spring or well water tested before using it to see if it is safe.

Bancha tea is the most frequently consumed beverage in most macrobiotic households. It is picked in midsummer from the large and mature leaves, stems, and twigs of the tea bush. These are called respectively bancha leaf tea, bancha stem tea, and bancha twig tea. Traditionally picked by hand in the high mountains of Asia, the bancha leaves, stems, and twigs are roasted and cooled up to four separate times in large iron caldrons. This procedure, as well as the late harvest when the caffeine has naturally receded from the tea bush, makes for a tea containing virtually no caffeine or tannin, especially in the stem and twig parts. Also, unlike other teas, which are acidic, bancha is slightly alkaline and thus has a soothing, beneficial effect on digestion, blood quality, and the mind. Bancha twig tea is also known as *kukicha tea*, from the Japanese term for "twig tea."

A delicious, calming beverage can be made by roasting whole cereal grains and preparing them like ordinary tea. Roasted barley tea, or mugicha as it is known in Japan, is very cooling to the body and commonly enjoyed during the hotter weather. Roasted brown rice tea has a unique nutty flavor. Other grain teas, such as millet tea, oat tea, and buckwheat tea, may also be made in this way. All wholegrain teas are suitable for daily use. For variety, they may be mixed with bancha tea in various proportions.

Juice made from fresh fruits or vegetables can be enjoyed on occasion, on average several times per week. However, since juice is a very concentrated product, it is used very sparingly and in small amounts. Apple juice or apple cider is the most balanced of the fruit juices, though other temperate-climate fruit juice such as grape juice, pear juice, apricot juice, cranberry juice, and others may also be prepared.

Light alcoholic beverages that have been naturally fermented and made with high-quality ingredients may be enjoyed, if desired, at parties, on holidays, and on special occasions. Most commercially available beer, wine, sake, and other alcoholic beverages contain sugar and other highly refined ingredients as well as preservatives, artificial coloring, and other chemical additives. Mild alcoholic beverages with more naturally fermented quality are preferred, such as brown rice sake, unsweetened grape or plum wine, and beer made without additives or other harmful ingredients. Hard liquor is generally avoided at macrobiotic food gatherings.

7
SHOPPING FOR NATURAL FOODS

Most people find shopping for natural foods a relaxing and enjoyable experience, one that offers the chance to learn about new foods and their uses. Going once or twice a week to a natural foods market can be fun. Of course, it is important to shop at a store that maintains high standards of quality.

Some people who are just starting on a macrobiotic diet prefer to stock their kitchens with natural foods all at once. Others prefer to do it gradually. Either way, incorporating new foods into your diet can be an exciting adventure.

Most cities and towns in North America and Europe have stores and co-ops where you can shop for quality natural foods. Moreover, many supermarkets have added natural foods sections where products like rice cakes, tofu, tempeh, miso, tamari soy sauce, and others are available. Some stock fresh organic produce. If you have trouble locating some of the items mentioned in this book, the Kushi Foundation in Boston (see "Macrobiotic Resources" at the back of the book) can provide you with a list of natural food suppliers that offer mail order services.

There are several steps that can help you to locate foods if you find it difficult. First, call the Kushi Foundation in Boston for a list of macrobiotic educational centers and friends who live near you. Several hundred educational centers of various sizes are located in all 50 states, while hundreds of thousands of individuals and families practice the macrobiotic way of life in this country and abroad. A listing of centers and individuals is featured in the *World-*

wide Macrobiotic Directory published by the Kushi Foundation. If you call the foundation, the staff will be happy to provide you with names and addresses close to you or tell you how to order the directory.

Then, once you receive the names of macrobiotic friends in your area, don't hesitate to call and ask where to locate high-quality foods. Macrobiotic friends often know which stores offer the highest-quality items and how to find produce and other foods that are not readily available. They may also know about cooking classes or other educational programs in your area.

Another possibility is to visit natural or health foods stores near you and talk with salespeople about the macrobiotic-quality foods they carry. If some items are not available in the store, ask where you can find them. Seasonal produce, for example, is often available directly from farmers. Macrobiotic friends and friends in the natural foods business would be the best persons to ask about this.

If, after checking these possibilities, you still have trouble locating some items, you can mail-order them from several mail order companies in the United States. They normally stock all of the macrobiotic staples used in our recipes, including specialty items that may be difficult to find.

Whenever possible, try to obtain organic produce and other staples. If you have the space, start a backyard organic garden. It will help ensure a steady supply of vegetables throughout the summer. High-quality organic seeds can be ordered by mail from companies such as Johnny's Selected Seeds, Foss Hill Rd., Albion, ME 04910. When necessary, your organic staples can be supplemented with nonorganic produce from local markets. Just be sure to thoroughly wash nonorganic foods to reduce potentially toxic residues.

Your staples can be bought in small quantities to suit your needs on a weekly basis or in larger bulk quantities at reduced prices to last for a month or more. Perishable items—such as fresh vegetables and fruit, tofu, tempeh, amasake, and others that need refrigeration—can be purchased as needed.

SHOPPING SCHEDULE

Staple, nonperishable items such as grains, beans, sea vegetables, seeds, nuts, miso, tamari soy sauce, and sea salt as well as prepackaged items like noodles and fu can be purchased in small quantities on a weekly basis to suit your needs, or they can be purchased in larger bulk quantities at a reduced price once or twice a month. As these are nonperishable, they store very well for several months in sealed glass jars or ceramic containers. Perishable items that need refrigeration, such as fresh vegetables, fruits, tofu, tempeh, bread, amasake, and others, are best purchased once or twice a week. Tofu, tempeh, bread, and amasake will store well for 7 to 10 days.

Freshly picked vegetables and fruits are brightly colored, crisp, and firm and will last for five to seven days. If the vegetables and fruits are not fresh, they may be limp, soft, and yellowed and will keep for only two or three days. Vegetables and fruits store well if kept in a vegetable drawer or in small paper bags in the refrigerator. Vegetables stored in plastic bags spoil more easily as moisture builds up. Vegetables such as watercress and parsley store well if the stems are placed in a cup or jar filled with fresh cold water. Vegetables and fruits that are sold at reduced prices in markets are usually not fresh and should be used soon after purchasing.

BASIC SHOPPING LIST

When you enter a natural foods store for the first time, you may be overwhelmed by the vast selection of cosmetics, herbs, spices, processed snacks, baked goods, and, in many cases, vitamins and supplements found there. To save time and avoid distractions, it helps to know what you are looking for. Below is a basic starter list for your convenience. (The food list in Chapter 6 can be used when buying vegetables and fruits or if you want more variety in the other food groups.) If desired, photocopy these pages and use them as a checklist.

Whole Grains (Prepackaged or in Bulk)

_____ Short-grain brown rice

_____ Medium-grain brown rice

_____ Long-grain brown rice

_____ Barley

_____ Pearl barley (hato mugi)

_____ Millet

_____ Sweet brown rice

_____ Whole oats

_____ Whole wheat berries

_____ Whole buckwheat (kasha)

_____ Corn on the cob (in season)

_____ Other whole grains

Noodles and Pasta (Prepackaged or in Bulk)

_____ Whole-wheat udon

_____ Whole-wheat somen

_____ Whole-wheat shells

_____ Ramen noodles (whole wheat, rice, or buckwheat)

_____ Whole-wheat spaghetti

_____ Buckwheat noodles (soba)

_____ Other whole-grain noodles and pasta

Cracked Grains (Prepackaged or in Bulk)

_____ Rolled or steel-cut oats

_____ Bulgur

_____ Couscous

_____ Cracked wheat

_____ Other cracked or rolled grains

Beans (Prepackaged or in Bulk)

_____ Azuki beans

_____ Chick-peas

_____ Green lentils

_____ Black soybeans

_____ Soybeans

_____ Kidney beans

_____ Black turtle beans

_____ Pinto beans

_____ Navy beans

_____ Great northern beans

_____ Split peas

_____ Whole green peas

_____ Red lentils

_____ Lima beans

_____ Other beans

Bean Products (Available in the Refrigerator Case)

_____ Fresh tofu

_____ Dried tofu (dried and prepackaged)

_____ Tempeh

_____ Other soy foods

Wheat Products (Ready-made)

_____ Seitan (available in the refrigerator case)

_____ Unyeasted sourdough bread

_____ Fu

_____ Other whole-wheat products

Sea Vegetables (Prepackaged or in Bulk)

_____ Arame

_____ Hijiki

_____ Kombu

_____ Wakame

_____ Nori

_____ Dulse

_____ Agar-agar

_____ Sea palm

_____ Other sea vegetables

Condiments and Seasonings (Prepackaged or in Bulk)

_____ Barley (mugi) miso

_____ Hatcho (soybean) miso

_____ Tamari soy sauce

_____ White sea salt

_____ Umeboshi plums

_____ Umeboshi paste

_____ Natural vinegar (umeboshi, brown rice, sweet brown rice)

_____ Gomashio (can also be made at home)

_____ Fresh gingerroot

_____ Sesame–sea vegetable powders and other natural sprinkling condiments (can also be made at home)

_____ Mirin

_____ Shiso leaf condiment

_____ Green nori flakes

Sweeteners (Prepackaged or in Bulk)

_____ Rice syrup

_____ Barley malt

_____ Dried chestnuts

_____ Amasake

_____ Dried fruit (raisins, apples, apricots, etc.)

_____ Apple cider and other northern fruit juices

_____ Other natural sweeteners

Seeds and Nuts (Prepackaged or in Bulk)

_____ Sesame seeds (black and white)

_____ Pumpkin seeds

_____ Sunflower seeds

_____ Walnuts

_____ Almonds

_____ Roasted peanuts

_____ Other low-fat nuts

Oils (Bottled or in Bulk)

_____ Unrefined dark sesame oil

_____ Light sesame oil

_____ Corn oil

_____ Other natural cold-pressed oils

Beverages (Prepackaged or in Bulk)

_____ Bancha twig tea (kukicha)

_____ Roasted barley tea (mugicha)

_____ Cereal grain coffee

_____ Spring water

Flours (Prepackaged or in Bulk)

_____ Whole-wheat bread flour

_____ Whole-wheat pastry flour

_____ Corn flour

_____ Cornmeal

_____ Other whole-grain flours

Pickles (Prepackaged)

_____ Natural sauerkraut

_____ Ginger pickles

_____ Pickled daikon (takuan)

_____ Other naturally fermented nonspicy pickles

Snacks (Prepackaged or in Bulk)

_____ Rice cakes

_____ Popping corn

_____ Puffed whole-grain cereals

_____ Other natural snacks

Special Items (Prepackaged or in Bulk)

_____ Kuzu

_____ Arrowroot flour

_____ Shiitake and other wild mushrooms (dried and fresh)

_____ Mochi

_____ Dried daikon

_____ Lotus root seeds

_____ Others

Fresh Produce

When shopping for fresh organic produce use these guidelines to determine quality and freshness:

- Select fruits or vegetables that have a beautiful color,
  balanced shape, and a fresh vital appearance. Try to
  choose those that are neither too big or small nor irregularly shaped. Vegetables and fruits that are limp, soft, or
  dull in color are less tasty and will spoil more rapidly.
- Greens that are turning yellow were picked too late, have
  aged, or have been stored at too high a temperature. They
  are stale and musty-tasting and are best avoided.
- Check the ends of root and stalk vegetables for long fibers
  that show toughness.
- Browning and hardening at the bottoms of stem vegetables are also signs of aging.
- Wrinkles and soft spots on round-shaped vegetables and
  on fruits show a loss of moisture.

SHOPPING TIPS

- In many outlets, organic produce is marked clearly
  and certified by an organic growers' association or
  state agency that periodically tests soil conditions
  and monitors cultivation standards.
- Produce that is not prepackaged or tied in bunches is
  less likely to spoil.

THE COMPLETE QUICK AND NATURAL SHOPPING LIST

The shopping list presented below is for the recipes and menus in Part III.

Whole Grains (Prepackaged or in Bulk)

_____ short-grain brown rice—10 pounds

_____ barley—½ pound

_____ pearl barley (hato mugi)—½ pound

_____ millet—2 pounds

_____ whole wheat berries—½ pound

_____ fresh corn—2 ears

Noodles and Pasta (Prepackaged or in Bulk)

_____ whole-wheat udon—2½-pound package

_____ soba (buckwheat noodles)—1 ½-pound package

Cracked or Milled Grains (Prepackaged or in Bulk)

_____ rolled or steel-cut oats—2 pounds

_____ yellow corn grits—½ pound

Beans (Prepackaged or in Bulk)

_____ azuki beans—1 pound

_____ chick-peas—1½ pounds

_____ green lentils—1 pound

Bean Products (Available in the Refrigerator Case)

_____ fresh tofu—4
1-pound packages

_____ tempeh—2 ½-pound
packages

Wheat Products (Ready-made)

_____ unyeasted
sourdough bread
(whole-wheat or
rye)—2 loaves

_____ seitan—½ pound

Flours (Prepackaged or in Bulk)

_____ whole-wheat pastry
flour—2 pounds

Fresh Vegetables (Available in the Produce Section)

_____ alfalfa sprouts—1
package

_____ bok choy—1 small
bunch

_____ broccoli—2 small
bunches

_____ burdock—1
medium-sized piece

_____ buttercup squash—1
small

_____ butternut squash—1
small

_____ cabbage—1 small
head

_____ carrots—3 pounds

_____ cauliflower—2 large
heads

_____ celery—1 bunch

_____ Chinese cabbage—1
large head

_____ collard greens—1
small bunch

_____ cucumbers—4
medium-sized

_____ daikon—2 medium-
sized

_____ daikon greens—1 small bunch

_____ radish (red) greens—1 bunch

_____ green peas—½ pound

_____ red onion—1 small

_____ green string beans— ½ pound

_____ scallions—3 medium-sized bunches

_____ kale—2 small bunches

_____ snow peas—½ pound

_____ leeks—1 medium-sized

_____ summer squash (yellow)—1 medium

_____ lettuce—2 small heads

_____ turnip greens—2 small bunches

_____ onions—3 pounds

_____ watercress—4 bunches

_____ parsley—1 small bunch

_____ radishes (red)—2 packages or bunches

Fresh Fruit (Available in the Produce Section)

_____ apples—3 medium-sized

_____ peaches—2 medium-sized

_____ lemons—2 medium-sized

Sea Vegetables (Prepackaged or in Bulk)

_____ agar-agar—1 package

_____ arame—1 package or 2 ounces

_____ hijiki—1 package or 2 ounces

_____ nori—1 package (10 sheets)

_____ kombu—1 package or 2 ounces

_____ wakame—1 package or 2 ounces

Condiments and Seasonings (Prepackaged or in Bulk)

_____ barley miso—1 pound

_____ tamari soy sauce—1 pint

_____ white sea salt—½ pound

_____ umeboshi plums—½ pound

_____ umeboshi vinegar—1 5-ounce bottle

_____ brown rice vinegar—1 5-ounce bottle

_____ mirin—1 5-ounce bottle

_____ shiso leaf condiment—1 package

_____ gingerroot—1 small piece

Sweeteners (Prepackaged or in Bulk)

_____ brown rice syrup—1 16-ounce jar

_____ dried chestnuts—½ pound

_____ amasake—1 quart

_____ raisins—½ pound

_____ apple juice—1 quart

Oils (Bottled or in Bulk)

_____ dark sesame oil—1 pint

_____ corn oil—1 pint

_____ light sesame oil—2 pints

Seeds and Nuts (Prepackaged or in Bulk)

_____ sesame seeds, black—½ pound

_____ sesame seeds, white—½ pound

_____ pumpkin seeds—½ pound

_____ sunflower seeds—½ pound

_____ walnuts—½ pound

_____ almonds, slivered—½ pound

_____ tahini (organic)—1 16-ounce jar

Beverages (Prepackaged or in Bulk)

_____ bancha twig tea (kukicha)—1 package or ¼ pound

_____ cereal grain coffee—1 16-ounce jar

_____ roasted barley tea (mugicha)—1 package

Pickles (Prepackaged)

_____ natural sauerkraut—1 16-ounce jar

_____ natural dill pickles—1 16-ounce jar

Special Items (Prepackaged or in Bulk)

_____ kuzu—½ pound

_____ mochi—1 1-pound package

_____ kanpyo—1 package

_____ shiitake, dried—1 package or about 15 mushrooms

_____ dried daikon—1 package

Fresh Fish

——— fillet of sole—1
pound

FOOD STORAGE

When you return home from the store, unpack your whole grains, beans, condiments, sea vegetables, pasta and noodles, seeds and nuts, dried fruits, kuzu, and other dry goods and put them in clean glass, ceramic, or wood containers (see Chapter 8 for more information on containers). Glass containers are fairly inexpensive and make it easy to locate the items you need while cooking. If you buy in really large quantities, such as 50-pound sacks of short-grain brown rice, you can store the sacks in the pantry and take what you need directly from them.

Store containers in a fairly cool place, such as a pantry, and occasionally stir the foods in them to permit air to circulate and to reduce heat in warm weather. Some items, like umeboshi plums and paste, barley malt, rice syrup, and others, are packaged in glass jars and can be placed as is in the cupboard or pantry.

A handy tip when storing food:

Place your jars of whole grains side by side in one section of your pantry or cupboard, beans in another, seeds and nuts in another, and dried fruits, condiments, special items, and snacks in another. By arranging your foods according to type, you'll find it much easier to plan meals and find what you need when cooking.

How to Store Particular Foods

- Sea salt can be stored in a tightly sealed glass jar to prevent the absorption of moisture and kept near the stove for easy access.

- Barley and soybean miso can be placed in tightly sealed glass jars and kept in a shaded, cool place, such as a cupboard or pantry. Other varieties of miso, especially quick-fermented misos, are best stored in the refrigerator.
- Tamari soy sauce can be left in the bottle, stored in the cupboard or pantry, and used as needed. You can also fill your tamari dispenser and keep it on a shelf or counter near the stove.
- Sesame, corn, and other oils can be stored in a cool cupboard, preferably in tinted glass bottles that will protect them from light. Naturally processed cold-pressed oils keep longer than chemically processed varieties.
- Tofu, tempeh, seitan, amasake, and other items from the store's refrigerator case are best kept in the refrigerator. Fruit juices can be either refrigerated or stored in a cupboard or pantry.
- Snacks, including rice cakes, puffed cereals, and popping corn, can be kept in the cupboard or pantry.
- Sauerkraut, pickles, and fresh shiitake mushrooms can be kept in the refrigerator. Dried shiitake, daikon, and tofu can be stored in the pantry or cupboard.
- Before storing fruits and vegetables, cut out and discard any bad spots. The remaining portions are fine for later use. Removing yellowing leaves or other aging parts helps prevent spoilage from spreading. Try to store your vegetables, especially squashes, slightly separated from each other, as their pressure on each other can lead to spoilage. Most root and round-shaped vegetables can be stored in the pantry, the basement, or a root cellar. Leafy greens and other soft vegetables can be refrigerated until they are used. Keep them separately in closed brown paper bags that allow the produce to breathe and help it retain freshness.

8
THE QUICK AND NATURAL KITCHEN

In many respects the kitchen is the most important room in the house. What occurs there has a profound influence on the health and well-being of each member of the household.

Today, however, the kitchen is losing that central place. The hearth has been abandoned, with far-reaching consequences. According to recent surveys, Americans now eat every other meal away from home. No wonder family unity seems more elusive than ever before. Food is the basic material out of which we create our lives daily, and eating together creates biological, emotional, and spiritual bonds. For family unity and stability in society, as much as possible, it is important to restore the tradition of cooking and eating at home.

If we close our eyes and imagine the ideal kitchen, the image of a country house often comes to mind. The kitchen has plenty of counter space with room for cutting, a large sink, and a pantry stocked with fresh natural foods. The walls are brightly painted, with natural wood cabinets and finishings and windows that let in plenty of light. Cool breezes keep it comfortable in warm weather, and in winter it is warm and cozy. The atmosphere in the kitchen reflects the changing of the seasons outside. Brightly colored curtains frame the windows, and the counters aren't cluttered with high-tech gadgets. Utensils are kept neatly in the most convenient place, ready for use. The kitchen is located on the ground floor of the house, and outside is a backyard garden where fresh vegetables are ready to be picked all summer long. There are no canned, frozen, or artificially processed foods in the pantry or cupboards. Everything is fresh and natural.

Of course, kitchens come in a variety of shapes, sizes, and colors. It doesn't matter whether you live in the city, in the suburbs, or in the country. What does matter is that you are comfortable in your kitchen and feel inspired and creative every time you cook in it.

Soft, bright colors promote a positive and cheerful state of mind. A clean, bright kitchen makes us happy while cooking. Proper lighting is important: natural full-spectrum lighting is best, since fluorescent lights create an unnaturally harsh feeling in a room. Moreover, they contribute to fatigue and have been linked to higher rates of skin cancer.

THE JOY OF CLEANING

Keeping your kitchen clean creates a positive state of mind, makes cooking easier and more enjoyable, and helps save time. If you put all of your energy into cleaning, washing dishes, and the other chores that revolve around cooking and eating, these activities will become a source of joy. Wash your dishes and utensils and put them away after each meal. Clean the countertops, tabletops, and cutting boards. Sweep the floor and mop if necessary. Keep your stovetop clean and shiny. If you wash and put your utensils away after each use, they will be ready the next time you need them.

Always keep your cupboards, drawers, refrigerator, pantry, and other cooking, eating, and storage areas clean and shiny. Remember, your kitchen is both the source and the reflection of your health and vitality.

It helps tremendously if your pantry, cupboards, and refrigerator are organized for maximum accessibility and convenience. It also helps to store your pots, pans, and other utensils in the most convenient places. Keep the equipment you use to prepare food separate from the dishes and tableware used for serving and eating. Knowing at all times where your foods and utensils are makes cooking quicker and more enjoyable.

If possible, arrange your refrigerator, tables, and cutting space for optimal speed and convenience when you cook. For example, it is convenient to place your cutting board next to your sink, so that you can wash and cut foods without wasting time or energy.

A NATURAL SOURCE OF ENERGY

Fire and water are the primary influences used in cooking. Each changes food in a way that is opposite the other, and the quality of both influence the quality of food. As we discussed, natural spring or well water is preferred for cooking and drinking. However, tap water, which is usually chemically processed, can be used for washing foods and utensils. Now let us consider the quality of the fire, or heat, that we use in the kitchen.

Fire changes food by making it more yang or contracted. For example, if we place food over an open flame, it becomes dry and black and eventually turns into ashes. When we roast grains, seeds, or other foods in a dry skillet, they become harder, drier, and darker in color. When fire, or heat, is the only factor applied—as it is in dry roasting—the food becomes more contracted. Water produces the opposite effect. It draws the minerals out of foods, causing them to become softer and more expanded.

In cooking, we balance these opposite energies. Cooking is a form of predigestion in which food is energized, broken down, and condensed so that we are better able to extract energy and nutrients from it. Cooking methods such as boiling, steaming, and pressure-cooking combine the effects of water and fire to varying degrees: the drying and contracting influence of fire are offset somewhat by the expanding influence of water or steam.

A pinch of sea salt, or a small amount of miso, tamari, umeboshi, or other natural seasoning is usually added during cooking. The minerals in sea salt cause foods to contract, further balancing the expanding effects of water or steam. Cooking methods that combine the contracting effects of fire, salt, pressure, and time with the expanding effects of water are generally more balanced than dry roasting or grilling, in which fire is the primary factor used. Vegetable foods become sweeter, softer, and more energized when cooked in a balanced manner.

Drying or pickling foods accelerates their contracting energy. If we compare a fresh apple with a dried apple, we see that the dried apple has lost much of its moisture and its sweetness has become more concentrated. If we compare fresh daikon with daikon that has been aged in rice bran and sea salt for several years, as it is in the pickle known as takuan, we see that the daikon has become harder, drier, saltier, and more contracted. On the other hand, oil creates expansive and upward energy. Only a small amount is needed from time to time to conduct heat and release the energy in food. On average, high-quality sesame oil is used in sautéing two to three times per week in most macrobiotic households.

Without exception, the best natural food cooks around the world prefer cooking with a natural gas flame rather than with electricity, for several reasons. First, it is very hard to fine-tune cooking with electricity. It is a conductive heat that first warms the coils and then the pot and its contents from the bottom up. The temperature cannot be changed quickly when the control is turned to high or low because it takes some time to cool or heat the pot. Electricity makes it difficult to cook uniformly, and it is possible that ingredients at the bottom of the pan can burn while those at the top need more cooking. A gas flame heats the surrounding air. Food thus cooks much more evenly, and the temperature can be adjusted immediately (a pot of water will instantly stop boiling when the flame is turned off, for example). Meals are cooked better. Interestingly, too, many of our students have reported improvements in their energy levels and overall well-being after converting from electric to gas cooking.

Because of these drawbacks, you may not feel satisfied with a meal cooked with electricity and may experience strong cravings. Eating in a naturally balanced manner becomes more of a struggle.

If you can't convert to gas cooking right away you can purchase inexpensively a small portable gas stove for home use. Brown rice, miso soup, and other staples can then be prepared on the gas burner, and the electric stove can be used for side dishes.

Similarly, microwave ovens have not found acceptance among whole foods cooks, including the cooking and teaching staff of the Kushi Institute, our macrobiotic educational center in Boston. Writing in the *Natural Foods Cookbook: Vegetarian Dairy-Free Cuisine*, Mary Estella, a gourmet natural foods cook, states, "Whole foods kitchens have no use for these appliances. I choose to avoid foods cooked or heated in them." Annemarie Colbin, founder of the Natural Gourmet Cookery School in New York, expresses a similar idea in her book *Food and Healing*. She states, "Very little research has been done on the health effects of microwave cooking; however, food tastes peculiar when prepared that way, and I share my students' intuitive feeling that something is not quite right."

The trend toward artificially high-speed cooking can easily be carried to extremes. Recently, for example, a food processor came up with a suggestion to build microwave ovens in the glove compartments of automobiles. In this way the millions of people who spend hours each day commuting to work could simply place a can of ready-to-eat soup in their glove compartment and "enjoy" breakfast while sitting in rush-hour traffic. The way we cook and eat plays a vital role in our health. Can eating microwaved canned food alone in a moving car be more appealing and healthful than taking time to eat in a calm and relaxed manner at home in the company of friends and family? We don't think so.

QUALITY EQUIPMENT AND UTENSILS

The tools and utensils used in cooking are just as important as the foods selected. High-quality, natural cookware and utensils enhance the flavor and appearance of food and help transform daily cooking into an art. Below are important items we suggest having in your kitchen.

For Storage

Containers Glass, ceramic, or wood containers are recommended for storing your grains, beans, seeds, sea vegetables, condiments, and other foods. Storing food in glass makes it easier to find the items you want when cooking. It is better to store food in containers made from natural materials than to use those made of plastic, as plastic affects the taste of food.

Ceramic Crocks Heavy earthenware crocks are useful when preparing homemade pickles that require aging. One or two medium-sized (4-quart) crocks should be enough for a steady supply of pickles.

Tamari Dispenser These small dispensers come in very handy when you want to season a dish with a few drops of tamari soy sauce or add a small amount of it at the table. Tamari dispensers are available at natural foods stores.

For Food Preparation

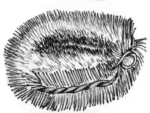

Vegetable Brushes Vegetable brushes made from natural bristles are very good for scrubbing carrots, burdock, squash, and other vegetables. They are available at natural foods stores. We suggest purchasing several.

Colanders and Strainers Strainers are used to wash grains, beans, seeds, and other foods; colanders are used for rinsing noodles and vegetables. One colander and two strainers (a large-meshed and a fine-meshed strainer), preferably stainless steel, are usually sufficient. They are sold in natural foods and department stores.

Vegetable Knives Japanese-style vegetable knives with square-edged blades are especially recommended for cutting vegetables smoothly and elegantly. Stainless-steel, carbon-steel, and high-grade carbon-steel varieties are available. We recommend the high-grade carbon-steel variety as it does not rust easily and holds a sharp edge longer than the others. The blade does not chip easily and will last many years when well cared for. These high-quality vegetable knives are available at most natural foods stores. They are generally 10½ to 12 inches long in total, with about a 6-inch blade. Two knives would be ideal to start with.

TAKING CARE OF YOUR KNIVES

To protect the blade, wash the knife in warm, soapy water and dry it immediately after use. If rust starts to appear, use a steel-wool scrubber to scrape it off. Coating the blade with a little sesame oil after use provides additional protection.

Sharpening Stone Your knife will need regular sharpening in order to maintain its cutting edge. Sharpening stones can be bought at natural foods or hardware stores. Keep your knife properly sharpened, as this is essential for quick and efficient cooking.

Graters Flat metal graters from Japan are especially useful for grating vegetables such as daikon radish, ginger, carrots, and others. They produce very fine gratings. Flat graters can be found in most natural foods stores. Regular stainless-steel graters are also useful, although we don't use them as often as the flat grater.

Hand Food Mill A hand mill is useful for pureeing foods, such as for soups, dips, or baby foods. Electric blenders disrupt the natural energy of foods. Instead of using one on a regular basis, save it for parties or special occasions when working with large volumes. Hand food mills are available in natural foods and kitchen specialty shops.

Suribachi A suribachi is a grooved earthenware bowl used to puree and grind foods by hand. It can be used when making gomashio and other condiments, dips, spreads, and sauces or when pureeing baby foods or other special dishes. Suribachis come in several sizes and can be found in natural foods stores. Small (6-inch) or medium-sized (8-inch) bowls are usually sufficient for home use. They come with a wood pestle called a *surikogi.*

Pickle Press These large plastic jars are imported from Japan and are used to make quick pickles and pressed salads. They come with a special lid with a screw-down pressure plate in the center. They are available in several sizes; small (2-quart) ones are adequate for most uses. They can be found in natural foods stores.

Pressure Cooker Pressure-cooking is the preferred way to cook short-grain brown rice and can be used to prepare other whole grains as well. This more concentrated form of boiling cooks each grain thoroughly and reduces nutrient loss. Pressure-cooked rice is easy to digest and becomes sweeter the longer you chew it.

Pressure cookers come in a variety of sizes and models and are sold in many natural foods stores. They are very safe. Ask the salesperson for advice on which model is best for your needs. A small (5-liter) cooker is usually sufficient for home use. Stainless-steel models are preferred; aluminum varieties are not recommended for optimal health.

Cutting Boards   Wood cutting boards, widely available, are also very useful. If you include fish in your diet, it is a good idea to use two boards—one for cutting vegetables and fruits and the other for fish and seafood—so as not to mix odors and juices from animal and vegetable foods. A wood cutting board also needs to be seasoned before use (see box).

PROTECTING YOUR CUTTING BOARDS

Quality hardwood cutting boards last many years when cared for properly. First season your board: Rub sesame or corn oil into the surface. Let the board absorb the oil for several hours and wipe it dry with paper towels. Repeat every month or so to prevent the board from absorbing the juices from foods and from warping or buckling.

To clean your board, simply wipe it with a damp sponge after each use. We do not recommend immersing wood boards in water. Do not use soap on wood utensils as it is easily absorbed into the wood and detracts from the flavor of foods that come in contact with it.

Sushi Mats   These mats made of thin strips of bamboo tied together with string can be used to cover leftovers or keep your dishes warm before serving. They allow air to circulate, help keep foods from drying out, and reduce spoilage. We also use them when making sushi. They can be found in natural foods and Oriental markets, and it is well worth purchasing several.

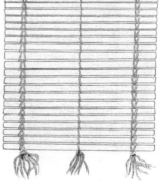

Cookware   High-quality stainless-steel cookware is also very useful. Aluminum, nonstick, and plastic-coated pots are not recommended. Aluminum scratches easily and is absorbed into foods, and this can cause a variety of health problems. Nonstick surfaces also scratch easily, and tiny fragments occasionally break off. Plastic-coated cookware is chemically processed and changes the taste and quality of foods.

You can begin with the following pots:

- A large (6-quart) or medium-sized (4-quart) pot for making soups, stews, grain, and bean dishes
- Two or three small (1-, 2-, and 3-quart) saucepans
- One or two stainless-steel, 10- or 12-inch skillets for frying and sautéing
- A 10-inch cast-iron skillet for frying and sauteing.
  New skillets should be seasoned before you cook with them (see box).

SEASONING AND CLEANING CAST-IRON SKILLETS

If you treat your cast-iron skillet well, it will give you many years of service. Roast a small amount of sea salt in the skillet, for a few minutes. Then brush it with sesame oil and sauté an onion in it. Remove and discard the onion. Then place the skillet, now coated with oil, in an oven and bake it for several hours at 300–350°F. It will turn dark or black when it is ready. Remove the skillet, allow it to cool, and wash it under cold water. Place it on the stove, turn the flame to low, and let it sit until completely dry. This procedure helps prevent rusting, and your skillet is now ready to use.

When washing a cast-iron skillet, don't use metal scrubbers as these can cause the protective seasoning to come off. Don't plunge a hot skillet into cold water or soak it in hot, soapy water as this can cause tiny holes to form in the cast iron. Wait until the skillet is completely cool before you wash it: dry it thoroughly over a low flame after washing.

- A small set of stainless-steel bakeware for natural baking needs
- A deep cast-iron pot (Dutch oven) for deep-frying vegetables and other foods
- One or two earthenware pots for baking beans, casseroles, and other dishes

Electric skillets and cooking pots are not recommended for optimal health. Foods heated by electricity are not as delicious as those cooked over more natural energy sources such as gas or wood, and they often require more seasoning.

Wood Utensils   Wood utensils have a nice natural look and feel. They have the best quality for interacting with food and are gentler to pots, pans, and bowls. They help prevent metal cookware from scratching. The following utensils are especially useful and can be purchased at natural foods and kitchenware stores:

- Several bamboo rice paddles of different sizes for removing cooked brown rice and other grains from cooking pots and transferring them to serving bowls and individual dishes
- Large (10½-inch) cooking chopsticks for sautéing and stirring. These are longer than the table variety
- A roasting paddle for use when roasting seeds, nuts, grains, and other foods
- Wood spoons for stirring, mixing, scooping, and serving food before and after cooking
- One or two soup ladles

Flame Deflector   These lightweight metal disks have wooden handles and are used to distribute the heat evenly under cooking pots, allowing foods to cook evenly and reducing the chance of burning. They can be placed under the pressure cooker when preparing rice or other grains or under pots that are simmering on the stove when you wish to heat food but not boil it. Metal flame deflectors are sold in natural foods stores and many other stores that sell kitchen supplies.

Steamer Baskets   Two varieties of steamer baskets are used in macrobiotic cooking: stainless-steel models that fit inside your cooking pots and Oriental-style bamboo steamers that fit on top of your pots. We recommend purchasing one of each. Stainless-steel steamers can be found in natural foods and department stores, while the bamboo models are available at natural foods and Oriental markets. It is helpful to season a bamboo steamer before using it to prevent the taste of wood from getting into food. To season, steam the odds and ends of vegetables in it several times.

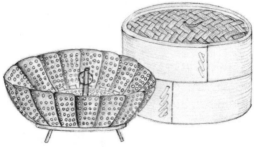

For Serving

Serving Bowls   Large wood bowls are ideal for serving brown rice and other grains. Wood is porous and lets food breathe. It absorbs water and retards spoilage. Keeping cooked whole grains in bowls made of wood helps them stay fresh. Buy at least one medium-sized (8- to 10-inch) bowl at the beginning and others as you need them. They come in a variety of sizes and are made from different types of wood. Your bowls will need to be seasoned from time to time in the same manner as your cutting board to ensure many years of use (see box). Porcelain and glass bowls can be used to wash, mix, and serve other foods.

Glass Teapot   Glass teapots are very good for making bancha tea and other beverages. Glass does not affect the flavor of the tea, and tea can be left in the pot, kept on the stove, and conveniently reheated when desired.

Tea Strainer Since bancha tea is made up of the loose twigs, stems, and leaves of the tea bush, it needs to be strained before drinking. Bamboo tea strainers, which come in different sizes, are preferred. They are held over each cup when pouring tea to strain off twigs and stems.

Miscellaneous Utensils

Other useful utensils include:

- Baking containers, including pie plates, bread pans, muffin tins, and so on. Again, don't use aluminum.
- A wok (Chinese-style skillet; optional). Cast-iron skillets are adequate for most sautéing needs, but a wok is wonderful for making light, fast-cooked vegetables and fish.
- A grain mill for grinding grains and nuts into flour. Flour is best when used soon after grinding. After being cracked, grain immediatcly starts to oxidize and begins to lose nutrients. Flour is most delicious when freshly ground.
- A bread knife. The best knife for cutting bread has a long, thin blade with a serrated edge.
- A vegetable peeler, good for removing skins of cucumbers, apples, and so on, when necessary.
- An oil skimmer for lifting small bits of batter and food from tempura oil as well as for lifting vegetables from a pot of water.
- Several stainless-steel, porcelain, or glass bowls of different sizes for washing and mixing food.
- A rubber spatula for scraping batter, pureed food, and the like from clean bowls.
- A metal spatula for turning food over.
- A rolling pin.
- Measuring cups and spoons.
- Organic soap. High-quality, organically made dishwashing soap is helpful in removing oil from skillets after frying, but is often not necessary for other utensils. A simple washing in hot water usually suffices.

9
FOOD PREPARATION

Several important steps come before the actual cooking. First, foods need to be washed thoroughly. Then vegetables, sea vegetables, fruits, and other foods need proper cutting. And certain foods need to be soaked, diluted, or pureed before they can be added to your dishes.

Efficient preparation can make the difference between a delicious and an average meal, between one that is ready on time and one that keeps everyone waiting. In this chapter we look more closely at each of the steps leading up to cooking. Please refer to these sections when you start the recipes in Part III.

STEP 1: WASHING

The vegetable kingdom is our intermediary with the world of nature. Vegetables transform inorganic elements—air, water, and soil—and energy from the sun into organic nutrients. We can't live by eating inorganic substances only; we need plants to synthesize them for us.

Grains, vegetables, beans, and other foods that come from the earth sometimes have soil or tiny stones mixed in with them. This is perfectly natural. Therefore, these plant foods need to be washed thoroughly before they are cooked. Below are helpful suggestions for washing these foods properly.

Grains

Before washing grains, place them a handful at a time on a plate. Look for small stones, clumps of soil, or broken or damaged grains. Sort and remove these. Then place the grains in a bowl or cooking pot, put it in the sink, and add enough cold water to cover. Gently stir the grains in one direction with your fingers. Pour the water off and again put water in the pot. Repeat the quick, gentle stirring motion and pour the water off again. Place the grains in a strainer and rinse quickly but thoroughly under a stream of cold water from the faucet. This helps remove dust or minute particles that may still be attached to the grains. Your grains are now ready to be cooked. Once they have been washed, do not let them sit for too long before you cook them, as this will cause them to absorb the water and lose freshness. This procedure can be used for all loose grains. Corn on the cob can be rinsed under cold water from the faucet after being husked.

Beans

Place your beans on a plate and remove any broken or damaged ones as well as small stones or clumps of soil. Place the beans in a bowl or cooking pot in the sink and cover them with cold water. Stir as you would grains and pour off the water. Add fresh water and repeat these steps. Place the beans in a strainer and run cold water over them. Your beans can now be cooked or presoaked. This procedure can be used for all beans except Japanese black soybeans. The method for washing these beans is explained in Part III.

Bean Products

Prepackaged soy foods such as tofu and tempeh normally don't require washing. Tempeh can be used as is from the package. When you buy tofu prepackaged in containers, simply pour off the water before slicing.

Vegetables

It is better not to cut vegetables and fruits before you wash them, as this causes them to lose vitamins, minerals, and other nutrients and diminishes their flavor. It is also easier to wash whole vegetables than it is to wash slices.

Vegetables can be divided into three categories: leafy greens, round-shaped varieties, and roots. To wash leafy greens such as daikon, turnip, and carrot tops, collards, watercress, kale, and Chinese cabbage, first sort and remove yellowed, damaged, or stale leaves. Then place the remaining leaves in a large bowl or pot and cover them with cold water. Swish them around with your fingers. Then remove and wash each leaf separately under a stream of cold water. Tightly curled leaves, such as kale, or minute leaves such as carrot greens, may require a little more effort than collard greens, Chinese cabbage, or other smooth leaves. Once the leaves have been washed thoroughly, they are ready to be cut.

Root, round, and most ground vegetables (as opposed to green, leafy vegetables) are best washed with a special natural-bristle vegetable brush. Place the vegetables one at a time under a stream of cold running water and scrub gently but firmly. Try not to damage or remove the nutrient-rich skin. Onions need to be peeled first and then washed for a few seconds under cold water until they are squeaky-clean. If vegetables such as cucumber, rutabaga, or squash have been waxed, wash them first (to prevent nutrient loss) with a vegetable brush and then peel the skin before cooking. Green cabbage can be washed with the leaves still attached to the head or a leaf at a time. Fresh mushrooms can usually be cleaned without a vegetable brush; simply rinse them thoroughly under cold water.

Fruits

Fruits can usually be washed without a vegetable brush. Simply rinse each piece thoroughly under a stream of cold water before slicing. Berries can be placed in a colander and rinsed under a stream of cold water.

Sea Vegetables

Each sea vegetable can be washed in a slightly different way. Kombu, for example, doesn't need to be washed. You can simply dust it off with a clean, damp sponge. Nori, which comes in the form of flat dried sheets, also doesn't need washing and can be used as is. Arame and hijiki both have a stringy, wiry form. Before you wash them, first remove any hard clumps, as these may contain small stones or shells. Then place the sea vegetable in a bowl and cover with water.

Rinse and pour off the water as you would with grains or beans, repeating once or twice. Then place the sea vegetable in a strainer and rinse quickly under a stream of cold water. Once hijiki has been washed, soak it for 3 to 5 minutes before slicing. Arame doesn't need to be soaked; simply let it drain for 3 to 5 minutes before you slice it. Wakame, dulse, and sea palm can simply be placed in a bowl, covered with cold water, and rinsed. Pour the water off and repeat once or twice. The sea vegetables are now ready to be soaked.

Seeds

Seeds can be washed in much the same manner as grains or beans. Sort and remove any stones, sticks, or hard shells. Then place the seeds in a bowl and cover with cold water. Stir and pour off the water. When washing sesame seeds, some seeds may float to the top. These can be skimmed off and discarded. Repeat the rinsing process. Then place the seeds in a strainer and rinse quickly under a stream of cold water. Sesame seeds are very small and require a very fine-meshed strainer for the final rinsing or they will fall through the strainer.

STEP 2: SOAKING AND DILUTING

Soaking

Some of the dried foods used in macrobiotic cooking need to be soaked before being added to dishes.

Sea Vegetables After washing kombu, wakame, hijiki, dulse, or sea palm as described earlier, place it in a bowl and add just enough water to cover. Let it soak for 3 to 5 minutes, then remove it a handful at a time, squeeze out excess liquid, and place it on your cutting board. Discard the soaking water if it is very salty. If not, you can use it as part of the water measurement in the recipe.

Shredded Daikon Place the dried shredded daikon in a bowl, add enough cold water to cover, and swish it around with your fingers. Place it in a strainer and rinse quickly under a stream of cold water. Then place it in a clean bowl, add enough water to cover, and let it soak for 5 to 10 minutes. Remove and squeeze out excess liquid. The dried daikon can now be placed on the cutting board. If the soaking water has turned dark, discard it. If it is still light-colored, you can use it as a part of the water measurement in the recipe.

Dried Tofu
Place dried tofu in a bowl and add *warm* water to cover. Let it soak for 7 to 10 minutes. Pour off the soaking water. Then add cold water to cover, quickly rinse, and pour off. Stack two or three pieces on top of each other, squeeze out excess liquid, and place on your cutting board.

Dried Shiitake Place the dried mushrooms in a bowl and add *warm* water to cover. Let them soak for 10 to 15 minutes. Remove several at a time and squeeze out excess liquid. Place on a cutting board and cut away the stems with a vegetable knife. The stems may be saved and used in making soup stock. The soaking water can be used as part of the water measurement in the recipe.

Dried Lotus Seeds Place the seeds in a bowl, cover with cold water, rinse quickly, and pour off the water. Place them in a strainer and rinse quickly under a stream of cold water. Then put them in a bowl and add cold water to cover. Let them soak for 30 to 60 minutes. Remove and use as directed. The soaking water can be used as a part of the water measurement.

Dried Fu Fu comes in round doughnut shapes and flat sheets. Place either variety in a bowl, add enough cold water to cover, and soak for 5 to 10 minutes. If you are using round fu, remove two or three pieces at a time, squeeze out excess liquid, and place on a cutting board. If you are using flat sheets, pick them up with both hands, squeeze out excess liquid, and place on a cutting board.

Dried Chestnuts Place the chestnuts in a bowl, add cold water to cover, rinse quickly, and drain. Then place them in a dry skillet, turn the flame to medium-low, and roast until golden brown, stirring constantly to prevent burning. Place them in a bowl and add just enough cold water to cover. Let them soak for 10 to 15 minutes. Remove and use as directed. The soaking water can be used as part of the water measurement.

Dried Fruit Place dried fruit in a colander and rinse quickly under a stream of cold water. Place in a bowl and add just enough water to cover. Soak for 10 to 15 minutes until soft. Remove them a handful at a time, squeeze out excess liquid, and place on a cutting board. The soaking water can be used in the recipe.

Whole Grains In certain recipes we recommend soaking whole grains before cooking them. First wash the grains as directed earlier and place them in a pressure cooker or cooking pot. Add the amount of water called for in the recipe and soak for 6 to 8 hours without adding salt. Then place them on the stove and cook in the soaking water.

Beans With few exceptions, beans need to be soaked before cooking. First wash them as directed above. Then place them in a bowl, add enough cold water to cover, and soak for 6 to 8 hours. After they have finished soaking, place them in a strainer and rinse quickly under a stream of cold water. The soaking water from azuki beans, chick-peas, or black soybeans can be added to the recipe (lentils don't require soaking), while the water used to soak other beans should be discarded.

Diluting

Some foods come in a powdered or concentrated form and need to be diluted before being added to your dishes.

Miso Diluting miso before adding it to soup stock helps it dissolve and mix thoroughly into the broth. Place miso in a suribachi and add the same—or a slightly larger—volume of water or soup broth from the pot. Mash it in a circular motion with the wooden pestle until it is dissolved thoroughly and has a smooth consistency. It is now ready to add to your soup.

Kuzu Kuzu, a white chalklike substance, needs to be diluted before being used in cooking. Place the required amount in a measuring cup and add an equal amount of cold spring or well water. Mash with a spoon and stir quickly until it is dissolved completely. It is now ready to be added to the recipe.

Arrowroot Flour Arrowroot flour, a white powdery substance, also needs diluting. Place the flour in a measuring cup and add a slightly larger volume of water. Stir until it dissolves completely and add it to the recipe as directed.

STEP 3: CUTTING

For vegetables, fruits, soy foods, and special items like fu and seitan, cutting is the final step before cooking. Cutting is an art that requires patience and skill to master. As with other skills, the best way to develop your cutting ability is to practice it.

Keeping your knife properly sharpened is essential for efficient cutting (see box).

HOW TO SHARPEN A KNIFE

To sharpen your knife, first moisten or oil your sharpening stone. Next, hold the handle of your knife in your right hand and place your left thumb, middle, and index fingers firmly against the left side of the blade. Tilt the blade so that it comes to about a 25- to 30-degree angle to the stone. Slide the entire length of the blade gently but firmly across the length of the stone. Remove the blade and slide it across again. Repeat several times until the blade is sharp. Then, to remove any burrs, flip the blade over and run it very gently over the entire length of the stone.

Once your knife has been sharpened, wash it to remove any metal filings and oil. It is now ready to use or to put away. Before putting it away, though, be sure to dry it. To store your knife, either place it in a special wood knife rack or wrap it in a clean kitchen towel (to protect the blade) and place it in a drawer. It is convenient to keep your knife rack near your cutting board.

Cutting Vegetables

Vegetables can be cut in a practically endless variety of ways. You can cut them into different shapes, sizes, and thicknesses. Cutting vegetables artistically adds to the over-all balance and enjoyment of a meal.

When cutting vegetables, hold them with the fingers curled slightly. Tilt the blade of your knife slightly away from the fingers, with the top of the blade resting against the middle or end joint. Then place the front part of the blade on the vegetable and slide it firmly but gently forward with a slight downward pressure. Cut through the vegetable with the entire length of the blade. It is best not to saw or to push down to the extent that the knife tears through the vegetable. This produces jagged cuts that are not very attractive.

Below are illustrations and brief explanations of the basic cutting styles.

Rounds

Vegetables may be cut into thick or thin rounds, depending on the dish being prepared. Thin rounds are more appropriate for quickly cooked dishes, thicker rounds for longer cooking times.

Diagonal Slices

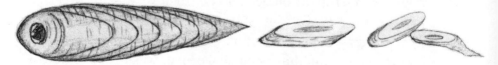

Hold the knife at an angle to slice your vegetables on the diagonal. The length of the pieces can be determined by the angle of the blade.

Irregular Wedges

Vegetables are cut on the diagonal and rotated toward you 90 degrees after each cut. The pieces are roughly the same size but are irregularly shaped.

Rectangles

First cut the vegetables into large rounds 1 to 2 inches thick. Stand each round on end and slice into 4 to 5 pieces ¼ to ⅓ inch thick. Then cut each section into thin rectangles.

Half-Moons

Cut each vegetable lengthwise through the middle into 2 halves. Then cut each half into thin rounds.

Quarters

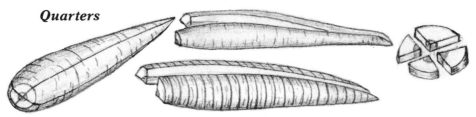

First slice each vegetable lengthwise into halves. Then cut each half down the center again. Slice the quarters crosswise.

Matchsticks

Cut each vegetable on the diagonal and then slice the diagonal pieces into thin matchsticks.

Shavings

Shave the vegetable from the bottom end as if you're sharpening a pencil. Rotate it slightly after each cut. Changing the angle of the knife makes for thinner or thicker shavings.

Dicing and Cubing

Cut the vegetables into 1- to 2-inch chunks. Stand each chunk on end and cut into ¼- to ½-inch cubes by slicing vertically, then horizontally, then crosswise. When dicing onions, cut them in half horizontally. Then cut thin parallel slices vertically, leaving the onion attached to the root base. Then cut in the opposite direction toward the base. Finally dice the root base into small pieces.

Cutting Squash

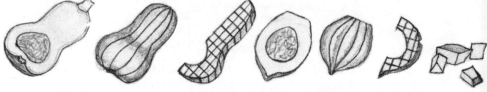

Cut the squash in half and remove the seeds. Place each half on the cutting board so that the cut surface faces downward. Slice each half into thick wedges and then slice each wedge into cubes or thin slices. (When cutting squash for sweet vegetable drink, slice each half into very thin wedges, then slice each wedge into very thin slices.)

Wedge Slices

Slice onions or other round vegetables lengthwise in half. Then cut each half into ¼- to ½-inch-thick wedges.

Slicing Cabbage

Cut the cabbage lengthwise into quarters. Cut away the attached core. Slice the core thin on the diagonal. Then slice the leaves on the diagonal into either thick or thin slices. (When cutting cabbage for sweet vegetable drink, slice the leafy portion into very thin slices.)

Flower Shapes

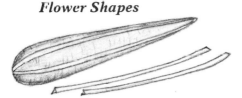 

Cut 4 or 5 grooves around the vegetable lengthwise at equal distances. Then slice the vegetable into thin rounds.

Slicing Large Leafy Greens

Place 2 or 3 leaves on top of each other. Slice through the center along both sides of the spine. Cut the halves either straight or on the diagonal into strips ⅛ to ¼ inch thick. Then chop the spine very fine.

Slicing Fine Leafy Greens

Place the bunch of greens on the cutting board. Cut straight across or on the diagonal. Each slice can be from ¼ to 2 inches in length, depending on your preference for the dish.

Cutting Sea Vegetables

Sea vegetables can be cut in basically the same way that land vegetables are cut. However, with the exception of nori, they are usually soaked prior to slicing, which makes them soft and slippery. They need to be handled a little differently from land vegetables. Also, if you soak them too long (more than 5 minutes), they become very slippery and difficult to hold while cutting. This is especially true of kombu and wakame. Below are guidelines for slicing kombu, wakame, dulse, hijiki, and arame. Instructions for cutting nori are presented in the recipes.

Kombu Squares   Spread the kombu on the cutting board and slice lengthwise strips about an inch wide. Then slice each strip crosswise into 1-inch squares.

Kombu Rectangles   Spread the kombu flat on the cutting board and slice it lengthwise into strips about 2 inches wide. Then slice each strip crosswise into ¼- to ½-inch strips.

Kombu Matchsticks   Spread the kombu flat on the cutting board. Then roll it up into a tight cylinder and slice it on the diagonal or straight across into very thin slices.

Wakame   Spread the wakame on a cutting board as you would leafy green vegetables. Cut away the hard stem as with leafy greens and slice it very fine as with leafy greens. Stack the leafy portions on top of each other and slice straight across or on the diagonal.

Hijiki, Arame, or Dulse   Place the hijiki, arame, or dulse on a cutting board. Slice thin or thick on the diagonal.

Cutting Fruits

Round melons can be sliced in the same manner as squash (into wedges or wedges that are sliced into chunks). Apples, pears, peaches, apricots, plums, nectarines, and similar fruits can be either sliced in half or quartered. Remove the seeds and then slice the sections into wedges, half-moons, or cubes. Strawberries can be halved, quartered, or sliced lengthwise; other berries can be left whole. Dried fruit can be diced or sliced on the diagonal after soaking or in some cases left whole.

Cutting Other Foods

Foods such as tofu, dried tofu, tempeh, seitan, and shredded daikon also need to be cut. Guidelines are presented below.

Tofu   To cut tofu into rectangular slices, place it on a cutting board and cut it crosswise into ¼- to ½-inch slices. If you wish to make cubes, after cutting the tofu crosswise, cut it lengthwise into ½- to 1-inch strips. Then cut 2 or 3 strips at a time into 1-inch cubes.

Dried Tofu or Tempeh   Place on the cutting board and slice lengthwise into ¼- to 1-inch strips. Then cut the strips, 2 or 3 at a time, into 1-inch cubes.

Seitan   Seitan can simply be sliced on the diagonal or cubed.

Fu   Round: Place the rounds one at a time on the cutting board. Cut in half and then cut each into quarters.

Flat: Place on a cutting board, cut lengthwise into halves or thirds, and then cut crosswise into strips.

Shredded Daikon   Squeeze out excess liquid and place on a cutting board. Cut on the diagonal into ¼- to 1-inch lengths.

PART III
QUICK AND NATURAL
MEALS

In this section we present a full week of macrobiotic breakfasts, lunches, and dinners. The recipes in this book are part of a coordinated meal plan in which each menu flows into the next. The instructions in the recipes are designed to help you save time in the kitchen.

Our week begins with dinner. These quick and natural meals include a wide selection of whole grains, soups, bean and soybean product dishes, and vegetables from land and sea. Natural, sugar-free desserts and low-fat, white-meat fish are also featured in several menus. Most of these full-course dinners can be prepared in about an hour and a half.

The meals we present serve three or four adults. Adjust the quantities in the recipes if you are cooking for more or fewer people. On days when dinner leftovers are the main ingredients in breakfast and lunch on the following day, the quantity of food in the recipes will be enough for these extra meals. So, for example, pressure-cooked brown rice can serve as the main dish at dinner and then be used on the following day to make a soft porridge for breakfast and rice balls for lunch. Similarly, the soups, and the bean and vegetable dishes prepared at dinner can also be used to prepare other meals. In general, however, try to use leftovers within a day or so. If you refrigerate or store them for longer than that, they start to lose freshness and vitality. Any leftovers that are not specifically called for on the following day can simply be reheated and eaten along with the meal.

The breakfasts and lunches in this section each take about 20 to 30 minutes to prepare. You have several options when preparing these meals. One option, for those who need to take a lunch to work, is to cook both meals in the morning. On average, both meals can be prepared in about 40 minutes to an hour. Breakfast can be enjoyed at home, and lunch can be packed in a lunch box and thermos. If you don't have time to cook lunch in the morning, a second option is simply to pack leftovers from the night before in your lunch box. This takes only a few minutes. We recommend using a stainless-steel lunch box, preferably with dividers to keep each dish separate. Soups, beverages, stews, and other liquid or semiliquid dishes can be kept in a thermos. In some cases foods can be taken to work in glass jars. Arrange your foods attractively in the lunch box and store it at room temperature or in a refrigerator until lunchtime. As stated earlier, we don't recommend heating foods in a microwave oven.

Along with the foods suggested in the lunch menu, any of the natural snacks listed in Chapter 6 can be included. (It might be a good idea to keep a supply of natural snacks at your workplace.) They can be enjoyed at lunch or any time during the day.

Another option, for those who are home during the day, is to prepare breakfast in the morning and lunch later in the day. Whichever option you choose, the suggestions in this chapter will help you cook quickly and efficiently.

Keep in mind that only a small amount of the total cooking time usually is spent in actual preparation. Preliminary steps such as washing, soaking, pureeing, and cutting take only a fraction of the total time needed for most dishes. Once a dish has been set up, often the best thing to do is to let it cook by itself. This leaves you free to start other dishes, set the table, or attend to other chores.

It is important to prepare complete meals when you begin eating macrobiotically. The recipes in this section are presented as a part of complete, naturally balanced meals. The complete menu is presented first, followed by the recipe for each dish. The recipes start with those that take the longest time to cook and finish with those that take the least amount of time.

When eating, however, we recommend starting with soup and then moving on to the main dishes. Whole grains can be eaten throughout the meal, and side dishes can be finished one by one or according to each person's desire. Fish is generally eaten along with the meal, and dessert and beverage are saved for the end. In more formal macrobiotic practice, we suggest eating the side dishes—interspersed with mouthfuls of the main grain dish—from the most yang (contracted) to the most yin (expanded). Therefore, a dish containing burdock root would be eaten at the beginning, while a pressed cucumber salad would come toward the end. Please see the discussion about the yin and yang qualities of foods in Part I to determine which dishes are more yin or yang. For everyday practice, however, we don't need to be as careful about the order of eating.

Each recipe includes a list of utensils and ingredients and step-by-step instructions for preparing the dish. (Basic kitchen equipment, such as vegetable brushes, sponges, and cutting boards, is not listed in each recipe, nor are containers for storing leftovers.) The sizes we specify for pots and bowls are approximate; a larger or smaller one will do in many cases. With practice you'll be able to determine the right sizes for preparing a dish. We also include suggestions for putting the dishes together in a complete meal, as well as tips on storing leftovers and preparing for the meals that follow.

Each menu includes the total length of time needed to prepare the complete meal, and each recipe notes the total cooking time for the dish, along with the approximate time for actual hands-on preparation. Kitchen cleanup is not included in these times.

Feel free to adapt the meal plan to your needs. The quick and natural meal plan is presented as a general guide and not as a program to be followed inflexibly. For example, you can follow the menus in order from Day One through Day Seven to familiarize yourself with the foods and cooking methods, or you can select individual meals and prepare them one at a time. Any of the recipes can be prepared individually as a part of your own meal plan. As you will discover, there are many ways to use the menus and recipes in this section.

Variety is an essential element in a healthful way of eating. Don't stick with the same dishes day in and day out; change them around. You can try any of the following if you feel you need more variety in your cooking:

1. Change the ingredients you cook with.
2. Vary your cooking methods.
3. Cut your vegetables in new ways.
4. Vary the amount of water used in cooking.
5. Increase or decrease the amounts of condiments and seasonings you use.
6. Change the type of condiments and seasonings you use.
7. Vary the amount of time used in preparing your dishes.
8. Try different intensities of heat; for example, vary the height of the flame used in cooking.
9. Change the combinations of foods and dishes.
10. Vary your foods and cooking methods in harmony with the changing of the seasons.

Once you have mastered the basic techniques and dishes in this section, please create your own recipes and menus. You can use any of the macrobiotic cookbooks listed in the "Recommended Reading" as a source of ideas. Also, we recommend that you attend macrobiotic dinners and cooking classes presented at educational centers near you. In this way your cooking will always be dynamic, new, and creative.

For instructions for washing, soaking, pureeing, and cutting foods, please refer to Chapter 9. Also, many of the dishes are garnished with chopped scallions or parsley (see box).

- To prepare scallions for garnish, first wash them under a stream of cold water (remove any damaged or aged leaves) and slice them very thin on the diagonal.
- Parsley can be washed under a stream of cold water and then chopped fine or minced.

You can use any of the condiments, pickles, and beverages listed in Chapter 6 with your meals. Before planning your meals, refer to the following section, in which we give recipes for some of these staples. Gomashio and sea vegetable powders are best when made at home and can be kept on the table. A variety of other condiments—some homemade and others store-bought—are delicious on whole grains and other dishes. Pickles can be stored in the pantry or refrigerator and included with meals. Bancha, barley, and brown rice tea can also be served at each meal, and the other beverages listed in Chapter 6 can be enjoyed on occasion. Rather than specifying which varieties to use, we simply include the heading "Condiments and Beverage" in each menu. Please select the ones that appeal to you.

Our principal aim in setting up the recipes as we have is to make them as quick and easy to use as possible. Therefore, we've departed from standard recipe format somewhat. We note the necessary preparation of foods in the ingredients list, and then we repeat the instructions for preparation in the recipe steps. This allows you to determine, from a glance at the ingredients, what preparation is called for, while the recipe directions tell you in what order to perform each task to make preparation as smooth as it can be. Again, refer to Chapter 9 for detailed explanations of these preliminaries.

STAPLES TO MAKE AHEAD

A few basic items can be made before you begin preparing meals. Although staple condiments such as gomashio and sea vegetable powders can be bought at the store, they are most nutritious and flavorful when made at home. Home-made condiments can be stored in the cupboard or kept on the table. Staple beverages such as bancha and cereal grain teas can be made in advance, kept on the stove, and then reheated whenever you want tea. Other condiments, including umeboshi plums, tekka, shiso leaves, and green nori flakes, can be bought ready-made and kept in small jars for convenient use.

The recipes that follow provide about a week's supply of condiments for four people. We suggest that you prepare them fresh every week or so.

C O N D I M E N T S

GOMASHIO
Approximate preparation time: 20–25 minutes

UTENSILS
small (8-inch) stainless-steel skillet
bamboo rice paddle
suribachi and pestle
medium (2-quart) porcelain or glass bowl
fine-meshed strainer
small (2-cup) jar or container with lid for storing

INGREDIENTS
1½–2 tablespoons (to taste) sea salt

1 cup black or white sesame seeds

PREPARATION
1. Place sea salt in the skillet.
2. Turn the flame to medium and roast for 1–2 minutes, stirring constantly with the rice paddle.
3. Pour the roasted salt into the suribachi. Grind it with a slow circular motion until it is crushed into a fine powder. Leave the crushed salt in the suribachi.
4. Wash and drain seeds.
5. Wash, rinse, and dry the skillet and place the seeds in it. Roast the seeds over a medium-low flame, stirring constantly with the rice paddle to prevent burning. Shake the skillet from time to time so that the seeds roast evenly.
6. When the seeds give off a nutty fragrance, darken in color, and begin popping, take a seed between your thumb and index finger and crush it. If it crushes easily, the seeds are done. If not, continue to roast them a little longer.
7. When the seeds are done, pour them into the suribachi. (The seeds will burn if left in the skillet after the flame has been turned off.)
8. Slowly grind the seeds and mix them with sea salt, using a steady circular motion. Continue until the seeds are

about half crushed. (Gomashio should not be ground too fine.) After letting it cool, pour it into a jar or container. Tighten the lid and place it in the cupboard or on the table.

KOMBU POWDER
Approximate preparation time: 20–25 minutes

UTENSILS
baking sheet
suribachi and pestle
small (2-cup) jar or
    container with lid for
    storing

INGREDIENTS
4–5 strips of kombu, about
    10–12 inches long

PREPARATION
1. Place unwashed kombu on the baking sheet and place in the oven.
2. Set the oven at 350°F and bake for 15–20 minutes, until the kombu becomes dark and crisp but not burned or charred.
3. Remove the kombu and allow it to cool slightly.
4. Crumble the roasted kombu in your fingers and let it drop into the suribachi.
5. Slowly grind the kombu with a steady circular motion of the pestle until it becomes a fine powder.
6. Pour into a jar or container. Tighten the lid and place in the cupboard or on your table.

GOMA-WAKAME (SESAME-WAKAME) POWDER
Approximate preparation time: 20–25 minutes

UTENSILS

baking sheet
fine-meshed strainer
small (8-inch) stainless-steel
  skillet
bamboo rice paddle
small (1-quart) porcelain or
  glass bowl

suribachi and pestle
small (2-cup) jar or
  container with lid for
  storing

INGREDIENTS

4–5 strips of wakame, about
  10 inches long (see note
  below)

½ cup white sesame seeds

PREPARATION

1. Place unwashed wakame on the baking sheet and place in the oven.

2. Set the oven at 350°F and bake for 15–20 minutes, until the wakame becomes dark and crisp but not burned or charred.

3. While the wakame is baking, wash and drain the sesame seeds.

4. Place the sesame seeds in the skillet and roast over a medium-low flame, stirring constantly with the rice paddle to prevent burning. Shake the skillet from time to time so that the seeds roast evenly.

5. When the seeds give off a nutty fragrance, darken in color, and begin to pop, crush a seed between your thumb and index finger. If it crushes easily, the seeds are done. If not, continue to roast a little longer.

6. When the seeds are done, pour them into the bowl.

7. Remove the wakame from the oven and use your fingers to crumble it into the suribachi. Then slowly grind the wakame with a steady circular motion of the pestle until it becomes a fine powder.

8. Pour the roasted seeds into the suribachi and grind

together with the powdered wakame until the seeds are half crushed. Allow to cool, pour into the jar or container, tighten the lid, and place in the cupboard or on the table.

Note: After the wakame is baked and ground to a powder, the powder should be approximately 40 to 50 percent of the total volume; this takes about 4 to 5 strips.

B E V E R A G E S

BANCHA TEA
Approximate preparation time: 10–15 minutes

UTENSILS

measuring cup
small (8-inch) stainless-steel
  skillet
bamboo rice paddle
small (2-cup) glass jar for
  storing

glass teapot
tablespoon
bamboo tea strainer

INGREDIENTS

1 cup bancha twigs
1½ quarts spring or well
  water

PREPARATION

1. To preroast bancha, place the twigs in the skillet and dry-roast over a medium flame for 2 minutes, stirring constantly with the rice paddle and shaking the pan to prevent the twigs from burning.

2. Remove the twigs from the skillet, allow them to cool, and store in an airtight jar.

3. To prepare bancha, fill the teapot with 1½ quarts of water and add 2 tablespoons of roasted twigs. Place the lid on the teapot.

4. Place the teapot on the stove, turn the flame to high, and bring to a boil.

5. Turn the flame to low and simmer for 2–5 minutes for a mild tea or 7–10 minutes for a stronger beverage.

6. After the tea has finished cooking, strain through a bamboo tea strainer into individual cups.

Note: Bancha twigs can be reused. Simply add fresh spring or well water and heat as above. A bunch of twigs can generally be used to make two or three pots of tea.

PREROASTED BARLEY TEA (MUGICHA)
Approximate preparation time: 10 minutes

UTENSILS

glass teapot   tablespoon
measuring cup

INGREDIENTS

1½ quarts spring or well   2 tablespoons preroasted
  water   packaged barley tea

PREPARATION

1. Fill the teapot with water, add the preroasted barley tea, and bring to a boil over a high flame.

2. Turn the flame to low and simmer for 2–5 minutes for mild tea or 7–10 minutes for a stronger beverage.

3. Strain through a bamboo tea strainer into individual cups.

HOMEMADE GRAIN TEAS

Brown rice and barley can be roasted at home and used to make deliciously refreshing tea. Other beverages, such as grain coffee and spring or well water, can be made or used as needed. Instructions for preparing other beverages are presented with the recipes (see index).

Approximate preparation time: 20–25 minutes

UTENSILS

measuring cup
small (1-quart) porcelain or
  glass bowl
strainer
small (8-inch) stainless-steel
  skillet

bamboo rice paddle
glass teapot
bamboo tea strainer
small (2-cup) jar or
  container with lid for
  storing

INGREDIENTS

1 cup barley or short-grain
  brown rice

1½ quarts spring or well
  water

PREPARATION

1. Wash, rinse, and drain the rice or barley in the bowl and strainer.

2. Place in the skillet, turn the flame to medium, and dry-roast for 10 minutes, stirring constantly to prevent burning and shaking the pan from time to time.

3. Place the water in the teapot and add ¼ to ½ cup roasted grain, depending on how strong you like your tea. Place the cover on the teapot and bring to a boil.

4. Reduce the flame to low and simmer for 10–15 minutes.

5. Strain the tea through a bamboo tea strainer into individual cups.

6. The unused grain can be stored in an airtight jar and used whenever you desire grain tea.

P I C K L E S

A variety of homemade pickles add flavor and balance to your meals. Some pickles—such as those presented in the recipes—can be made in an hour or so. Others require a longer time to age and ferment. Below are recipes for quick pickles that are ready in several days. They can be made in advance, stored in the refrigerator, and eaten along with meals whenever you like. On average, about a tablespoon or so of pickles can be eaten daily. If your pickles have a strong salty taste, simply rinse them under cold water for a few seconds.

UMEBOSHI PICKLES
Approximate time until ready: 3–5 days

UTENSILS
large (3- to 4-quart) glass jar with lid
measuring cup
vegetable knife

cotton cheesecloth
string or a rubber band
strainer (when serving)

INGREDIENTS
7–8 (to taste) umeboshi plums
2 quarts spring or well water
1 ½-pound package red radishes, washed and ends trimmed off (1 cup)

1 medium onion, peeled, washed, and sliced into thick half-moons (1 cup)

PREPARATION
1. Place the umeboshi plums in the glass jar (use 7 for a less salty pickle, 8 for a saltier pickle) and add the water.
2. Fasten the lid securely on the jar and shake it well. Then let the plums sit in the water for 3–5 hours, until the water turns pink.
3. Wash the vegetables and slice the onion as directed.
4. Remove the lid and place the radishes in the jar.

5. Place a small piece of cotton cheesecloth over the top of the jar. Fasten it tightly with string or a rubber band.

6. Place the jar in a cool place (such as a cupboard or pantry) and let it sit for 3–5 days (3–4 days in warm weather, 4–5 in cool weather).

7. When the pickles are ready, remove the cheesecloth and replace with the lid. Place the jar in the refrigerator.

8. The pickles can be kept for 3–4 weeks in the refrigerator. Simply rinse in a strainer for several seconds under a stream of cold water before serving.

TAMARI SOY SAUCE PICKLES
Approximate time until ready: 3–5 days

UTENSILS

measuring cup

large (2-quart) glass jar
  with lid

vegetable knife

cotton cheesecloth

string or a rubber band

strainer (when serving)

INGREDIENTS

2 cups spring or well water

2 cups tamari soy sauce

¼ bunch of broccoli,
  washed and sliced into
  flowerets (1 cup)

1 medium onion, peeled,
  washed, and sliced into
  thick half-moons (1 cup)
  or enough small whole
  onions to make 1 cup

1 medium carrot, washed
  and sliced on the
  diagonal (1 cup)

PREPARATION

1. Place the water and tamari soy sauce in a jar. Fasten the lid and shake the jar well to mix. Remove the lid.

2. Wash and slice the vegetables. Place the sliced vegetables in the jar with the tamari and water.

3. Cover the jar with the cotton cheesecloth and fasten tightly with string or a rubber band.

4. Place the jar in a cool place (such as a cupboard or pantry) and let it sit for 3–5 days (3–4 days in warm weather, 4–5 days in cool weather).

5. When the pickles are ready remove the cheesecloth and replace with the lid; store in the refrigerator. They will last for about a month but become saltier the longer they stay in the tamari soy sauce mixture.

6. Remove and rinse in a strainer under a stream of cold water before serving.

BRINE PICKLES
Approximate time until ready: 2–3 days

UTENSILS

measuring cup
medium (4-quart) stainless-
   steel cooking pot
large (4-quart) glass jar
   with lid

vegetable knife
cotton cheesecloth
strainer (when serving)

INGREDIENTS

1½ quarts spring or well
   water
2–3 teaspoons (to taste) sea
   salt
¼ small head of cauliflower,
   washed and sliced into
   small flowerets, then
   sliced in half lengthwise
   (1 cup)
2 unwaxed pickling
   cucumbers, washed and
   sliced lengthwise into
   quarters (1 cup)

1 medium onion, peeled,
   washed, and sliced into
   thin half-moons (1 cup)
½ cup thinly sliced daikon
½ medium carrot, washed
   and sliced thin on the
   diagonal (½ cup)
1 strip of kombu, about 5–6
   inches long, dusted with a
   clean, damp sponge

PREPARATION

1. Place the water and sea salt in the pot and bring to a boil.

2. When the water comes to a boil, remove the pot from the burner.

3. Let the water sit until it becomes completely cool.

4. Pour the cool salt water into the glass jar.

5. Wash and slice the vegetables.

6. Place the vegetables and kombu in the salt water.

7. Cover the jar with cotton cheesecloth and fasten tightly with string or a rubber band.

8. Place the jar in a cool dark place for 2–3 days.

9. When the pickles are ready (they should taste salty and slightly sour and will be crispy), remove the cheesecloth, replace with the lid, and refrigerate them. The pickles will keep for 2–4 weeks.

10. Rinse in a strainer under a stream of cold water before serving to remove any strong salty flavor.

DAY ONE

PRESSURE-COOKED BROWN RICE
LENTILS AND VEGETABLES
QUICK RED RADISH PICKLES
MISO SOUP WITH DAIKON AND SHIITAKE
WATER-SAUTEED CARROTS
BLANCHED WATERCRESS
CONDIMENTS AND BEVERAGE
Approximate preparation time: 1 hour and 15 minutes

Putting the Meal Together: Once the rice has started cooking on the stove, you can begin to set up the lentil-vegetable dish. Once that dish has started cooking, proceed to the radish pickles and to the other dishes in the order presented. If you follow this progression and move from one dish to the next, your dishes will finish cooking at about the same time and the meal can be finished in the amount of time indicated above.

As you place your foods in serving bowls, garnish them as suggested and arrange them on your dining table. Place the brown rice in the center of the table and the other dishes around or on either side of it. Arrange your dishes so that the colors balance and complement each other. Serve the meal with condiments and beverage of your choice.

165

PRESSURE-COOKED BROWN RICE

Pressure-cooked brown rice is a staple in most macrobiotic households. Please experiment and discover the best method for making delicious brown rice.

Approximate cooking time: 65–70 minutes (about 10 minutes preparation time)

UTENSILS

measuring cup
medium (2-quart) porcelain
  or glass bowl
strainer
5-liter pressure cooker

flame deflector
chopstick
bamboo rice paddle
wood serving bowl

INGREDIENTS

4 cups short-grain brown
  rice
5⅓ cups spring or well
  water

4 small pinches of sea salt
1 sprig of parsley, washed

PREPARATION

1. Place the rice in the bowl and wash.

2. Place the washed rice in the pressure cooker. Add the water and place the uncovered cooker over a low flame until the water just begins to boil.

3. Add the sea salt. Place the lid on the cooker and turn the flame to high. This will cause the pressure to come up.

4. When the pressure is up, place the flame deflector under the cooker and reduce the flame to medium-low.

5. Let the rice cook on a medium-low flame for about 50 minutes. Then remove the cooker from the burner (it can be placed on a cold burner) and gently place the narrow tip of a chopstick under the pressure gauge to allow steam to escape more rapidly. When the pressure has come down completely, remove the lid and let the rice sit for 4–5 minutes.

6. Remove the rice with the rice paddle and place it in a wood serving bowl.

7. Rinse a sprig of parsley under a stream of cold water and place it in the center of the rice as a garnish.

LENTILS AND VEGETABLES

Approximate cooking time: 1 hour and 10 minutes (about 10 minutes preparation time)

UTENSILS

measuring cup
medium (2-quart) porcelain
  or glass bowl
strainer
vegetable knife
tablespoon
medium (4-quart) cooking
  pot with lid

teaspoon
serving spoon
porcelain (preferably light-
  colored) or glass serving
  bowl

INGREDIENTS

2 cups green lentils
1 strip of kombu, 3–4
  inches long, soaked and
  diced
1 cup spring or well water
  for soaking kombu
1 quart spring or well water

2 cups diced onion (about 2
  medium onions)
1 ear of sweet corn
1 tablespoon chopped
  parsley
½ teaspoon sea salt

PREPARATION

1. Place the lentils in the bowl and wash them. Set them aside to drain.

2. Wipe both sides of the kombu with a clean, damp sponge. Place it in a bowl with 1 cup of water and let it soak for 3–5 minutes. Remove, place it on the cutting board, and dice. Save the soaking water.

3. Peel and wash the onions and then dice them into large pieces.

4. Remove the husk from the ear of corn and wash the corn under a stream of cold water. Place it on the cutting board and remove the kernels with the vegetable knife. Set them aside.

5. Wash the parsley under a stream of cold water, chop it very fine, and set it aside.

6. Place the kombu, onions, lentils, and water, including

the kombu soaking water, in a pot. Bring to a boil, place the lid on the pot, and reduce the flame to medium-low.

7. Cover and simmer on a medium-low flame for 45 minutes. Then add the corn kernels and sea salt. Cover and simmer for another 10–15 minutes.

8. Remove the lid, add the chopped parsley, and cook, uncovered, for another 3–5 minutes. Remove from the pot and place in a serving bowl.

QUICK RED RADISH PICKLES

When pickles are prepared with a meal, it is unnecessary to serve other varieties.

Approximate time to make: 1 hour and 15 minutes (about 15 minutes preparation time)

UTENSILS

vegetable knife
measuring cup
pickle press
tablespoon

strainer (optional)
glass or porcelain serving
bowl or plate

INGREDIENTS

1 cup sliced red radish (1 or 2 bunches of radishes with the greens attached), greens reserved
2 cups finely chopped radish greens (trimmed from the radishes)

2–2½ tablespoons (to taste) umeboshi vinegar

PREPARATION

1. Place the radishes (with greens attached) on the cutting board. Slice off the greens. Wash the radishes and greens separately.

2. Chop the greens fine and place them in the pickle press.

3. Slice the radishes into thin rounds and place them in the press.

4. Add the umeboshi vinegar (use 2 tablespoons if you like it less salty, 2½ if you like it saltier) and thoroughly mix it with the radishes and greens.

5. Place the lid on the press and tighten the pressure plate to apply pressure. Let the vegetables sit under pressure for about 1 hour.

6. Disengage the pressure plate, remove the lid, pour off excess liquid, and take the vegetables out of the press. Squeeze out the remaining liquid with your hands. If the vegetables taste too salty, place them in a strainer and rinse quickly under a stream of cold water.

7. Place the pressed vegetables in a serving dish.

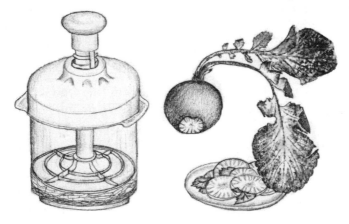

MISO SOUP WITH DAIKON AND SHIITAKE

This basic miso soup is a staple in macrobiotic cooking. It is simple, nourishing, and delicious.

Approximate cooking time: 30–35 minutes (about 10–15 minutes preparation time)

UTENSILS

measuring cup
medium (4-quart) stainless-
   steel cooking pot with lid
2 small (1-quart) porcelain
   or glass bowls for soaking

vegetable knife
teaspoon
ladle

INGREDIENTS

1½ quarts spring or well water

¼ cup soaked and sliced wakame

5–6 shiitake mushrooms, soaked, stems removed, and sliced

2 cups shiitake soaking water

1 cup wakame soaking water (optional)

1 medium daikon root, 6–8 inches long, washed and sliced into thin half-moons (2 cups)

2–2½ teaspoons (to taste) barley miso, pureed in ¼ cup spring or well water

2 tablespoons chopped scallion

PREPARATION

1. Place the cooking water in the pot, cover, turn the flame to high, and bring to a boil.

2. Wash, soak, and slice the wakame.

3. Soak and slice the shiitake. (Whether you use 5 or 6 depends on whether you're serving 3 or 4 people. Generally 1–1½ shiitake are sufficient for each person.)

4. Add the shiitake soaking water to the cooking water and bring to a boil again.

5. If the wakame soaking water has an overly salty taste, discard it. If the water is only mildly salty, you can add it to the cooking water. Simply pour it in and let the water come to a boil again.

6. When the water begins to boil, add the sliced shiitake, cover the pot, and reduce the flame to medium. Let the broth simmer for 5–7 minutes.

7. Add the wakame. Cover the pot and simmer for 3–5 minutes.

8. Add the sliced daikon, cover, and simmer for another 3–5 minutes.

9. Turn the flame to low.

10. Put the miso in the measuring cup. Add ¼ cup of water and puree with a teaspoon. (Whether you use 2 or 2½ teaspoons miso depends on how salty you want the dish to be.)

11. Place 3 cups of the unseasoned broth in a glass jar. Fasten the lid and refrigerate until the following morning.

12. Add the pureed miso to the remaining broth and let it simmer for 2–3 minutes.

13. Wash the scallions and chop fine.

14. Ladle the soup into individual serving bowls and garnish each with a few chopped scallions.

WATER-SAUTEED CARROTS
Approximate cooking time: 15–18 minutes (about 7–8 minutes preparation time)

UTENSILS

measuring cup	fine-meshed strainer
vegetable knife	tablespoon
medium (10-inch) stainless-steel skillet with lid	small (8-inch) stainless-steel skillet
teaspoon	chopsticks or wood spoon
small (1-quart) porcelain or glass bowl	porcelain serving bowl

INGREDIENTS

About 8 medium carrots, washed and sliced thin on the diagonal (5 cups)	1½ teaspoons tamari soy sauce
1 cup spring or well water	2 tablespoons black sesame seeds
Small pinch of sea salt	

PREPARATION

1. Wash the carrots and cut them into thin diagonal slices.

2. Place ½ cup of the water in the 10-inch skillet, turn the flame to high, and bring to a boil.

3. Add the carrots and sauté for 2–3 minutes, stirring constantly to ensure even cooking.

4. Add the remaining ½ cup of water and a pinch of sea salt. Put the lid on the skillet and bring to a boil again.

5. Reduce the flame to medium-low and simmer for 5–7

minutes. Remove the lid and add the tamari soy sauce. Place the cover on the pot and cook for another 1–2 minutes.

6. Remove the lid and cook for another minute or so, until all the liquid evaporates.

7. While the carrots are simmering, wash, drain, and dry-roast the sesame seeds as described in the recipe for gomashio (see index).

8. When the carrots have finished cooking, sprinkle the roasted seeds over them and mix in. Place the sesame-coated carrots in a serving bowl.

BLANCHED WATERCRESS
Approximate cooking time: 4–5 minutes (about 3–4 minutes preparation time)

UTENSILS

medium (4-quart) stainless-steel cooking pot with lid	chopsticks or wood spoon
	colander
small (1-quart) porcelain or glass bowl	vegetable knife
	porcelain serving plate

INGREDIENTS
Spring or well water
2 bunches watercress, washed

PREPARATION
1. Place about an inch of water in the cooking pot. Place the lid on the pot and bring the water to a boil.

2. Wash and drain the watercress.

3. Place the watercress in the boiling water, cover the pot, and bring to a boil again.

4. Remove the cover, stir the watercress with cooking chopsticks or a wood spoon to cook evenly, and simmer for about 45–50 seconds.

5. Remove the watercress and place it in the colander. Rinse quickly under a stream of cold water and let it drain in the sink for 1–2 minutes.

6. Divide the watercress in half. Put one portion in a tightly sealed container and store it in the refrigerator for use on the following day.

7. Cut the remainder into $\frac{1}{2}$-inch slices. Arrange on a plate and serve.

Preparing for the Following Day: By the time you finish cooking, you should have 3 cups of unseasoned soup broth set aside in the refrigerator for use in the morning. The watercress that you put aside can be used in making lunch. After you have eaten dinner you should have enough rice, lentils, carrots, and radish pickles leftover to use on the following day. Some people prefer to store most leftovers unrefrigerated in the kitchen or pantry in covered bowls. (The bowls are usually covered with bamboo sushi mats.) However, some leftovers may need to be stored in the refrigerator, especially in hot weather. To store foods in the refrigerator, after they have cooled slightly, place them separately in covered glass or ceramic containers until the following day.

DAY TWO

SOFT RICE PORRIDGE WITH UMEBOSHI
MISO SOUP WITH MOCHI
STEAMED BROCCOLI
CONDIMENTS AND BEVERAGE

In this simple breakfast we create new dishes from the brown rice and soup broth left over from dinner and add a fresh, quickly steamed vegetable dish to round out the meal.
Approximate preparation time: 15 minutes

Putting the Meal Together: The soft rice porridge takes the longest time to cook and should be started first. After you place the rice on the stove, start the soup and then proceed to the broccoli. The porridge and soup can be ladled directly from the cooking pot into individual serving bowls and then garnished, while the broccoli can be placed in a serving bowl on the table. Sprinkle condiments are especially delicious on soft rice, while roasted barley tea is especially nice in the morning.

SOFT RICE PORRIDGE WITH UMEBOSHI

There are many ways to use leftover brown rice in the morning. It can be quickly boiled, pressure-cooked, or mixed with oats or other whole grains to make creamy breakfast cereals. It can also be steamed or eaten as is. In this recipe we explain how to make a quick-boiled rice porridge.
Approximate cooking time: 10–15 minutes (about 2–3 minutes preparation time)

UTENSILS

measuring cup
medium (4-quart) stainless-
  steel pot with lid

ladle or serving spoon
individual serving bowls

INGREDIENTS

1 cup leftover cooked
  brown rice
3 cups spring or well water

½ umeboshi plum
Chopped scallion or other
  condiment for garnish

PREPARATION

1. Place the leftover rice, water, and umeboshi in the cooking pot.

2. Put the lid on the pot and place over a high flame.

3. Bring to a boil and reduce the flame to medium-low.

4. Let the rice cook over a medium-low flame for 10–15 minutes.

5. When the rice has finished cooking, remove the cover, spoon the porridge into serving bowls, and garnish with a few chopped scallions or sprinkle one of your favorite condiments on top.

MISO SOUP WITH MOCHI

Mochi, or pounded sweet brown rice, can be bought ready-made at natural foods stores. It is delicious when puffed in a dry skillet or in the oven and added to morning miso soup.
Approximate cooking time: 12–15 minutes (about 5 minutes preparation time)

UTENSILS

measuring cup

small (1- to 3-quart)
stainless-steel saucepan
with lid

small (8-inch) stainless-steel
or cast-iron skillet with
lid

vegetable knife

teaspoon

ladle

individual serving bowls

INGREDIENTS

3 cups leftover unseasoned
daikon-shiitake soup
broth

3 pieces of mochi, 2 inches
wide by 3 inches long

2–2½ heaping teaspoons (to
taste) barley miso, pureed
in ¼ cup spring or well
water

2 teaspoons finely chopped
scallion

PREPARATION

1. Remove the leftover broth from the refrigerator and place it in a saucepan. Turn the flame to high and bring to a boil.

2. Place the skillet on the stove and turn the flame to medium-low.

3. If the mochi is not precut, place it, unwashed, on the cutting board, then slice it into three 2- by 3-inch rectangles.

4. When the water comes to a boil, turn the flame to low.

5. Puree the miso and add it to the simmering broth.

6. Let the miso simmer in the broth without boiling for 2–3 minutes.

7. Place the cut mochi in the heated skillet, cover, and pan-fry on one side for about 3 minutes. Turn the mochi over and pan-fry on the other side for 3–4 minutes or until each piece begins to puff up.

8. Place a piece of mochi in each serving bowl and ladle hot soup over it.

9. Wash and slice scallion and garnish each bowl with some.

STEAMED BROCCOLI
Approximate cooking time: 5–7 minutes (about 2 minutes preparation time)

UTENSILS
vegetable knife
measuring cup
small (1- to 3-quart)
   cooking pot with lid
stainless-steel steamer
   basket

chopsticks
porcelain or glass serving
   bowl

INGREDIENTS
2 cups broccoli flowerets
   (about 1 bunch of
   broccoli)

Spring or well water

PREPARATION
1. Wash and cut the broccoli into flowerets.
2. Place about ½–1 inch of water in the pot and put the steamer basket inside the pot.
3. Turn the flame to high, put the pot on the burner, and place the cut broccoli in the steamer.
4. Cover the pot and let the water come to a boil.
5. Boil for 3–5 minutes, until the broccoli becomes tender but is still crisp and bright green. Remove the broccoli with chopsticks and place in a serving bowl.

L U N C H

LENTIL SOUP
WATERCRESS NORI ROLL
SESAME-COATED RICE BALLS
FRESH GARDEN SALAD WITH UME-TAHINI DRESSING
CONDIMENTS AND BEVERAGE

In this quick, light lunch, we make use of leftovers from dinner. The brown rice can be used to make sesame rice balls, the lentils make a wonderful soup, the carrots and watercress are wrapped in nori, and the radish pickles are used in the salad. This menu illustrates how versatile natural foods are and how leftovers can be used on the following day to create an entirely new meal.
Approximate preparation time: 20–25 minutes

Putting the Meal Together: The lentil soup takes the longest time to cook and should be started first. Then proceed to the watercress nori roll and the sesame rice balls and finish with the garden salad. These rice balls and salad can be arranged attractively on serving dishes, and the soup can be ladled directly into individual bowls. If you are packing lunch, place several rice balls in one section of your lunch box and the salad in another. (Take the dressing in a small jar or bottle.) The soup can be placed in a thermos or glass jar. Serve the meal with the condiments and beverage of your choice.

LENTIL SOUP

Hot lentil soup is especially delicious on cool autumn or winter days.

Approximate cooking time: 20 minutes (about 5 minutes preparation time)

UTENSILS

vegetable knife
measuring cup
medium (4-quart) stainless-
  steel cooking pot with lid

teaspoon
ladle
individual serving bowls or
  thermos

INGREDIENTS

¼ cup thinly sliced carrot (1 small carrot)

¼ cup diced celery (½ celery stalk)

2 cups leftover cooked lentils

3½ cups spring or well water

2½–3 teaspoons (to taste) tamari soy sauce

2 teaspoons finely chopped scallion

PREPARATION

1. Wash and slice the carrot and celery.
2. Place the leftover lentils in the saucepan and add the sliced carrots, celery, and water.
3. Cover and bring to a boil.
4. Reduce the flame to medium-low and simmer for 15–20 minutes.
5. Add the tamari soy sauce, cover, and simmer for another 4–5 minutes.
6. Chop the scallion fine.
7. Ladle the soup into serving bowls or in a thermos.
8. Garnish with chopped scallion.

WATERCRESS NORI ROLL

This recipe yields approximately 12–14 bite-sized pieces of watercress roll (with 2–4 oddly shaped end pieces, which you may serve separately another time).

Approximate preparation time: 7–10 minutes

UTENSILS

bamboo sushi mat
measuring cup
vegetable knife

porcelain or glass serving
platter or lunch box

INGREDIENTS

2 sheets nori, toasted
2 cups leftover cooked
   watercress

1 cup leftover cooked
carrots

PREPARATION

1. Take 2 sheets of nori from the package. Turn the flame to medium and hold the sheets, one at a time, over the flame, rotating slowly to toast them evenly.

2. Place the bamboo sushi mat on the cutting board.

3. Place a sheet of toasted nori on the sushi mat.

4. Separate the watercress into two equal bunches. Spread one bunch on the sheet of nori, covering the lower half of the sheet (the half closer to you).

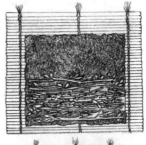

5. Stack ½ cup of the carrots lengthwise across the center of the watercress, forming a straight line.

6. Use the sushi mat to roll up the nori tightly. Press the mat firmly against the nori and watercress until you completely roll it up into a round log shape.

7. Place the watercress roll on the cutting board.

8. Slice the roll in half. Then slice each half into four equal pieces.

9. Stand the individual pieces on end in a lunch box or serving platter.

10. Repeat the steps above for the remaining sheet of nori and remaining vegetables.

SESAME-COATED RICE BALLS

Rice balls can be made at any time as a snack or quick, light meal. They are a wonderful way to use leftover brown rice. This recipe yields approximately 8 small rice balls.

Approximate preparation time: 10 minutes

UTENSILS

measuring cup

small (1-quart) porcelain or
   glass bowl

fine-meshed strainer

small (8-inch) stainless-steel
   skillet

bamboo rice paddle

dinner plate

porcelain or glass serving
   platter or lunch box

INGREDIENTS

¼ cup white sesame seeds

2 cups leftover cooked
   brown rice

PREPARATION

1. Wash and drain the sesame seeds.

2. Place the sesame seeds in the skillet and dry-roast them as described in the recipe for gomashio (see index).

3. Remove the seeds and place them on the plate.

4. Wet your hands very slightly with cold water and mold the leftover rice into 8 balls about 1–1½ inches in diameter.

5. Roll each ball in the toasted sesame seeds until completely covered.

6. Place the rice balls on a serving platter or in a lunch box.

FRESH GARDEN SALAD WITH
UME-TAHINI DRESSING
Approximate preparation time: 10–15 minutes

UTENSILS

measuring cup

vegetable knife

medium (2-quart) porcelain
 or glass bowl

fork or chopsticks

small (6-inch) suribachi
 with pestle

tablespoon

teaspoon

porcelain or glass serving
 bowl or lunch box

small (1-cup) bottle or
 container for dressing

INGREDIENTS

Salad:

1½ cups torn lettuce

2 tablespoons thinly sliced
 (on the diagonal) celery

¼ cup sliced unwaxed
 pickling cucumber

1 teaspoon minced red
 onion

½ cup leftover pressed red
 radishes

Dressing:

1 teaspoon very finely
 chopped scallion or
 parsley

1 teaspoon tahini

1 teaspoon umeboshi
 vinegar

¼ cup spring or well water

PREPARATION

1. Wash lettuce and tear it into bite-sized pieces with your fingers.

2. Wash and slice the celery, cucumber, and red onion.

3. Place the lettuce, celery, cucumber, red onion, and leftover radishes in a mixing bowl and toss with a fork or chopsticks.

4. Chop scallion or parsley very fine and place it in the suribachi together with the tahini and umeboshi vinegar. Puree until smooth and creamy. Then add the water and puree again. Place the finished dressing in a small bottle or container.

5. Place the salad in a serving bowl or lunch box and pour the dressing over it just before serving

D I N N E R

PRESSED SALAD
MILLET WITH CAULIFLOWER
OATMEAL-RAISIN COOKIES
UDON (WHOLE-WHEAT NOODLES) IN BROTH
FRIED TOFU WITH KUZU SAUCE
BOILED KALE
CONDIMENTS AND GRAIN COFFEE
Approximate preparation time: 1½ hours

Putting the Meal Together: When you include a pressed salad with your meal, we suggest setting it up before starting your other dishes. Once set up, it requires no attention and can be left to press longer than indicated if your other dishes take longer to prepare than expected. Then proceed to the millet and cauliflower. (Garnish the millet with a sprig of fresh bright green parsley, as this adds a beautiful color contrast to the dish.) The oatmeal cookies, which take about half an hour to prepare, can be started next. Once they are in the oven, proceed to the noodles in broth. (Noodles are quick and easy to make and can be enjoyed as a snack whenever you are pressed for time.) Once the noodles are cooking, prepare the fried tofu dish. The kale, which cooks fairly quickly, can be prepared last. Arrange your dishes attractively on the table, with the millet in the center, so that the colors complement and balance each other. Serve the meal with condiments of your choice and grain coffee.

PRESSED SALAD

Pressed salads can take the place of pickles at a meal. They are light and crispy and easy to digest.

Approximate preparation time: 45 minutes (about 5 minutes to set up)

UTENSILS

vegetable knife

measuring cup

small (1-quart) porcelain or glass mixing bowl

teaspoon

pickle press

strainer (optional)

porcelain or glass serving bowl

INGREDIENTS

2 cups very finely chopped Chinese cabbage

¼ cup thinly sliced (on the diagonal) celery

¼ cup thinly sliced red radish (5–6 radishes)

¼ cup brown rice vinegar

½ teaspoon sea salt

PREPARATION

1. Wash and slice the vegetables.

2. Place all of the sliced vegetables in the mixing bowl and add the brown rice vinegar and sea salt.

3. Mix the ingredients thoroughly with your fingers and place them in the pickle press.

4. Tighten the lid and pressure plate. Let the vegetables sit under pressure for 30 minutes.

5. Remove the lid, disengage the pressure plate, and remove the vegetables. Squeeze out excess liquid with your hands.

6. If the vegetables are too salty, place them in a strainer and rinse them quickly under a stream of cold water.

7. Place the pressed salad in a serving bowl.

MILLET WITH CAULIFLOWER

Together with rice, millet is often used as a staple in macro-biotic households.

Approximate cooking time: 35–40 minutes (about 5 minutes preparation time)

UTENSILS

measuring cup
medium (2-quart) porcelain
  or glass bowl
fine-meshed strainer
vegetable knife

5-liter pressure cooker
flame deflector
bamboo rice paddle
wood serving bowl

INGREDIENTS

3 cups millet
1 small head of cauliflower,
  sliced into 2-inch pieces
  (3½ cups)

5½ cups spring or well
  water
3 small pinches of sea salt

PREPARATION

1. Wash the millet and allow it to drain in the sink.

2. Wash the cauliflower and slice it, as you would cabbage, into 2-inch pieces.

3. Place the millet in the pressure cooker and add the cauliflower, water, and sea salt.

4. Place the cover on the cooker and turn the flame to high.

5. When the pressure comes up, place a flame deflector under the cooker and reduce the flame to medium-low.

6. Pressure-cook over a medium-low flame for 15–20 minutes.

7. Remove the cooker from the flame and allow the pressure to come down by itself.

8. Take the lid off the cooker and let the millet sit for 3–4 minutes.

9. Remove the millet with a rice paddle and place it in the serving bowl.

OATMEAL-RAISIN COOKIES

These sugar-free natural cookies are quick and easy to make.
They are wonderful in lunch boxes or as an anytime snack.
Approximate time to make: 30–35 minutes (about 10
minutes preparation time)

UTENSILS

measuring cup
medium (2-quart) porcelain
or glass bowl
teaspoon
tablespoon
wood spoon

baking sheet
paper towels
metal spatula
porcelain or glass serving
platter

INGREDIENTS

1½ cups rolled oats
¾ cup whole-wheat pastry
flour
⅛ teaspoon sea salt
½ cup chopped walnuts
½ cup raisins

2 tablespoons corn oil
1 cup cold spring or well
water
1 teaspoon corn oil for
baking sheet

PREPARATION

1. Place the rolled oats in the mixing bowl and add the flour, sea salt, walnuts, and raisins. Mix well.

2. Place the oil in the bowl and mix with a wood spoon.

3. Add the water and mix thoroughly until you have a thick batter.

4. Set the oven at 375°F and let it preheat for 1–2 minutes.

5. While the oven is heating, place a teaspoon of oil on the baking sheet and spread it evenly on the surface with a paper towel.

6. Spoon the batter, a tablespoonful at a time, onto the oiled sheet. Pat it down to form patties that are about 2 inches across and ¼ inch thick. (Since there is no leavening agent in the batter, the cookies will not spread, so you don't have to leave more than ½–1 inch space between them.)

7. Place in the heated oven and bake for 25–30 minutes, until golden brown.

8. Remove with the spatula and place on a serving plate.

UDON IN BROTH

Many delicious noodle dishes are used in macrobiotic cooking. This one is quick and simple and can be made as a snack or a quick mini-meal.

Approximate cooking time: 30–35 minutes (about 10 minutes preparation time)

UTENSILS

measuring cup

2 medium (4-quart) stainless-steel pots with lids

small (1-quart) porcelain or glass bowl

vegetable knife

chopsticks

colander

ladle

individual serving bowls

INGREDIENTS

Noodles:

3–4 quarts spring or well water

2½-pounds whole-wheat udon

Broth:

1 quart spring or well water

1 strip of kombu, about 3–4 inches long, soaked and sliced into thin matchsticks

1 cup spring or well water for soaking kombu

¼ cup tamari soy sauce

2 tablespoons chopped scallion

PREPARATION

1. Place the noodle cooking water (3–4 quarts) in one of the pots, cover, and bring to a boil.

2. Place the water for the broth (1 quart) in the other pot, cover, and bring to a boil.

3. While the water is heating, soak the kombu in 1 cup water for 3–5 minutes and slice it into thin matchsticks.

4. When the water for the broth has started boiling, add the kombu and soaking water.

5. Put the lid on the pot and simmer over a low flame for 10–15 minutes.

6. When the noodle water has come to a boil, add the

udon, quickly stir with chopsticks, and cook for about 7–10 minutes or until the noodles are tender.

7. Season the broth with tamari, cover, and simmer for another 4–5 minutes.

8. When the noodles have finished cooking, remove and place them in the colander. Rinse under a stream of cold water and let them drain in the sink.

9. Place the noodles in individual serving bowls and ladle hot broth over them.

10. Chop the scallion and garnish each bowl with some.

FRIED TOFU WITH KUZU SAUCE

In this recipe we see how versatile tofu is and how it can be adapted to a variety of cooking methods.

Approximate cooking time: 20–25 minutes (about 5–7 minutes preparation time)

UTENSILS

medium (10-inch) cast-iron pot for deep-frying
vegetable knife
paper towels
wire-mesh oil skimmer
measuring cup
medium (4-quart) stainless-steel pot with lid
tablespoon
flat grater
teaspoon
wood spoon
porcelain or glass serving dish

INGREDIENTS

About 1 quart light sesame oil
1 1-pound cake tofu
2 cups spring or well water
1 medium carrot, washed and sliced into thin matchsticks (½ cup)
½ leek, washed and sliced thin on the diagonal (1 cup)
2 heaping tablespoons kuzu, diluted in ¼ cup spring or well water
3½ tablespoons tamari soy sauce
1 teaspoon grated gingerroot

PREPARATION

1. Place about 2–3 inches of oil in the cast-iron pot and heat over a medium-high flame.

2. Slice the tofu into ½-inch-thick slices and place on paper towels to drain.

3. To test whether the oil is hot enough, take a small piece of tofu and drop it into the hot oil. If the tofu sinks to the bottom of the pot and then resurfaces almost immediately, the oil is ready. If it remains at the bottom for several seconds before rising, the oil is not yet hot enough. On the other hand, if the oil begins to smoke, it has become too hot, so lower the flame somewhat.

4. Place several slices of tofu in the hot oil and deep-fry until both sides are golden brown.

5. Remove with a wire-mesh oil skimmer and drain on paper towels.

6. Repeat the steps above until all of the tofu has been deep-fried.

7. While the tofu is frying, put 2 cups of water in the stainless-steel pot, place the pot over a high flame, and bring to a boil.

8. While the water is coming to a boil, wash the vegetables and slice them.

9. When the water has come to a boil, place the slices of fried tofu in it.

10. Put the lid on the pot, reduce the flame to medium-low, and simmer for about 5 minutes.

11. Add the vegetables, place the lid back on the pot, and simmer for 2–3 minutes.

12. Dilute the kuzu in ¼ cup of water and add it to the tofu and vegetables, stirring constantly to prevent it from lumping. Continue stirring until the water becomes a thick sauce.

13. Add the tamari soy sauce, place the lid on the pot, and simmer for another 3–4 minutes.

14. Grate the ginger on the flat grater. Then place the gratings in your hand and squeeze out ½ teaspoon ginger juice; add the juice to the broth. Stir in with a wood spoon.

15. Remove and place in the serving bowl.

BOILED KALE
Approximate cooking time: 5–7 minutes (about 2–3 minutes preparation time)

UTENSILS

medium (4-quart) stainless-
  steel pot with lid
vegetable knife
measuring cup

chopsticks
colander
porcelain or glass serving
  bowl

INGREDIENTS

Spring or well water
1 medium bunch of kale (6–
  7 cups), washed and
  sliced on the diagonal

PREPARATION

1. Place an inch of water in the pot, cover, turn the flame to high, and bring to a boil.

2. Wash and slice the kale.

3. Add the kale to the boiling water and simmer for 3–5 minutes over a high flame, until tender but bright green and slightly crisp.

4. Remove the kale using the chopsticks, place in a colander, and rinse under a stream of cold water. Let it drain in the sink.

5. Place the kale in the serving bowl.

GRAIN COFFEE

Grain coffee is a cereal beverage that can be enjoyed any-time. It's quick and easy to make.

Approximate preparation time: 3–4 minutes (about 1–2 minutes to set up)

UTENSILS

measuring cup   teaspoon
small (1- to 3-quart)   individual serving cups
   stainless-steel saucepan

INGREDIENTS

3–4 cups (1 cup per serving)   3–4 teaspoons (1 teaspoon
   spring or well water   per serving) grain coffee

PREPARATION

1. Place the water in a saucepan and bring to a boil.
2. Spoon the grain coffee into serving cups.
3. When the water comes to a boil, pour it over each cup, stir, and serve.

Preparing for the Following Day: When you have finished eat-ing, place your leftovers in covered jars or containers in the refrigerator. The following leftovers will be needed for breakfast: 1 cup of cooked millet with cauliflower, 4 cups of cooked udon, and enough kale for 3–4 people.

DAY THREE

B R E A K F A S T

KALE
SOFT MILLET WITH CAULIFLOWER
QUICK MISO SOUP WITH UDON
CONDIMENTS AND BEVERAGE

In this quick, light breakfast, we use the millet, udon, miso soup, and kale left over from the night before.
Approximate preparation time: 20 minutes

Putting the Meal Together: This meal is very simple and quick to prepare, as it is based on leftovers from the night before. Although the leftover kale requires no preparation, it can be removed from the refrigerator when you begin cooking so as to allow time for it to warm up. Start the millet first and then proceed to the quick miso soup with udon. Serve the meal with condiments and beverage of your choice.

KALE

Approximate preparation time: 10 minutes (to let the kale warm up to room temperature)

UTENSILS

porcelain or glass serving bowl

individual serving bowls or plates

INGREDIENTS

3–4 cups leftover cooked kale

PREPARATION

Take the leftover kale out of the refrigerator and place it in a serving bowl or plate. Let it sit for 10 minutes at room temperature to warm up before serving.

SOFT MILLET WITH CAULIFLOWER

Soft millet makes a delicious morning cereal.
Approximate cooking time: 20 minutes (about 1–2 minutes preparation time)

UTENSILS

measuring cup
5-liter pressure cooker

serving spoon
individual serving bowls

INGREDIENTS

1 cup leftover cooked millet with cauliflower

5 cups spring or well water

PREPARATION

1. Place the leftover millet with cauliflower in the pressure cooker and add the water.

2. Put the lid on the cooker and place it over a high flame.

3. When the pressure comes up, reduce the flame to low.

4. Let the millet cook for 10–20 minutes over a low flame.

5. Remove the cooker from the hot burner and let the pressure come down.

6. Remove the lid and spoon the porridge into individual serving bowls.

QUICK MISO SOUP WITH UDON

In this quick miso soup we add udon left over from the night before. Udon and other noodles make a wonderful addition to miso and other soups.

Approximate time to make: 10 minutes (about 2 minutes preparation time)

UTENSILS

measuring cup
medium (4-quart) cooking
  pot with lid
teaspoon

vegetable knife
ladle
individual serving bowls

INGREDIENTS

1 quart spring or well water
3½–4 teaspoons (to taste)
  barley miso, pureed in
  3½–4 teaspoons spring
  or well water

4 cups leftover cooked udon
2 sheets nori, toasted and
  cut into squares
¼ cup very finely chopped
  scallion

PREPARATION

1. Place 1 quart water in the pot, cover, and bring to a boil over a high flame.

2. Turn the flame to low.

3. Put the miso in the measuring cup, add the 3½–4 teaspoons water, and puree. Add the pureed miso to the water in the pot.

4. Take the udon out of the refrigerator and add it to the broth.

5. Simmer for 2–3 minutes over a low flame (without boiling).

6. Toast the nori as described in the recipe for watercress nori roll (see index) and cut it into 1-inch squares.

7. Wash the scallions and chop them very fine.

8. Add the chopped scallion and nori squares to the soup.

9. Simmer for about 1 minute (without boiling).

10. Ladle into individual serving bowls.

Preparing for Dinner: Wash and soak ¾ cup dried chick-peas in 2 cups spring or well water for 6–8 hours or until dinner-time.

L U N C H

CHINESE CABBAGE ROLLS
SEITAN SANDWICHES
DILL PICKLES
BEVERAGE

In this easy-to-make lunch we use a variety of prepackaged natural foods. Unyeasted sourdough bread can be found in natural foods stores or can be made at home. Many stores also carry prepackaged seitan (wheat gluten), or wheat meat, in the refrigerator case, while naturally processed cucumber pickles are also widely available. Try to find pickles that are made without spices, chemicals, or artificial vinegar.
Approximate preparation time: 20 minutes

Putting the Meal Together: While the cabbage is cooking, start to prepare some of the items used in the sandwiches. You can interrupt your sandwich preparation when the cabbage is ready and go on to make the cabbage rolls. When you have finished, continue with your sandwiches and then slice the pickles. No condiments are necessary because this meal is a sandwich, not a whole-grain dish. Serve the beverage of your choice.

CHINESE CABBAGE ROLLS
This recipe yields approximately 24–32 bite-sized slices of cabbage roll.
Approximate cooking time: 15–20 minutes (about 10 minutes preparation time)

UTENSILS

vegetable knife
medium (4-quart) stainless-
  steel cooking pot
colander

bamboo sushi mat
porcelain or glass serving
  plate or lunch box

INGREDIENTS

8 medium-large Chinese
  cabbage leaves
1 carrot, about 8–10 inches
  long, sliced into
  lengthwise quarters

Spring or well water

PREPARATION

1. Separate 4 leaves from a head of Chinese cabbage and wash them by hand under a stream of cold water. Wash and slice the carrot.

2. Place an inch of water in the cooking pot and bring to a boil over a high flame.

3. Place the cabbage leaves in the boiling water, cover, and cook for 1–2 minutes.

4. Remove the leaves, place them in a colander, and rinse under cold water. Let the leaves drain in the sink.

5. Place the carrot slices in the same boiling water, cover, and cook for 2–3 minutes. Remove, rinse in the colander, and drain.

6. Spread one of the leaves out on the bamboo sushi mat. Place another leaf on top of it so that it overlaps about halfway above the bottom leaf.

7. Place a carrot slice about 2 inches from the bottom edge of the leaves.

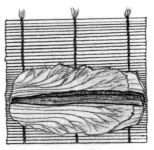

8. Use the sushi mat to roll up the leaves tightly.

9. Repeat these steps until you have four cabbage rolls.

10. Slice each roll in half and then slice each half into three or four equal pieces.

11. Stand the cabbage rolls on end on a serving plate or in a lunch box with the cut side facing up.

SEITAN SANDWICHES

These sandwiches are real lunchtime favorites. Naturally processed miso mustard or mayonnaise made from tofu (without eggs, sugar, dairy products, or chemicals) can be used on occasion by those in good health. These ingredients are listed below as optional. The recipe yields either 3 or 4 seitan sandwiches, one per person.

Approximate preparation time: 5-7 minutes

UTENSILS

bread knife
vegetable knife
colander

table knife
porcelain or glass serving
   platter or lunch box

INGREDIENTS

Enough unyeasted whole-
   wheat bread to make 6-8
   thin slices
½ pound prepackaged
   cooked seitan, cut into
   thin slices
½ medium onion, peeled,
   washed, and sliced into
   thin rings

3-4 lettuce leaves
½ cup alfalfa sprouts
Prepared miso mustard or
   tofu mayonnaise
   (optional)

PREPARATION

1. Cut the whole-wheat bread into 6-8 thin slices.
2. Slice the seitan, then wash and slice the onion.
3. Place the lettuce in a colander and wash quickly under a stream of cold water. Let it drain in the sink. Then do the same with the sprouts.
4. Spread a small amount of miso mustard or tofu mayonnaise on 3-4 slices of bread.
5. Place two to three slices of seitan, one to two slices of onion, a few sprouts, and a lettuce leaf on the prepared slices of bread.
6. Place another slice of bread on top of each sandwich.
7. Cut each sandwich in half.
8. Place on a serving platter or wrap and place in a lunch box.

DILL PICKLES

In this recipe we use ready-made natural pickles that can be found at most natural foods stores.

Approximate preparation time: 1–2 minutes

UTENSILS

vegetable knife
porcelain or glass serving
  plate or lunch box

INGREDIENTS

4 jarred naturally
  processed dill pickles,
  sliced into lengthwise
  quarters

PREPARATION

1. Slice the pickles.
2. Arrange on a serving plate or wrap and place in a lunch box.

D I N N E R

BROWN RICE WITH WHEAT BERRIES AND
CHICK-PEAS
PRESSED CUCUMBERS AND WAKAME
DRIED DAIKON WITH KOMBU
PUREED CAULIFLOWER SOUP
BOILED TURNIP GREENS
CONDIMENTS AND BEVERAGE

Approximate preparation time: 1 hour and 15 minutes

Putting the Meal Together: This meal features a wide variety of beautiful colors that complement each other nicely. The chick-peas and wheat berries add a nice tan color to the brown rice, while the soft, pale green cucumbers and the dark green kombu contrast with the bright orange carrots. The cauliflower soup with its pure white color and pale yellow lemon garnish is especially attractive when presented in a dark bowl. The bright green turnip greens add vibrantly fresh energy to the meal. The dishes in the meal can be prepared in the order presented below for maximum speed and efficiency. Serve the meal with condiments and beverage of your choice.

BROWN RICE WITH WHEAT BERRIES AND CHICK-PEAS

In this recipe we combine brown rice with other ingredients for variety. Whole wheat berries add a wonderful chewy consistency to the brown rice dish.

Approximate cooking time: 1 hour and 15 minutes (about 10 minutes preparation time)

UTENSILS

measuring cup

small (1-quart) porcelain or glass bowl

colander

medium (10-inch) stainless-steel skillet

wood paddle or spoon

medium (2-quart) porcelain or glass bowl

5-liter pressure cooker

flame deflector

chopstick

bamboo rice paddle

wood serving bowl

INGREDIENTS

¾ cup dried chick-peas, washed and soaked in 2 cups spring or well water for 6–8 hours

¼ cup wheat berries, washed, drained, and dry-roasted

3 cups short-grain brown rice, washed

6½ cups spring or well water

4 small pinches of sea salt

PREPARATION

1. The chick-peas that were soaked in the morning are now ready to use. Drain off the soaking water.

2. Wash and drain the wheat berries. Place them in a dry skillet and roast for about 5 minutes over a medium-low flame, stirring constantly to prevent burning. Remove from the skillet and place in a small bowl.

3. Wash the rice and place it, together with the wheat berries and chick-peas, in the pressure cooker.

4. Add the water and place the cooker over a low flame for 7–10 minutes.

5. Add the sea salt, place the lid on the cooker, and turn the flame to high.

6. Let the pressure come up.

7. When the pressure has come up, place a flame deflector under the cooker and reduce the flame to medium-low.

8. Let the dish cook for 50 minutes, then remove the cooker from the burner, place the tip of a chopstick under the pressure gauge to let steam escape, and wait until the pressure has come down.

9. Remove the cover from the cooker and let the dish sit for 4 minutes.

10. Use the rice paddle to transfer the rice dish from the cooker to the serving bowl.

PRESSED CUCUMBERS AND WAKAME
Approximate preparation time: 50 minutes (about 5 minutes to set up)

UTENSILS

vegetable knife
measuring cup
large (3-quart) porcelain or glass bowl
small (1-quart) porcelain or glass bowl
small (1-quart) stainless-steel saucepan
colander
tablespoon
teaspoon
pickle press
porcelain or glass serving bowl

INGREDIENTS

4 cups peeled and sliced cucumber (about 2–3 medium cucumbers)
4 cups sliced lettuce (1 small head)
½ cup washed, soaked, and sliced wakame
¼ cup washed and thinly sliced red radish
1 cup spring or well water for soaking wakame
1½ tablespoons mirin
6 tablespoons brown rice vinegar
½–¾ teaspoon (to taste) sea salt
Spring or well water for cooking wakame

PREPARATION

1. Wash and slice the vegetables.
2. Place the sliced vegetables in the mixing bowl.
3. Wash, soak (for 3–5 minutes), and slice the wakame.
4. Place about ½ inch water in the saucepan and bring to a boil.
5. Place the wakame in the saucepan and simmer over a medium flame for 5–7 minutes.

6. Remove the wakame and place it in the colander.

7. Rinse the wakame under a stream of cold water and let it drain in the sink.

8. Place the wakame in the mixing bowl with the vegetables.

9. Add the mirin, vinegar, and sea salt and mix thoroughly.

10. Place the ingredients in the pickle press.

11. Tighten the lid and pressure plate and let the vegetables sit under pressure for about 45 minutes.

12. Remove the pressed salad, squeeze out excess liquid with your hands, and place in the serving bowl.

DRIED DAIKON WITH KOMBU
Approximate cooking time: 55 minutes (about 10 minutes preparation time)

UTENSILS

measuring cup
2 small (1-quart) porcelain
  or glass bowls
vegetable knife
medium (10-inch) stainless-
  steel skillet with lid

teaspoon
cooking chopsticks
porcelain or glass serving
  bowl

INGREDIENTS

1 strip of kombu, 6 inches
  long, soaked and sliced
  into thin matchsticks
1 cup spring or well water
  for soaking kombu
2–2½ ounces dried daikon,
  washed, soaked, and
  sliced into 1-inch-long
  pieces (1 cup)

2 cups spring or well water
  for soaking dried daikon
2–3 teaspoons (to taste)
  tamari soy sauce
Additional spring or well
  water if needed
½ carrot, sliced into flowers

PREPARATION

1. Wash the kombu and soak it in 1 cup water for 3–5 minutes. Wash and soak the dried daikon in 2 cups water and then slice, reserving the soaking water for both.

2. Place the kombu in the skillet.

3. Set the dried daikon on top of the kombu.

4. Add enough soaking water to half cover the kombu and dried daikon.

5. Cover, place over a high flame, and bring to a boil.

6. Reduce the flame to medium-low and simmer for 30–35 minutes.

7. While the dish is cooking, you may occasionally need to add more soaking water and some plain water to prevent burning. Add only enough to half cover the ingredients each time. Do not stir the dish while cooking.

8. Add the tamari soy sauce, cover, and simmer for another 7–10 minutes.

9. Remove the cover and cook until any remaining liquid evaporates.

10. Mix the ingredients using the chopsticks and place in the serving bowl.

11. Wash the carrot and make three or four raw carrot flowers for garnish.

PUREED CAULIFLOWER SOUP
Approximate cooking time: 30–35 minutes (about 5 minutes preparation time)

UTENSILS

measuring cup	large (3-quart) porcelain or
medium (4- to 5-quart)	glass bowl
stainless-steel cooking pot	ladle
with lid	teaspoon
vegetable knife	individual serving bowls
stainless-steel hand food	
mill	

INGREDIENTS

2 quarts spring or well
   water
2 heads of cauliflower (10
   cups), washed and sliced
   as thin as possible
Small pinch of sea salt

¼–½ teaspoon (to taste) sea
   salt
3–4 slices (1 slice per
   serving) of lemon, cut
   into half-moons

PREPARATION

1. Place the water in the cooking pot, cover, and bring to a boil.

2. Slice the cauliflower as thin as possible, as for cabbage.

3. Place the cauliflower and a pinch of sea salt in the boiling water.

4. Cover, reduce the flame to medium-low, and simmer for 15–20 minutes or until soft.

5. Transfer the cauliflower and cooking water to a hand food mill and puree.

6. Ladle 3–4 cups (1 cup per serving) of the cauliflower puree into a covered glass jar or container for use the following morning.

7. Place the remaining puree back in the cooking pot.

8. Bring to a boil, add the ¼–½ teaspoon sea salt to taste, and reduce the flame to low.

9. Simmer for 10 minutes over a low flame.

10. Ladle into individual serving bowls.

11. Slice the lemon and garnish each bowl of soup with a half-moon slice.

BOILED TURNIP GREENS
Approximate cooking time: 6 minutes (about 2 minutes preparation time)

UTENSILS

medium (4-quart) stainless-
  steel cooking pot with lid
measuring cup
slotted spoon or chopsticks

colander
vegetable knife
porcelain or glass serving
  bowl

INGREDIENTS

Spring or well water
6–7 cups (2 bunches) turnip
  greens

PREPARATION

1. Place 1–2 inches of water in the cooking pot, cover, and bring to a boil.

2. Wash the turnip greens and leave them whole.

3. Place the greens in the boiling water, cover, and cook for 4–5 minutes.

4. Remove the greens with a slotted spoon or chopsticks and place them in the colander.

5. Quickly rinse under a stream of cold water to cool the greens, then drain.

6. Slice the greens into 1- to 2-inch pieces and place in a serving bowl.

Preparing for the Following Day: For breakfast we will use 2 cups of turnip greens and 3–4 cups of unseasoned cauliflower soup. At lunch we will use 4 cups of leftover brown rice with chick-peas and wheat berries and 2 cups of leftover pressed cucumbers and wakame. Place these leftovers in covered jars or containers and keep them in the refrigerator overnight.

DAY FOUR

B R E A K F A S T

OATMEAL WITH RAISINS
LEFTOVER TURNIP GREENS
CAULIFLOWER MISO SOUP
CONDIMENTS AND BEVERAGE

Although whole-grain porridges are preferred for breakfast, oatmeal (made from rolled oats) can be used on occasion by those in general good health. In fact, oats have become one of America's trendiest new health foods. According to News- week, *"the lowly oat has become* haute*" among health- conscious consumers who value it for its cholesterol-lower- ing properties. The cauliflower soup and turnip greens from the night before are used to round out the menu.*
Approximate preparation time: 20 minutes

Putting the Meal Together: As the turnip greens are cold after being refrigerated overnight, place them in a serving bowl and let them sit while you cook the other dishes in the meal. The oatmeal can be started first, and while it is cooking you can start to prepare the miso soup. Gomashio (see index) is an especially nice condiment with oatmeal. Serve the bever- age of your choice.

OATMEAL WITH RAISINS
Approximate cooking time: 20 minutes (about 2 minutes preparation time)

UTENSILS
measuring cup
medium (4-quart) stainless-
  steel cooking pot with lid

serving spoon
individual serving bowls

INGREDIENTS
2 cups rolled oats
¼ cup raisins

1 quart spring or well water
Small pinch of sea salt

PREPARATION
1. Place the rolled oats and raisins in the cooking pot.
2. Add the water and a pinch of sea salt.
3. Cover and bring to a boil.
4. Reduce the flame to low and simmer for 15 minutes.
5. Remove the lid and spoon the oatmeal and raisins into individual serving bowls.

LEFTOVER TURNIP GREENS
Approximate preparation time: 10 minutes (to let the greens warm up)

UTENSILS
chopsticks
porcelain or glass serving
  bowl

INGREDIENTS
2 cups leftover cooked
  turnip greens

PREPARATION
1. Remove the turnip greens from the refrigerator and place in a serving bowl.
2. Let them sit for 10 minutes or so to warm them to room temperature.

CAULIFLOWER MISO SOUP
Approximate cooking time: 5–7 minutes (about 2 minutes preparation time)

UTENSILS

measuring cup
medium (4-quart) stainless-
 steel saucepan with lid
vegetable knife

teaspoon
scissors
ladle
individual serving bowls

INGREDIENTS

3–4 cups leftover
 cauliflower soup,
 unseasoned
1–1¼ heaping teaspoons (to
 taste) barley miso, pureed
 in an equal amount of
 spring or well water

½ sheet nori, toasted and
 cut into thin strips
2 teaspoons finely chopped
 scallion

PREPARATION

1. Place the leftover cauliflower soup in the saucepan.

2. Cover the pot, turn the flame to high, and bring to a boil.

3. While the soup is heating up, wash and chop the scallion.

4. Place the miso in the measuring cup, add the water, and puree.

5. Remove the cover from the saucepan and reduce the flame to low.

6. Add the pureed miso to the soup broth and simmer for 2–3 minutes.

7. Fold a sheet of nori in half lengthwise and tear or cut along the fold. Toast half the sheet over a medium flame for several seconds as described in the recipe for watercress nori roll (see index). (Store the other half for another use.)

8. Fold the toasted sheet in half lengthwise and cut it along the fold with the scissors.

9. Slice each strip of nori crosswise into thin strips.

10. Wash a scallion and chop about half of it fine to make 2 teaspoons.

11. Ladle the soup into individual serving bowls.

12. Garnish with some chopped scallion and several strips of nori.

Preparing for Dinner: Wash 1 cup hulled barley and let it soak in 2 cups spring or well water for 6–8 hours or until dinner.

L U N C H

FRIED RICE WITH WHEAT BERRIES AND CHICK-PEAS
BOILED COLLARD GREENS
LEFTOVER PRESSED CUCUMBERS AND WAKAME
CONDIMENTS AND BEVERAGE
Approximate preparation time: 20 minutes

Putting the Meal Together: If you are packing lunch, the dishes can be prepared in the order presented below. Put the pressed cucumbers and wakame in the lunch box after you have prepared the other dishes. This will help them stay fresh longer. If you are eating at home, take the cucumbers and wakame out of the refrigerator before you start to make the other dishes to allow time for them to warm up. Serve the meal with condiments and beverage of your choice.

FRIED RICE WITH WHEAT BERRIES AND CHICK-PEAS

Fried rice is an especially quick and delicious way to use leftover brown rice. It can be fried with tofu, vegetables, and a variety of other ingredients.

Approximate cooking time: 10–12 minutes (about 2 minutes preparation time)

UTENSILS

teaspoon

medium (10-inch) stainless-steel skillet with lid

measuring cup

vegetable knife

wood spoon or rice paddle

porcelain or glass serving bowl or lunch box

INGREDIENTS

1-2 teaspoons sesame oil, preferably dark

4 cups leftover cooked brown rice with wheat berries and chick-peas

¼ cup spring or well water

¼ cup finely chopped scallion

2 teaspoons tamari soy sauce

PREPARATION

1. Place the oil in the skillet (use the lesser amount if you need to restrict oil intake) and turn the flame to high.

2. When the oil is hot, place the rice in the skillet.

3. Add the water, cover the skillet, and turn the flame to medium low.

4. Let the rice fry for 6-8 minutes or until hot.

5. Wash the scallion and chop fine while the rice is frying.

6. Add the tamari soy sauce and the chopped scallion to the rice.

7. Cover and fry for another 2-3 minutes.

8. Remove the cover and, using the spoon or rice paddle, mix the rice. Fry for 1-2 minutes more.

9. Place the fried rice in a serving bowl or a lunch box.

BOILED COLLARD GREENS

Approximate cooking time: 5–7 minutes (about 3 minutes
preparation time)

UTENSILS

medium (4-quart) stainless-
    steel cooking pot with lid
vegetable knife
measuring cup

cooking chopsticks
colander
porcelain or glass serving
    bowl or lunch box

INGREDIENTS

Spring or well water
3 cups thinly sliced (on the
    diagonal) collard greens

PREPARATION

1. Place about an inch of water in the pot.
2. Cover the pot and bring the water to a boil over a high
flame.
3. While the water is boiling, wash the collard greens
and slice, thin on the diagonal.
4. Place the collards in the boiling water, cover, and
simmer for 3–4 minutes.
5. Remove the greens with the long chopsticks and place
in a colander.
6. Rinse under a stream of cold water and drain in the
sink.
7. Place in a serving bowl or lunch box.

LEFTOVER PRESSED CUCUMBERS AND WAKAME

Approximate preparation time: 1 minute to pack in a
lunch box or 10 minutes to warm up to room temperature

UTENSILS

chopsticks
porcelain or glass serving
    bowl or lunch box

INGREDIENTS

2 cups leftover pressed
  cucumbers and wakame

PREPARATION

  1. Remove the dish from the refrigerator and, using the
chopsticks, place the cucumbers and wakame in a serving
bowl.

  2. Place in a lunch box or let sit for several minutes at
room temperature if you are eating at home.

D I N N E R

BROWN RICE WITH BARLEY
ONION SOUP
ARAME WITH SNOW PEAS AND SESAME SEEDS
BLANCHED SALAD WITH TOFU DRESSING
AMASAKE PUDDING
CONDIMENTS AND BEVERAGE
Approximate preparation time: 1 hour and 25 minutes

Putting the Meal Together: Since the brown rice and barley
takes the longest time to cook, begin it first. While it is
cooking on the stove, you will have about an hour to finish
the other dishes in the meal. Start the onion soup next, then
proceed to the arame, blanched salad, and amasake pudding. The tofu dressing can be started last and spooned over
each serving of salad or mixed in with the salad just before
serving. Serve the meal with condiments and beverage of
your choice.

BROWN RICE WITH BARLEY

Cooking brown rice with barley is a wonderful way to add variety to your main grain dish.

Approximate cooking time: 1 hour and 15 minutes (about 5 minutes preparation time)

UTENSILS

measuring cup
medium (2-quart) porcelain
  or glass bowl
fine-meshed strainer
5-liter pressure cooker

flame deflector
chopstick
bamboo rice paddle
wood serving bowl
vegetable knife (optional)

INGREDIENTS

3½ cups short-grain brown rice
1 cup hulled barley, soaked for 6–8 hours in 2 cups spring or well water
4½ cups spring or well water (in addition to the 2 cups of barley soaking water)

4½ small pinches of sea salt
1 slice of lemon *or* 1 sprig of parsley, washed, for garnish (optional)

PREPARATION

1. Wash and drain the rice.
2. Place the rice, barley, and barley soaking water in the pressure cooker.
3. Add another 4½ cups of water to the pressure cooker.
4. Place the uncovered cooker on the stove, turn the flame to medium-low, and cook for 10–12 minutes.
5. Add the sea salt.
6. Place the lid on the cooker and turn the flame to high.
7. When the pressure comes up, reduce the flame to medium-low.
8. Place a flame deflector under the cooker and let the rice and barley cook for 50 minutes.
9. When the grains have finished cooking, remove the cooker from the flame and place a chopstick under the

pressure gauge to allow the pressure to come down more rapidly.

10. When all the steam has been released, remove the lid and let the grains sit for 4–5 minutes.

11. Remove the grains with a wood rice paddle and place them in a wood serving bowl.

12. The rice and barley can be garnished with a slice of lemon or a sprig of parsley.

ONION SOUP
Approximate cooking time: 35 minutes (about 10–15 minutes preparation time)

UTENSILS
2 small (1-quart) porcelain or glass bowls for soaking
vegetable knife
tablespoon
medium (4-quart) stainless-steel cooking pot with lid
chopsticks or wood spoon
teaspoon
ladle
individual soup bowls

INGREDIENTS
1 strip of kombu, 4 inches long, soaked and sliced into very thin matchsticks
1 cup water for soaking kombu
1 cup water for soaking shiitake
3 shiitake mushrooms
3 medium onions, peeled, washed, and sliced into thin half-moons (3 cups)
1 tablespoon dark sesame oil
3 cups spring or well water
small pinch of sea salt
½ teaspoon chopped scallion
3–3½ tablespoons (to taste) tamari soy sauce

PREPARATION
1. Dust the kombu with a clean, damp sponge.

2. Place 1 cup water in each of the soaking bowls and put the kombu in one and the shiitake in the other. Soak the kombu for 3–5 minutes and the shiitake for 10 minutes.

3. Peel, wash, and slice the onions.

4. Place the dark sesame oil in the cooking pot and heat over a medium flame.

5. Add the onions and sauté for 3–4 minutes, stirring with chopsticks or a wood spoon to cook evenly.

6. Take the kombu from the soaking water, place it on the cutting board, and slice it into very thin matchsticks.

7. Remove the shiitake from the soaking water, cut away the stems with a vegetable knife, and slice thin.

8. Add the kombu and shiitake soaking water, plus another 3 cups water, to the pot.

9. Add the sliced kombu and shiitake.

10. Add a pinch of sea salt, place the lid on the pot, turn the flame to high, and bring to a boil.

11. Reduce the flame to low and simmer for 20 minutes.

12. Wash and slice the scallion.

13. Season the soup with the tamari soy sauce and simmer for another 3–5 minutes.

14. Ladle the soup into individual soup bowls and garnish each serving with a few scallion slices.

ARAME WITH SNOW PEAS AND SESAME SEEDS

This nutritious sea vegetable can be used to prepare delicious side dishes.

Approximate cooking time: 30–35 minutes (about 5 minutes preparation time)

UTENSILS

measuring cup
small (1-quart) porcelain or
  glass bowl
colander
vegetable knife
medium (10-inch) stainless-
  steel skillet with lid
cooking chopsticks or wood
  spoon

teaspoon
fine-meshed strainer
small (8-inch) stainless-steel
  skillet with lid
medium porcelain or glass
  serving bowl

INGREDIENTS

2 cups (dry measurement)
   arame
1½–2 cups spring or well
   water
1 cup snow peas, washed
   and stems removed
1 tablespoon sesame seeds,
   washed and dry-roasted

1 small carrot, washed and
   sliced into matchsticks
   (¼ cup)
1½ teaspoons tamari soy
   sauce

PREPARATION

1. Wash, drain, and slice the arame.

2. Place ½ cup of the water in a skillet, turn the flame to high, and bring to a boil.

3. Add the arame and water-sauté it for 2 minutes, stirring occasionally with cooking chopsticks or a wood spoon.

4. Pour the remaining water into the skillet, and when the water starts to boil, place the lid on the skillet.

5. Reduce the flame to medium-low and simmer for 20–25 minutes.

6. While the arame is cooking, wash the snow peas and break off the stems with your fingers.

7. Wash, drain, and dry-roast the sesame seeds as described in the recipe for gomashio (see index).

8. Place the dry-roasted seeds in a small bowl.

9. Wash and slice the carrot.

10. Add the tamari to the simmering arame.

11. Place the cut carrots on top of the arame, put the lid on the skillet, and cook for 1 minute.

12. Place the snow peas on top of the carrots, cover, and cook for another 2 minutes.

13. Remove the cover and cook until almost all of the remaining liquid evaporates.

14. Mix the arame and vegetables with cooking chopsticks or a wood spoon.

15. Place the finished dish in a serving bowl and sprinkle the roasted sesame seeds over it.

BLANCHED SALAD

Blanched vegetables are delicious as is or with homemade dressings such as those made with tofu and other natural ingredients.

Approximate cooking time: 20 minutes (about 3–4 minutes preparation time)

UTENSILS

vegetable knife

4 small (2-cup) porcelain or glass bowls or plates

measuring cup

medium (4-quart) stainless-steel cooking pot with lid

wire-mesh or slotted spoon

colander

medium (2-quart) porcelain or glass bowl

wood spoon

medium ceramic or glass serving bowl

INGREDIENTS

¼ small bunch of broccoli, washed and sliced into flowerets (1 cup)

¼ small head of cauliflower, washed and sliced into flowerets, then cut in half lengthwise (1 cup)

1 medium summer squash, washed, sliced in half lengthwise, and then cut into ½-inch diagonal slices (1 cup)

½ cup halved red radishes (5–6 radishes)

Spring or well water

PREPARATION

1. Wash the broccoli and cauliflower by rinsing them under a stream of cold water. Then wash the summer squash and radishes under a stream of cold water with a vegetable brush. After washing the vegetables, slice them and place them separately on plates or in small bowls.

2. Put an inch of water in the pot, cover, turn the flame to high, and bring to a boil.

3. Put the summer squash in the boiling water, cover the pot, and cook for 2–3 minutes.

4. Remove the summer squash with a wire-mesh or slotted spoon, place it in a colander, allow it to drain, and place it in the mixing bowl.

5. Then place the broccoli in the boiling water, cover, and boil for 2–3 minutes.

6. Remove with the wire-mesh or slotted spoon, place in a colander, rinse under a stream of cold water, drain, and place in the mixing bowl.

7. Place the cauliflower in the boiling water, cover the pot, and boil for 3–4 minutes.

8. Remove as above, place in a colander, drain, and add to the mixing bowl.

9. Place the radishes in the water, cover the pot, and boil for 2 minutes.

10. Remove as above, place in a colander, drain, and add to the mixing bowl.

11. Gently mix the vegetables using the wood spoon and place the finished salad in a serving bowl.

TOFU DRESSING
Approximate preparation time: 8–10 minutes

UTENSILS

stainless-steel hand food mill
medium (2-quart) porcelain or glass bowl
wood spoon
suribachi and pestle
flat grater
teaspoon
tablespoon
measuring cup
vegetable knife
ceramic or glass serving bowl

INGREDIENTS

1 1-pound cake firm-style tofu
1½ tablespoons finely grated onion
1½ teaspoons tamari soy sauce
2 tablespoons umeboshi vinegar
⅓ cup spring or well water
1 tablespoon chopped parsley

PREPARATION
1. Place the hand food mill over the mixing bowl.
2. Put the tofu into the mill and puree it. Then place the pureed tofu in the suribachi.
3. Grate the onion fine and place the gratings in the suribachi.
4. Add the tamari, umeboshi vinegar, and water and puree with the wood pestle until the ingredients are mixed thoroughly.
5. Wash the parsley, place it on the cutting board, and chop fine.
6. Place the tofu in a serving dish and garnish with the chopped parsley.
7. Spoon the dressing over each serving of boiled salad.

AMASAKE PUDDING

This delicious natural dessert is very simple and easy to make. Prepared amasake, or rice milk, is now available in many natural foods stores.

Approximate time to make: 10 minutes (1–2 minutes preparation time)

UTENSILS

measuring cup	wood spoon
medium (4-quart) stainless- steel saucepan	individual glass or porcelain dessert cups or
teaspoon	a shallow serving bowl

INGREDIENTS

1 quart amasake	4 teaspoons raisins
4 heaping teaspoons kuzu, diluted in 5 teaspoons spring or well water	

PREPARATION
1. Place the amasake in the saucepan.
2. Dilute the kuzu and add it to the amasake. Stir to mix in well.

3. Place over a high flame, stirring often to prevent lumping, until it comes to a boil. Turn the flame to low and simmer for 1–2 minutes.

4. Spoon into individual dessert cups or into a shallow serving bowl.

5. Garnish with the raisins.

Preparing for the Following Day: Set aside 2 cups of rice and barley for lunch on the following day. Place the leftovers in a covered bowl in the refrigerator.

DAY FIVE

B R E A K F A S T

MISO SOUP WITH WAKAME AND ONIONS
WHOLE-WHEAT CREPES WITH PEACH-RAISIN SAUCE
CONDIMENTS AND BEVERAGE
Approximate preparation time: 20 minutes

Putting the Meal Together: Miso soup can be started first. While it is cooking, begin preparing the crepes. Similarly, serve the soup first, and after it is finished, the crepes can be enjoyed. The meal can be rounded out with hot bancha tea or grain coffee.

MISO SOUP WITH WAKAME AND ONIONS
Approximate cooking time: 15–20 minutes (about 5 minutes preparation time)

UTENSILS

measuring cup
medium (4-quart) stainless-
steel saucepan with lid
small (1-quart) porcelain or
glass bowl

vegetable knife
tablespoon
ladle
individual soup bowls

INGREDIENTS

4–5 cups spring or well water

¼ cup (6-inch strip) wakame, soaked and sliced

½ cup spring or well water for soaking wakame

1 medium onion, peeled, washed, and sliced into half-moons (1 cup)

1½–2 tablespoons (to taste) barley miso, pureed in an equal amount of water

1 tablespoon sliced scallion

PREPARATION

1. Place the water in a saucepan, cover, place over a high flame, and bring the water to a boil.

2. While the water is coming to a boil, wash and soak the wakame in ½ cup water for 3–5 minutes.

3. Peel, wash, and slice the onion as directed.

4. Slice the wakame and place it in the boiling water.

5. Reduce the flame to medium-low, cover the pot, and simmer for 1–2 minutes.

6. Add the onion, cover, and simmer for about 5 minutes.

7. Reduce the flame to low, puree the miso in the water, and add to the soup stock.

8. Simmer for 2–3 minutes.

9. Wash and slice the scallion while the soup is simmering.

10. Ladle the soup into individual bowls and garnish with chopped scallion.

WHOLE-WHEAT CREPES WITH PEACH-RAISIN SAUCE

These quick, light whole-wheat crepes are delicious when served with a natural sugar-free peach-raisin sauce. If peaches are not in season, you can make the same topping with fresh apples. This recipe makes about 9 crepes. Please enjoy!

Approximate cooking time: 20 minutes (about 10 minutes preparation time)

UTENSILS

vegetable knife
measuring cup
medium (4-quart) stainless-
   steel cooking pot with lid
medium (2-quart) porcelain
   or glass bowl
wood spoon
teaspoon

medium (10-inch) stainless-
   steel skillet or pancake
   griddle
metal spatula
tablespoon
porcelain or glass serving
   bowl
individual plates

INGREDIENTS

Batter:
2 cups whole-wheat pastry
   flour
2 cups spring or well water

$\frac{1}{4}$ teaspoon sea salt
3 teaspoons light sesame oil

Sauce:
2 peaches, washed and
   sliced into $\frac{1}{4}$- to $\frac{1}{2}$-inch
   wedges (2 cups)
$\frac{1}{4}$–$\frac{1}{3}$ cup raisins
2 cups spring or well water
small pinch of sea salt

1 heaping tablespoon kuzu,
   diluted in 2 tablespoons
   water
3–4 teaspoons (to taste)
   brown rice syrup

PREPARATION

1. Wash and slice the peaches. Then place them in a saucepan and add the raisins (use the larger amount if you want the dish to be sweeter), 2 cups water, and a pinch of sea salt.

2. Place the lid on the pot, turn the flame to high, and bring to a boil. Then turn the flame to medium-low and simmer for 10 minutes.

3. While the peaches are cooking, place the whole-wheat pastry flour, 2 cups water, and $\frac{1}{4}$ teaspoon sea salt in a bowl. Mix the ingredients thoroughly with the wood spoon.

4. Place 1 teaspoon of the oil in the skillet or griddle and heat for about 1 minute. When the oil is hot, ladle about $\frac{1}{3}$–$\frac{1}{2}$ cup of batter into the skillet, depending on the crepe size you prefer. As soon as the batter hits the hot skillet, smooth it

out, using the rounded bottom of a teaspoon to make a quick circular motion across the surface of the batter. This helps keep the crepe very thin.

5. Cook the crepe for 1 minute and then turn it over. Fry the other side for several seconds only. Repeat until the batter is used up. Lightly oil the skillet after every other crepe, using about a teaspoon of oil each time.

6. Stack the finished crepes on a serving plate.

7. Dilute the kuzu in 2 tablespoons of water. Then add the diluted kuzu and the rice syrup to the peaches. Stir constantly to prevent lumping and cook for about 1 minute. Transfer the sauce to a serving bowl.

8. Place each crepe on a serving plate and spoon 2–3 tablespoons of peaches and raisins over the center of each crepe. Then roll up the crepe and spoon 3–4 tablespoons of kuzu sauce over the crepe.

L U N C H

TEMPEH SANDWICHES
RICE, BARLEY, AND SQUASH SOUP
ROASTED PUMPKIN SEEDS
CONDIMENTS AND BEVERAGE

In this quick soup-and-sandwich meal, the rice with barley left over from the night before is transformed into a deliciously sweet soup.

Approximate preparation time: 20–25 minutes

Putting the Meal Together: This delicious natural sandwich can be served on whole-wheat or whole-grain bread. While the tempeh is cooking, start the soup. Then you can wash and cut the ingredients for the sandwiches. This step can save additional time when preparing the meal. The pumpkin seeds can be roasted as you finish cooking. Serve the meal with condiments and beverage of your choice.

TEMPEH SANDWICHES

Tempeh, a versatile fermented soy food, is wonderful in sandwiches. Tempeh sandwiches are easy to make and can be eaten anytime. This recipe makes either 3 or 4 sandwiches.

Approximate cooking time: 20 minutes (about 3–4 minutes preparation time)

UTENSILS

tablespoon
medium (10-inch) stainless-steel skillet
vegetable knife
stainless-steel spatula
measuring cup

3 small porcelain or glass plates
bread knife
porcelain or glass serving platter or lunch box

INGREDIENTS

1 tablespoon dark sesame oil
½ pound tempeh, sliced into 3–4 3-inch squares, ¼ inch thick
½–¾ cup spring or well water
3–4 slices of onion, separated into rings
6–8 thin diagonal slices of cucumber

3–4 whole lettuce leaves
Enough unyeasted, sourdough whole-wheat or other whole-grain bread to make 6–8 slices
1½–2 teaspoons (to taste) tamari soy sauce
⅓–½ cup sauerkraut

PREPARATION

1. Place the oil in the skillet, turn the flame to high, and heat for about a minute.

2. Slice the tempeh and place it in the skillet.

3. Fry the tempeh for 1–2 minutes on each side.

4. Place the water in the skillet, cover, and bring to a boil.

5. Reduce the flame to medium-low and simmer for 10 minutes.

6. While the tempeh is cooking, wash and slice the onion and cucumber. Place the sliced vegetables on separate plates.

7. Wash the lettuce leaves and place them on a plate.

8. Slice the bread.

9. Season the tempeh with tamari soy sauce, cover the skillet, and cook for another 2–3 minutes.

10. Remove the cover and cook for another minute or so, until all the liquid evaporates.

11. Place a piece of tempeh on each of 3 or 4 slices of bread.

12. Place 2 tablespoons of the sauerkraut, 2 slices of cucumber, 1 slice of onion, and 1 lettuce leaf on top of each piece of tempeh.

13. Place a slice of bread on top of each sandwich.

14. Slice in half and place on a serving plate or pack in a lunch box.

RICE, BARLEY, AND SQUASH SOUP
Approximate cooking time: 15–20 minutes (about 5 minutes preparation time)

UTENSILS

measuring cup
medium (4-quart) stainless-steel cooking pot with lid
vegetable knife
tablespoon

porcelain or glass dinner plate
ladle
individual serving bowls or thermos

INGREDIENTS

1 quart spring or well water
½ cup diced onion
¼ cup butternut squash
2 tablespoons chopped scallion

2 cups leftover cooked brown rice with barley
1 tablespoon tamari soy sauce

PREPARATION

1. Place the water in the pot and bring to a boil.

2. While the water is coming to a boil, wash and dice the vegetables. Place the diced vegetables in separate piles on the plate.

3. When the water comes to a boil, place the leftover rice and barley, diced onions, and squash in the pot.

4. Cover the pot, reduce the flame to medium-low, and simmer for about 10 minutes.

5. Season with tamari soy sauce, cover, and simmer for another 2–3 minutes.

6. Ladle the finished soup into individual serving bowls or a thermos.

7. Garnish each serving with some chopped scallion.

ROASTED PUMPKIN SEEDS

Roasted seeds can be eaten anytime as a snack. They are quick and easy to prepare.

Approximate preparation time: 5–7 minutes

UTENSILS

medium (10 inch) stainless-steel skillet

measuring cup

small (1-quart) porcelain or glass bowl

strainer

bamboo rice paddle or spoon

porcelain or glass serving bowl or lunch box

INGREDIENTS

1 cup hulled pumpkin seeds, washed and drained

PREPARATION

1. Heat the dry skillet over a medium flame for about a minute.

2. While the skillet is heating, wash and drain the seeds.

3. Place the damp seeds in the hot skillet.

4. Dry-roast for about 5–6 minutes, constantly stirring to roast evenly. When the seeds turn golden brown and begin to expand and pop, they are ready.

5. Remove and place in a serving bowl or pack in a lunch box.

D I N N E R

BROWN RICE WITH CHESTNUTS
HIJIKI WITH ONIONS
NISHIME-STYLE VEGETABLES
CLEAR BROTH SOUP
BLANCHED SALAD WITH UME-PARSLEY DRESSING
CONDIMENTS AND BEVERAGE
Approximate preparation time: 1½ hours

Putting the Meal Together: In this meal we emphasize the natural sweetness of grains and vegetables. Begin the meal by preparing the brown rice with chestnuts (a delicious, naturally sweet dish). While the main grain dish is cooking, start the hijiki, then proceed to the nishime-style vegetables. The clear broth soup can be started next, followed by the blanched salad and ume-parsley dressing. Arrange the finished dishes attractively on your table. (The dark-colored hijiki looks especially nice in a light-colored serving bowl.) Serve the meal with condiments and beverage of your choice.

BROWN RICE WITH CHESTNUTS

Cooking brown rice with dried chestnuts produces an incredibly rich, sweet grain dish. It is almost like eating dessert!

Approximate cooking time: 1 hour and 15 minutes (about 20 minutes preparation time)

UTENSILS

measuring cup
small (1-quart) porcelain or
　glass bowl
strainer
medium (10-inch) stainless-
　steel skillet

bamboo rice paddle or
　spoon
5-liter pressure cooker
flame deflector
chopstick
wood serving bowl

INGREDIENTS

1 cup dried chestnuts

3 cups short-grain brown
  rice

4½ cups spring or well
  water

3 small pinches of sea salt

PREPARATION

1. Place the chestnuts in the bowl and wash them.

2. Place the washed chestnuts in the strainer, rinse under a stream of cold water, and let them drain in the sink.

3. Place the skillet over a medium-high flame and heat for several seconds.

4. Place the chestnuts in the skillet and dry-roast, stirring constantly with a rice paddle or wood spoon, for 5–7 minutes or until they turn golden brown.

5. Place the roasted chestnuts in the pressure cooker.

6. Wash the rice and add it to the pressure cooker along with the water.

7. Place the uncovered cooker over a low flame and heat until the water just begins to boil.

8. Add the sea salt. Fasten the lid on the cooker and turn the flame to high.

9. When the pressure comes up, place the flame deflector under the cooker and turn the flame to medium-low.

10. Let the rice cook for 50 minutes. Remove the cooker from the hot burner and place the tip of a chopstick under the pressure gauge to allow steam to come out more rapidly. When the pressure has come down completely, remove the lid.

11. Let the finished dish sit for about 5 minutes, then remove the grains with a rice paddle. Place in a wood serving bowl.

HIJIKI WITH ONIONS

Hijiki is a highly nutritious sea vegetable that can be cooked with vegetables to make appetizing side dishes.

Approximate cooking time: 50–55 minutes (about 5 minutes preparation time)

UTENSILS

measuring cup
small (1-quart) porcelain or
  glass bowl
strainer
vegetable knife
medium (10-inch) stainless-
  steel skillet with lid

cooking chopsticks
teaspoon
porcelain or glass serving
  bowl

INGREDIENTS

1½ cups soaked and sliced
  hijiki (about 2 ounces dry
  weight), washed, soaked,
  and sliced
2 cups spring or well water
  for soaking hijiki
1 medium onion, peeled,
  washed, and sliced into
  thin half-moons (1 cup)

1 teaspoon dark sesame oil
About 1 cup spring or well
  water
1–1½ teaspoons (to taste)
  tamari soy sauce
1 tablespoon very finely
  chopped scallion

PREPARATION

1. Wash the hijiki, soak it for 3–5 minutes, and then slice it.

2. While the hijiki is soaking, peel, wash, and slice the onion.

3. Place the oil in the skillet and heat over a high flame for about 1 minute.

4. Add the onion slices and sauté for 1–2 minutes with the cooking chopsticks.

5. Set the hijiki on top of the onions. Do not mix.

6. Add enough water to just cover the onions (but not the hijiki).

7. Place the lid on the skillet, bring to a boil, and reduce the flame to medium-low. Simmer for 35–40 minutes.

8. Add the tamari soy sauce, place the cover on the skillet, and cook for another 5–10 minutes.

9. Remove the lid and cook for another couple of minutes until all remaining liquid evaporates.

10. Mix the ingredients and place the finished dish in a serving bowl.

11. Wash a scallion and chop it very fine. Use the chopped scallion to garnish the hijiki.

NISHIME-STYLE VEGETABLES

Nishime-style vegetables are mainly root or round vegetables cut into large bite-sized pieces, cooked slowly over a medium-low flame in a small amount of water, and then seasoned. This method is sometimes referred to as "waterless cooking" because the water is cooked off at the end. This nishime dish features naturally sweet vegetables. The vegetables should be soft and should practically melt in your mouth when they are finished.

Approximate cooking time: 50 minutes (about 10 minutes preparation time)

UTENSILS

2 small (1-quart) porcelain or glass bowls
vegetable knife
measuring cup
porcelain or glass dinner plate

medium (4-quart) stainless-steel saucepan with lid
teaspoon
wood spoon
porcelain or glass serving bowl

INGREDIENTS

1 strip of kombu, 4–6 inches long, washed, soaked, and cubed
1 cup spring or well water for soaking kombu
3–4 squares dried tofu, soaked, rinsed, and cut into 1-inch squares (½ cup)
1 cup warm spring or well water for soaking tofu
1 stalk of celery, washed and sliced thick on the diagonal (½ cup)
1 piece of daikon root, 4–5 inches long, washed and sliced into ½-inch-thick half-moons (1 cup)

½ medium carrot, washed and sliced into bite-sized chunks (½ cup)
¼ medium butternut or buttercup squash, washed, seeds removed, and sliced into bite-sized chunks (1 cup)
½ cup spring or well water
Small pinch of sea salt
1–1½ teaspoons (to taste) tamari soy sauce

PREPARATION

1. Wipe the kombu with a clean, damp sponge. Place it in a bowl and soak it in 1 cup water for 3–5 minutes. Remove and slice, reserving the soaking water.

2. Place the dried tofu in a second bowl, cover with warm water, and soak for 5 minutes. Drain, rinse under cold water, squeeze out water with your hands, and cut into squares.

3. While the kombu and dried tofu are soaking, separately wash and slice the celery, daikon, carrot, and squash. Arrange them neatly on a plate, keeping each vegetable separate.

4. Place the kombu in the pot. Then layer the other ingredients in the following order: dried tofu, celery, daikon, carrot, and squash.

5. Add the kombu soaking water, another ½ cup water, and a small pinch of sea salt. Cover the pot and bring to a boil. Reduce the flame to medium-low and cook for 30–35 minutes.

6. Add the tamari soy sauce, cover, and cook for another 5–10 minutes, until almost all of the liquid evaporates.

7. Mix the vegetables gently with a wood spoon and place in a serving bowl.

CLEAR BROTH SOUP

Approximate cooking time: 25 minutes (about 3–4 minutes preparation time)

UTENSILS

measuring cup
medium (4-quart) stainless-
    steel cooking pot with lid
small porcelain or glass
    plate
cooking chopsticks

vegetable knife
ladle
1-quart jar with lid for
    storing
tablespoon
individual serving bowls

INGREDIENTS

1 strip of kombu, 3–4
    inches long
2 quarts spring or well
    water
4 medium dried shiitake
    mushrooms
2 cups diagonally sliced
    Chinese cabbage

Greens from 1 bunch of
    scallions, washed and
    sliced crosswise into 2-
    inch lengths (1 cup)
2 tablespoons tamari soy
    sauce

PREPARATION

1. Wipe the kombu with a clean, damp sponge. Place the water in the pot and add the kombu and shiitake.

2. Cover and bring to a boil. Turn the flame to medium-low and simmer for 4–5 minutes.

3. Remove the kombu and set it aside on a plate. Put the lid back on the pot and simmer the shiitake for another 4–5 minutes.

4. Remove the shiitake with the chopsticks. Cut away and discard the stems.

5. Slice the shiitake into thin slices and put the cut mushrooms back into the boiling water. Simmer over a medium flame for another 2–3 minutes.

6. While the shiitake are cooking, wash and slice the Chinese cabbage and scallions.

7. Place the sliced cabbage in the pot, cover, and cook for 1 minute. Then remove 3 cups of unseasoned broth with

a soup ladle and put it in a jar in the refrigerator for use the following day.

8. Add the tamari soy sauce and the cut scallions. Cover the pot and cook for 2–3 minutes.

9. Ladle the hot soup into individual serving bowls.

BLANCHED SALAD

Approximate cooking time: 5–7 minutes (about 2 minutes preparation time)

UTENSILS

medium (4-quart) stainless-steel cooking pot with lid
vegetable knife
measuring cup
porcelain or glass dinner plate
wire-mesh spoon
colander
medium (2-quart) porcelain or glass bowl
medium porcelain or glass serving bowl

INGREDIENTS

Spring or well water (1 cup)
3 cups sliced bok choy or pak choy
1 ½-pound package red radishes, washed and sliced in half

PREPARATION

1. Place about 2 inches of water in a pot, cover, and bring to a boil.

2. While the water is coming to a boil, wash and slice the vegetables. Place the cut vegetables on separate sections of a plate.

3. Place the bok choy in the water, cover, and boil for 1–2 minutes. Remove with a wire-mesh spoon and place in a colander in the sink.

4. Rinse the greens quickly under cold water and place the colander inside a bowl to allow them to drain; discard the liquid. Then place the greens in a serving bowl.

5. Place the radishes in the boiling water, cover, and boil for 1–2 minutes.

6. Remove the radishes with the wire-mesh spoon, place them in the colander, and rinse under cold water. Then place them in the serving bowl and mix with the greens.

UME-PARSLEY DRESSING

The blanched salad is delicious as is or with this salad dressing.

Approximate preparation time: 2–3 minutes

UTENSILS

suribachi and pestle   teaspoon
vegetable knife   measuring cup

INGREDIENTS

2 umeboshi plums, pits   ½–¾ cup spring or well
   removed   water
½ teaspoon very finely
   chopped parsley

PREPARATION

1. Place the pitted plums in the suribachi and grind into a smooth paste.

2. Wash the parsley and chop it very fine. Add it to the umeboshi paste.

3. Grind for several seconds to mix the parsley and umeboshi.

4. Add the water (use the larger amount if you like the dressing less salty) and grind for another 1–2 minutes, until the ingredients are mixed thoroughly.

5. Spoon 1–2 tablespoons over each serving of salad.

Preparing for the Following Day: Put aside 1 cup of brown rice with chestnuts for the following day, along with 3 cups of unseasoned soup broth. They can be stored in the refrigerator until the following morning.

DAY SIX

B R E A K F A S T

SOFT RICE WITH CHESTNUTS
SCRAMBLED TOFU WITH VEGETABLES
MISO SOUP WITH CHINESE CABBAGE
CONDIMENTS AND BEVERAGE
Approximate preparation time: 20 minutes

Putting the Meal Together: The soft grain porridge can be started first. While it is cooking, begin preparing the scrambled tofu. The miso soup takes only a short time to prepare and can be started last. The soup and porridge can be left in the cooking pots and spooned or ladled directly into individual serving bowls. Serve the meal with condiments and beverage of your choice.

SOFT RICE WITH CHESTNUTS

The cooked chestnuts make this morning porridge wonderfully sweet.

Approximate cooking time: 10–15 minutes (about 3–4 minutes preparation time)

UTENSILS

measuring cup
medium (4-quart) stainless-
  steel pot with lid

serving spoon
individual serving bowls

INGREDIENTS

1 cup leftover cooked
  brown rice with chestnuts

3 cups spring or well water

PREPARATION

1. Place the leftover rice with chestnuts in the pot and add the water.

2. Put the lid on the pot and bring to a boil over a high flame.

3. Reduce the flame to medium-low and simmer, covered, for 10–15 minutes.

4. When the rice and chestnuts are ready, spoon into individual serving bowls. Serve hot.

SCRAMBLED TOFU WITH VEGETABLES

This quick and easy-to-prepare tofu dish is a real favorite in the morning.

Approximate cooking time: 10–12 minutes (about 3–4 minutes preparation time)

UTENSILS

vegetable knife
measuring cup
porcelain or glass dinner
  plate
teaspoon
medium (10-inch) stainless-
  steel skillet with lid

cooking chopsticks or wood
  spoon
porcelain or glass serving
  bowl

INGREDIENTS

1 piece of burdock, 3–4 inches long, washed and sliced into thin matchsticks (2 tablespoons)

½ cup diced onion

½ medium carrot, washed and sliced into thin matchsticks (½ cup)

1 cup sliced green cabbage

1½–2 teaspoons dark sesame oil

1 1-pound cake firm-style tofu

2 teaspoons tamari soy sauce

1 sprig of parsley, washed

PREPARATION

1. Wash and slice the vegetables. Arrange them separately on a plate.

2. Place the oil in the skillet (use the smaller amount if you need to restrict oil intake) and heat it for 1 minute over a medium-high flame.

3. Add the onion and sauté for 1–2 minutes. Add the carrot and cabbage and sauté for 1–2 minutes.

4. Crumble the tofu with your fingers and let the pieces drop into the skillet so that they evenly cover the vegetables.

5. Cover the skillet and turn the flame to medium-low. Cook for 4–5 minutes, until the tofu becomes fluffy and the vegetables are done.

6. Season with tamari soy sauce, cover, and cook for another 1–2 minutes.

7. Remove the cover and mix well.

8. Place in a serving dish and garnish with a sprig of fresh parsley.

MISO SOUP WITH CHINESE CABBAGE
Approximate cooking time: 10 minutes (about 2–3 minutes preparation time)

UTENSILS

measuring cup

medium (4-quart) stainless-
steel cooking pot with lid

tablespoon

vegetable knife

teaspoon

ladle

individual serving bowls

INGREDIENTS

3 cups leftover clear broth
soup, unseasoned

1 tablespoon chopped
scallion

2–2½ heaping teaspoons (to
taste) barley miso, pureed
in an equal amount of
spring or well water

PREPARATION

1. Place the unseasoned soup broth in the pot, cover, and bring to a boil.

2. While the broth is coming to a boil, wash and slice the scallion.

3. Puree the miso in the measuring cup.

4. When the broth comes to a boil, reduce the flame to low and add the pureed miso. Simmer over a low flame for 2–3 minutes.

5. Ladle the soup into individual serving bowls and garnish with a pinch of chopped scallion.

Preparing for Dinner: After you have finished breakfast, or during a lull in the cooking, wash 4 cups brown rice. Place it in a pressure cooker with 5⅓ cups spring or well water without adding sea salt. Let the rice soak until you start to prepare dinner. Then wash 2 cups azuki beans. Put the washed beans in a ceramic or glass bowl, add 6 cups spring or well water, and let them soak until dinner.

L U N C H

FRIED SOBA WITH VEGETABLES
STEAMED CABBAGE
CONDIMENTS AND BEVERAGE
Approximate preparation time: 20 minutes

Putting the Meal Together: Start the noodle dish first. While the water is coming to a boil, wash and slice the vegetables that will be used in the dish. You may also have time to wash and slice the cabbage before the noodles are cooked. The quickly cooked scallions used in the noodle dish retain their bright green color and freshness, so there is no need for additional garnish. Several drops of tamari soy sauce can be used as a condiment on the fried noodles if desired. Serve the meal with the beverage of your choice.

FRIED SOBA WITH VEGETABLES
Fried soba or udon are quick and easy to make. You can enjoy them as a snack or mini-meal any time of day.
Approximate cooking time: 20 minutes (about 10 minutes preparation time)

UTENSILS

measuring cup

medium (4-quart) stainless-
   steel cooking pot with lid

vegetable knife

porcelain or glass plate

cooking chopsticks

colander

teaspoon

medium (10-inch) stainless-
   steel skillet with lid

porcelain or glass serving
   bowl

INGREDIENTS

2 quarts spring or well water

1 small onion, peeled, washed, and sliced into thin half-moons (½ cup)

½ medium carrot, washed and sliced into thin matchsticks (½ cup)

¼ cup thinly sliced (on the diagonal) celery

½ cup thinly sliced scallion

1 ½-pound package soba (buckwheat noodles)

2 teaspoons dark or light sesame oil

2–3 teaspoons (to taste) tamari soy sauce

PREPARATION

1. Place the water in the pot, cover, turn the flame to high, and bring to a boil.

2. While the water is coming to a boil, wash and slice the vegetables. Arrange them separately on a plate.

3. When the water starts to boil, remove the lid and place the noodles in the pot. Stir them once or twice with chopsticks and let them cook for about 7 minutes or until the center of each noodle becomes the same color as the outside. To check whether the noodles are ready, break one in half. If the center is lighter than the outside, the noodles need to cook a little longer.

4. When the noodles have finished cooking, place the colander in the sink, pour the noodles and cooking water into it, and rinse under a stream of cold water until cool. Let them drain for a minute or so.

5. While the noodles are draining, place the oil in the skillet and heat for about 1 minute over a high flame.

6. Place the onion in the skillet and sauté, using the chopsticks, for 1 minute. Then add the carrots and celery and sauté for 1 minute.

7. Place the cool noodles on top of the vegetables. Add the tamari soy sauce, cover, and cook for 4–5 minutes. Do not mix.

8. Sprinkle the sliced scallion on top of the noodles. Cover and cook for another minute.

9. Remove the cover, mix thoroughly, and cook for another 1–2 minutes.

10. Remove the noodles and vegetables and place them in a serving bowl.

STEAMED CABBAGE
Approximate cooking time: 5–7 minutes (about 2–3 minutes preparation time)

UTENSILS
medium (4-quart) stainless-steel cooking pot with lid
stainless-steel steamer basket
vegetable knife

measuring cup
cooking chopsticks
porcelain or glass serving bowl

INGREDIENTS
2–3 cups thinly sliced green cabbage
Spring or well water

PREPARATION
1. Place an inch of water in the saucepan and set the steamer basket inside of it.

2. Wash and slice the cabbage.

3. Put the lid on the pan and bring the water to a boil. Then place the cabbage in the steamer basket and steam over a high flame for 2–3 minutes.

4. Remove with the chopsticks and place in a serving bowl.

D I N N E R

AZUKI BEANS WITH KOMBU AND SQUASH
PRESSURE-COOKED BROWN RICE
(SOAKING METHOD)
DAIKON, DAIKON GREENS, AND KOMBU
PRESSED SALAD
BURDOCK AND CARROT KINPIRA
WATERCRESS SOUP
CONDIMENTS AND BEVERAGE

In this meal we introduce another basic method of pressure-cooking brown rice. Soaking produces a softer, more easily digested grain dish. Azuki beans require the longest time to cook among the dishes in this menu, and that is why the meal takes longer than the others in this chapter.
Approximate preparation time: 2 hours–2 hours and
15 minutes

Putting the Meal Together: This special dinner takes a little longer to prepare than the others in this chapter. Like the azuki, kombu, and squash dish here, most beans take longer to cook than other dishes do. If you are pressed for time during the week, save your bean dishes for the weekend or whenever more time is available. (If necessary, the bean dish can be omitted from the menu.) If you prepare the full meal, begin by prepping the azuki beans. Then proceed to the brown rice, which has been soaking since morning. (Rice that is presoaked can be cooked in slightly less time than usual.) Then, while the rice and beans are cooking, proceed to the daikon, pressed salad, soup, and kinpira. Serve the meal with condiments and beverage of your choice.

AZUKI BEANS WITH KOMBU AND SQUASH

*Combining azuki beans with squash produces a wonderful,
naturally sweet dish rich in complex carbohydrates.*
Approximate cooking time: 2 hours–2 hours and 15
minutes (about 10 minutes preparation time)

UTENSILS

small (1-quart) porcelain or
 glass bowl
vegetable knife
medium (4-quart) cooking
 pot with lid

measuring cup
teaspoon
wood spoon
porcelain or glass serving
 bowl

INGREDIENTS

1 strip of kombu, 4–6
 inches long, wiped,
 soaked, and diced
1 cup spring or well water
 for soaking kombu
½ medium buttercup or
 butternut squash, washed
 and cut into bite-sized
 chunks (2 cups)

2 cups azuki beans, washed
 and soaked in 6 cups
 spring or well water for
 6–8 hours
¼ teaspoon sea salt

PREPARATION

1. Wipe the kombu with a clean, damp sponge and soak
it in the water for 3–5 minutes. Then dice the kombu, reserving the soaking water.

2. Place the diced kombu in the bottom of the pot.

3. Wash the squash, slice it in half, and remove the seeds
from one of the halves. Then slice that half into bite-sized
chunks.

4. Place the squash chunks on top of the kombu in the
pot.

5. Place the azuki beans on top of the squash, reserving
the soaking water.

6. Add enough azuki and kombu soaking water to just
cover the squash (but not the beans).

7. Put the lid on the pot, turn the flame to high, and

bring to a boil. Turn the flame to medium-low and simmer for about 1½–2 hours.

8. While the beans are cooking, check the water level from time to time. Keep the level of water just below the beans by occasionally adding more soaking water.

9. The beans should be almost ready after they have cooked for about 1½ hours. At this time, season them with sea salt.

10. Let the beans cook for about 10 minutes after seasoning them.

11. Remove the lid and let them cook for 5 minutes more.

12. Remove the beans and vegetables and place in a serving bowl.

PRESSURE-COOKED BROWN RICE (SOAKING METHOD)

Approximate cooking time: 1 hour and 5 minutes (about 10 minutes preparation time)

UTENSILS

5-liter pressure cooker
flame deflector
chopstick

bamboo rice paddle or
wood spoon
wood serving bowl

INGREDIENTS

4 cups short-grain brown rice, washed and soaked in 5⅓ cups spring or well water for 6–8 hours

4 small pinches of sea salt
1 sprig of parsley, washed

PREPARATION

1. Place the rice and soaking water in the pressure cooker. Place the pressure cooker on the stove and turn the flame to high.

2. Add the sea salt, fasten the lid on the cooker, and wait until the pressure comes up.

3. When the pressure comes up, turn the flame to medium-low. Place a flame deflector under the cooker and cook for 50 minutes.

4. Remove the cooker from the hot burner and place a chopstick under the pressure gauge to allow steam to escape more rapidly.

5. When all the steam has escaped, remove the lid and let the rice sit for about 5 minutes.

6. Remove the rice with a rice paddle and place in a wood serving bowl. Garnish with a sprig of fresh parsley.

DAIKON, DAIKON GREENS, AND KOMBU

Root vegetables such as daikon, carrots, and turnips are especially delicious when cooked along with their green tops. If daikon greens are not available, simply cook the daikon root along with the kombu.

Approximate cooking time: 40–45 minutes (about 10 minutes preparation time)

UTENSILS

small (1-quart) porcelain or glass bowl
measuring cup
vegetable knife
medium (4-quart) stainless-steel cooking pot with lid
teaspoon
wood spoon
porcelain or glass serving bowl

INGREDIENTS

1 strip of kombu, 4–6 inches long, soaked and cut into 1-inch squares
1 cup spring or well water for soaking kombu
1 piece of daikon root, 6–8 inches long, washed and sliced into $\frac{1}{4}$- to $\frac{1}{2}$-inch-thick rounds (2 cups)
$\frac{1}{2}$ cup spring or well water
Small pinch of sea salt
$\frac{1}{2}$ bunch of daikon greens (1 cup), washed and sliced into 1-inch lengths (1 cup)
$1\frac{1}{2}$ teaspoons tamari soy sauce

PREPARATION

1. Wipe the kombu with a clean, damp sponge. Place it in a bowl and cover with 1 cup water. Soak for 3–5 minutes and then slice it into squares, reserving the soaking water.

2. Place the kombu squares on the bottom of the pot.

3. Wash and slice the daikon. Then place it on top of the kombu.

4. Place the water, including the kombu soaking water, and a pinch of sea salt in the pot. Cover, bring to a boil, and reduce the flame to medium-low. Simmer for 30–35 minutes.

5. Wash and slice the daikon greens and place them on top of the daikon. Then add tamari soy sauce, put the lid on the pot, and cook for another 4–5 minutes.

6. Mix the ingredients with a wood spoon and place in a serving bowl.

PRESSED SALAD
Approximate cooking time: 25–30 minutes (about 3 minutes preparation time)

UTENSILS

vegetable knife

measuring cup

medium (2-quart) porcelain or glass mixing bowl

teaspoon

tablespoon

pickle press

porcelain or glass serving bowl

INGREDIENTS

2 cups thinly sliced (on the diagonal) Chinese cabbage

½ small red onion, peeled, washed, and sliced into very thin half-moons (¼ cup)

¼ cup very thinly sliced (on the diagonal) celery

½ teaspoon sea salt

2 tablespoons brown rice vinegar

2 teaspoons mirin

PREPARATION

1. Wash and slice the vegetables. Then place them in the mixing bowl.

2. Add the sea salt, brown rice vinegar, and mirin. Mix thoroughly with your fingers.

3. Place the vegetables and any liquid left in the bottom of the bowl into the pickle press. Fasten the lid on the press and tighten the pressure plate to apply pressure.

4. Let the vegetables sit for 20–25 minutes.

5. Release the pressure plate, remove the lid, and remove the pressed salad with your fingers. Squeeze out excess liquid with both hands and arrange the finished salad, a handful at a time, in an attractive pattern in the serving bowl.

BURDOCK AND CARROT KINPIRA

This dish is especially good for vitality. If you can't find burdock, you can use parsnips, fresh or dried lotus root, or turnips instead.

Approximate cooking time: 15–17 minutes (about 5 minutes preparation time)

UTENSILS

vegetable knife
measuring cup
porcelain or glass dinner
  plate
medium (10-inch) stainless-
  steel skillet

teaspoon
cooking chopsticks
porcelain or glass serving
  bowl

INGREDIENTS

1 cup shaved burdock
1 medium carrot, washed
  and sliced into
  matchsticks (1 cup)
2 teaspoons dark sesame oil

$\frac{1}{4}$–$\frac{1}{2}$ cup spring or well
  water
1–1$\frac{1}{2}$ teaspoons (to taste)
  tamari soy sauce

PREPARATION

1. Wash and slice the vegetables. Place the vegetables on separate sections of a plate.

2. Place the skillet over a high flame and add the oil. Heat for about 1 minute.

3. Add the burdock and sauté for 2–3 minutes, using the cooking chopsticks to stir.

4. Place the carrots on top of the burdock. Do not mix. Add enough water to barely cover the bottom of the skillet, put the lid on the skillet, and simmer for 5–7 minutes, until the vegetables are tender.

5. Add the tamari soy sauce, cover, and simmer for 1–2 minutes.

6. Remove the lid, mix the vegetables, and sauté for another 1–2 minutes, until all the liquid has evaporated.

7. Place in a serving bowl.

WATERCRESS SOUP
Approximate cooking time: 10 minutes (about 4–5 minutes preparation time)

UTENSILS
measuring cup
small (2-quart) stainless-
   steel cooking pot with lid
cooking chopsticks
small (1-quart) porcelain or
   glass bowl
tablespoon

medium (2-quart) porcelain
   or glass bowl
colander
vegetable knife
individual serving bowls
ladle

INGREDIENTS
3–4 cups spring or well
   water
1 strip of kombu, 2–3
   inches long

3 tablespoons tamari soy
   sauce
1 cup sliced watercress (1-
   inch lengths)

PREPARATION
1. Place enough water in the pot to cover the kombu, add the kombu, dusted with a clean, damp sponge, cover, and bring to a boil over a high flame. Turn the flame to medium-low and simmer for 4–5 minutes. Remove the kombu using the chopsticks and set it aside in a small bowl.

2. Season the cooking liquid with the tamari soy sauce, cover, and reduce the flame to low. Simmer for 2–3 minutes.

3. While the broth is simmering, place the watercress in

a bowl, wash it, and then place it in a colander to drain. Then slice the watercress.

4. Place ¼ cup of chopped watercress in each serving bowl. Ladle the hot broth over the watercress. The hot broth is sufficient to partially cook the watercress.

Preparing for the Following Day: After you finish cooking, set aside 3 cups of leftover brown rice and 2 cups of azuki beans with kombu and squash for lunch on the following day. They can be stored in containers in the refrigerator.

DAY SEVEN

B R E A K F A S T

CORN GRITS
BOILED TEMPEH WITH SCALLIONS
BOILED BROCCOLI
ROASTED SUNFLOWER SEEDS
CONDIMENTS AND BEVERAGE
Approximate preparation time: 20 minutes

Putting the Meal Together: Naturally processed yellow corn grits are quick and easy to prepare. Cook the grits first and then proceed to the tempeh and scallions, boiled broccoli, and roasted sunflower seeds. The seeds are especially nice as a topping or garnish for the corn grits. Serve the meal with the condiments and beverage of your choice.

CORN GRITS

Corn grits make a light and appetizing breakfast cereal.
Approximate cooking time: 20 minutes (about 5 minutes preparation time)

UTENSILS

measuring cup
medium (4-quart) stainless-
  steel cooking pot with lid

wood spoon
individual serving bowls

INGREDIENTS

3–4 cups spring or well
    water
small pinch of sea salt

1 cup organic yellow corn
    grits

PREPARATION

1. Place the water (use the smaller amount if you like the dish thicker in consistency) and sea salt in a saucepan. Put the lid on the pot, turn the flame to high, and bring to a boil.

2. Slowly add the corn grits to the boiling water, a little bit at a time, stirring constantly with the wood spoon to prevent lumping.

3. Bring to a boil again, turn the flame to low, cover, and simmer for 15 minutes.

4. Spoon the hot grits into individual serving bowls.

BOILED TEMPEH WITH SCALLIONS

Approximate cooking time: 20 minutes (about 3–4 minutes preparation time)

UTENSILS

vegetable knife
small (2-quart) stainless-
    steel saucepan with lid
measuring cup

teaspoon
wood spoon
porcelain or glass serving
    bowl

INGREDIENTS

1 ½-pound package tempeh,
    sliced into 1-inch squares
½ cup spring or well water
2 teaspoons tamari soy
    sauce

1 bunch scallions, washed
    and sliced into 1-inch
    lengths

PREPARATION

1. Slice the tempeh and place it in the saucepan. Add the water, cover the pot, and place over a high flame. Bring to a boil.

2. Turn the flame to medium-low and simmer for 10 minutes.

3. Add the tamari soy sauce, cover the pot again, and cook for another 5 minutes.

4. While the tempeh is cooking, wash and slice the scallions.

5. Place the scallion slices on top of the tempeh, cover, and cook for 1–2 minutes.

6. Remove the cover, turn the flame to high, mix the ingredients with the wood spoon, and cook until all the remaining liquid evaporates.

7. Place in a serving bowl.

BOILED BROCCOLI

Approximate cooking time: 5–7 minutes (about 2–3 minutes preparation time)

UTENSILS

measuring cup
small (2-quart) stainless-
   steel saucepan with lid
vegetable knife

wire-mesh spoon
porcelain or glass serving
   bowl

INGREDIENTS

2 cups spring or well water
½ bunch of broccoli,
   washed and sliced into
   flowerets (2 cups)

PREPARATION

1. Place the water in the pot, cover, and bring to a boil.

2. Wash and slice the broccoli.

3. Place the broccoli in the pot, cover, and boil for 3–4 minutes.

4. Remove with a wire-mesh spoon and place in a serving bowl.

ROASTED SUNFLOWER SEEDS

Sunflower seeds can be roasted and eaten as a snack several times a week.

Approximate preparation time: 5–7 minutes

UTENSILS

measuring cup
small (1-quart) porcelain or
  glass bowl
strainer
medium (10-inch) stainless-
  steel skillet

bamboo rice paddle
porcelain or glass serving
  bowl

INGREDIENTS

1 cup hulled sunflower
  seeds

PREPARATION

1. Place the seeds in a bowl and wash. Remove and place in a strainer. Rinse under a stream of cold water and drain.

2. Place the skillet over a medium-high flame for 1 minute. Then add the damp seeds.

3. Dry-roast for about 4–5 minutes, until the seeds turn golden brown, stirring constantly with the rice paddle to roast evenly and prevent burning.

4. Remove and place in the serving bowl. Eat anytime as a snack or sprinkle on top of the corn grits or other dishes.

L U N C H

AZUKI BEAN SOUP
HOMEMADE SUSHI
BOILED WATERCRESS
CONDIMENTS AND BEVERAGE

In this meal leftover brown rice is transformed into home-made sushi, and the leftover azuki beans with kombu and squash serve as the basis for a delicious and nourishing soup.

Approximate preparation time: 20 minutes

Putting the Meal Together: This meal is based around the brown rice and azuki bean dish left over from the previous dinner. Start the meal with the azuki bean soup, and while that is cooking, there should be enough time to make the sushi. The watercress, which cooks very quickly, can be made last. Homemade sushi is a real favorite. It is a convenient lunch box item or snack. Serve the meal with condiments and beverage of your choice.

AZUKI BEAN SOUP

Approximate cooking time: 20 minutes (about 5–7 minutes preparation time)

UTENSILS

vegetable knife
measuring cup
medium (4-quart) stainless-
  steel cooking pot with lid

teaspoon
ladle
individual serving bowls or
  thermos

INGREDIENTS

¼ cup diced onion
¼ cup diced celery
2 cups leftover cooked
  azuki beans with kombu
  and squash
3½ cups spring or well
  water

2½–3 teaspoons (to taste)
  tamari soy sauce
2 teaspoons very finely
  chopped parsley

PREPARATION

1. Peel the onion, wash the onion and celery, and then dice.

2. Place the leftover azuki beans in the saucepan and add the water, onion, and celery.

3. Put the lid on the pot, turn the flame to high, and bring to a boil.

4. Turn the flame to medium-low and simmer for 15 minutes.

5. Add the tamari soy sauce and simmer for another 4–5 minutes.

6. Wash the parsley and chop it very fine.

7. Ladle the hot soup into serving bowls or a thermos.

8. Garnish each serving with a pinch of chopped parsley.

HOMEMADE SUSHI

This is a wonderful way to use the leftover brown rice. Homemade sushi can be eaten any time of day as a snack or quick meal. Please experiment and discover new variations on this basic recipe. This recipe yields 24 bite-sized pieces of sushi.

Approximate preparation time: 10–15 minutes

UTENSILS

bamboo sushi mat
small (1-quart) porcelain or glass bowl
bamboo rice paddle
measuring cup

vegetable knife (preferably recently sharpened)
porcelain or glass serving platter or lunch box

INGREDIENTS

3 sheets of nori, toasted
Spring or well water
3 cups leftover cooked brown rice
6–9 strips of shiso leaves (the purplish leaves aged with umeboshi plums)

1 small cucumber, washed, peeled (if waxed), and sliced into matchsticks (1 cup)

PREPARATION

1. One at a time, toast the sheets of nori as described in the recipe for watercress nori rolls (see index).

2. Place the bamboo sushi mat on the cutting board.

3. Place a sheet of toasted nori on the mat.

4. Place a small amount of water in a bowl and moisten the rice paddle.

5. Spread 1 cup of the rice evenly over the entire lower half of the sheet of nori, pressing the rice down firmly with the moistened rice paddle.

6. Place 2–3 strips of shiso lengthwise in a straight line across the center of the rice.

7. Lay ⅓ cup of cucumber matchsticks on top of the shiso leaves, completely covering the leaves.

8. Use the sushi mat to tightly roll the nori around the rice. Press the mat firmly against the nori and rice until you completely roll it up into a round log shape.

9. Place the rice roll on the cutting board.

10. Moisten your vegetable knife (make sure it is sharp) with cold water.

11. Slice the roll in half. Then moisten the knife again and slice each half into four equal pieces.

12. Moisten the knife every time or every other time you cut so as to prevent the nori from tearing.

13. Repeat the steps above until you use up the rice and nori.

14. Stand the individual pieces of sushi on end in a lunch box or arrange them on a serving platter.

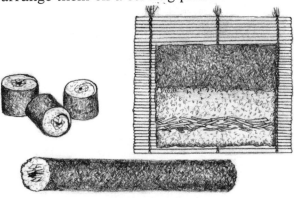

BOILED WATERCRESS
Approximate cooking time: 5 minutes (about 2 minutes preparation time)

UTENSILS

measuring cup

small (2-quart) stainless-
   steel saucepan with lid

medium (2-quart) porcelain
   or glass bowl

colander

wire-mesh spoon

vegetable knife

porcelain or glass serving
   bowl or lunch box

INGREDIENTS

2 cups spring or well water
1 large bunch of
   watercress, washed

PREPARATION

1. Place the water in the pot, cover, and bring to a boil over a high flame.

2. While the water is coming to a boil, place the watercress in a bowl and wash it. Then put it in a colander to drain.

3. Place the watercress in the boiling water, cover the pot, and bring to a boil again. Cook for 1 minute.

4. Remove the watercress with the wire-mesh spoon and place it in the colander.

5. Rinse under cold water. Squeeze the rinsed watercress with your hands to remove excess liquid.

6. Place the watercress on the cutting board and slice on the diagonal into 1-inch lengths.

7. Place in a serving bowl or lunch box.

D I N N E R

APPLE KANTEN
BROWN RICE WITH PEARL BARLEY (HATO MUGI)
KOMBU CARROT ROLLS
PUREED SQUASH SOUP
GREEN BEANS AMANDINE
BROILED SOLE
GRATED DAIKON
CONDIMENTS AND BEVERAGE

This special full-course dinner features broiled fish along with grains, soup, several vegetable dishes, garnish, and a kanten dessert. Friends who are vegetarian can omit the fish and still have a complete and balanced meal.

Approximate preparation time: 1½ hours

Putting the Meal Together: Begin the meal by preparing the kanten. Once you have put it aside to jell, move on to the brown rice with pearl barley. While the grains are cooking, move on to the sweet squash soup and then to the kombu carrot rolls. The green beans can be started next. While they are cooking, start the broiled sole. Other varieties of white-meat fish may be used in place of sole, but if the fillets are thicker, they may require a minute or two longer to cook. The daikon can be grated last and can be eaten with the seafood to aid digestion. Serve the meal with condiments and beverage of your choice.

APPLE KANTEN

Kanten is a wonderfully refreshing natural jellied dessert. A variety of fresh fruits can be prepared in kantens. In this recipe, we use apples and apple juice. Since the kanten takes time to jell, start it before the other dishes in the meal.
Approximate cooking time: 1 hour and 10 minutes (about 10–15 minutes preparation time)

UTENSILS

measuring cup
medium (4-quart) stainless-
  steel cooking pot with lid
tablespoon
vegetable knife

wood spoon
shallow (11¾" × 7½" × 1¾")
  glass baking or casserole
  dish

INGREDIENTS

1 quart organic natural
  apple juice *or* 2 cups
  spring or well water and
  2 cups juice
Small pinch of sea salt

6 tablespoons agar-agar
  flakes (read directions on
  package)
3 medium apples, sliced
  into thin half-moons (3
  cups)

PREPARATION

1. Place the juice or water and juice in the cooking pot, turn the flame to high, and add the sea salt and agar-agar flakes.

2. Wash and slice the apples and add them to the pot.

3. Stir several times until the flakes dissolve.

4. Cover the pot and bring to a boil.

5. Remove the cover, lower the flame, and simmer for 2–3 minutes.

6. Pour the hot liquid with sliced apples into the baking dish.

7. Place in the refrigerator or in a cool place for about 50–60 minutes or until the kanten solidifies.

BROWN RICE WITH PEARL BARLEY (HATO MUGI)

Pearl barley, or hato mugi, combines very nicely with brown rice. It can be added from time to time to your main rice dish for variety.

Approximate cooking time: 1 hour (about 10 minutes preparation time)

UTENSILS

measuring cup
medium (2-quart) porcelain
  or glass bowl
strainer
5-liter pressure cooker

flame deflector
chopstick
bamboo rice paddle
wood serving bowl

INGREDIENTS

3½ cups short-grain brown
  rice
½ cup pearl barley (hato
  mugi)

5⅓ cups spring or well
  water
4 small pinches of sea salt
1 sprig of watercress

PREPARATION

1. Place the brown rice in the bowl and wash.

2. After washing it, place the rice in the pressure cooker.

3. Put the pearl barley in the bowl used to wash the rice and wash. Then add it to the pressure cooker along with the rice.

4. Add the water and place the uncovered cooker over a low flame until the water just begins to boil.

5. Then add the sea salt, fasten the lid on the cooker, and turn the flame to high.

6. When the pressure comes up, place a flame deflector under the cooker, turn the flame to medium-low, and cook for 50 minutes.

7. When the rice has finished cooking, remove the cooker from the hot burner and gently place the narrow tip of a chopstick under the pressure gauge to allow steam to escape more rapidly. When the pressure has come down, remove the lid and let the rice sit for 4–5 minutes.

8. Remove the grains with the rice paddle and place them in a wood serving bowl.

9. Rinse a sprig of watercress under a stream of cold water and use as a garnish.

KOMBU CARROT ROLLS

This recipe makes 12 small kombu carrot rolls.
Approximate cooking time: 45–50 minutes (about 7–10 minutes preparation time)

UTENSILS

measuring cup
large (11¾" × 7½" × 1¾") glass baking or casserole dish
medium (2-quart) porcelain or glass bowl
vegetable knife

medium (4-quart) stainless-steel cooking pot with lid
tablespoon
chopsticks
porcelain or glass serving platter

INGREDIENTS

3 cups spring or well water for soaking kombu
2 strips of kombu, about 12 inches long by 3 inches wide, soaked and sliced in half crosswise
12 strips of kanpyo (dried gourd strips), 6 inches long, soaked

1 cup spring or well water for soaking kanpyo
4 medium carrots, washed and trimmed
1 tablespoon tamari soy sauce

PREPARATION

1. Place 3 cups of water in the casserole dish. Add the kombu and soak for 3–5 minutes.

2. Place the kanpyo in another bowl, add 1 cup of water, and soak for 5 minutes.

3. Wash the carrots and trim off the very top and the tip with a vegetable knife.

4. Place the soaked kombu on the cutting board and

slice each strip in half crosswise, reserving the kombu soaking water.

5. Place the kombu, a piece at a time, on the cutting board. Then place a carrot lengthwise in the middle of the kombu.

6. Roll the kombu around the carrot as tightly as possible so that it completely covers the carrot.

7. Tie a strip of kanpyo around the middle of the roll and a strip about an inch from each end. Tie the kanpyo as tightly as you can.

8. Repeat until all the kombu, carrots, and kanpyo are used up.

9. Place the tied rolls in the cooking pot and add the 3 cups of kombu soaking water. Discard the water left from soaking the kanpyo.

10. Place the cover on the pot, turn the flame to high, and bring the water to a boil. Then turn the flame to medium-low and simmer for 40 minutes.

11. Add the tamari soy sauce, put the lid back on the pot, and cook for another 5 minutes or so, until the kombu becomes tender.

12. Remove the rolls with chopsticks and slice each roll into three equal pieces. Cut between the kanpyo strips so that you have 12 small kombu carrot rolls, each with a strip of kanpyo in the center.

13. Place the tied rolls on a serving platter. The kanpyo can be eaten along with the roll.

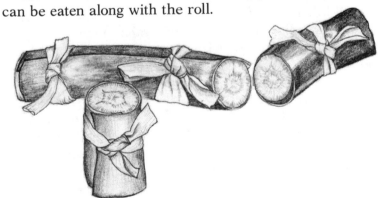

PUREED SQUASH SOUP

This deliciously sweet soup is a real autumn favorite but can be served at any time of year.

Approximate cooking time: 40 minutes (about 10 minutes preparation time)

UTENSILS

measuring cup
medium (4-quart) stainless-steel cooking pot with lid
vegetable knife
tablespoon
small (1-quart) porcelain or glass bowl
teaspoon
stainless-steel hand food mill
medium (2-quart) porcelain or glass bowl
wood spoon
ladle
individual serving bowls

INGREDIENTS

4–5 cups spring or well water
1 small unwaxed buttercup squash, washed, peeled, and sliced into 1-inch chunks (3 cups)
¼–½ teaspoon (to taste) sea salt
1 tablespoon chopped scallion

PREPARATION

1. Place the water in the pot (use the smaller amount if you like the soup thicker), cover it, and bring to a boil.

2. While the water is heating, scrub the squash, slice it in half, and remove the seeds with a tablespoon.

3. Peel the squash with a vegetable knife, put the skin in a bowl, cover it, and place it in the refrigerator.

4. Slice each half of the squash into wedges and then cut each wedge into 1-inch chunks.

5. Place the squash chunks in the boiling water and add a pinch of the sea salt. Cover and bring to a boil again.

6. Reduce the flame to medium-low and simmer for 10–15 minutes.

7. Place the food mill securely on top of the bowl. Use the wood spoon to transfer the squash to the mill, pouring

the cooking water, 1–2 cups at a time, into the mill along with it. Puree until smooth.

8. Pour the pureed squash back into the cooking pot. Add the remaining sea salt to taste, cover, turn the flame to high, and bring to a boil.

9. Turn the flame to medium-low and simmer for another 10–15 minutes.

10. While the squash is simmering, wash and chop the scallion.

11. Ladle the hot soup into individual serving bowls and garnish with the chopped scallion.

GREEN BEANS AMANDINE
Approximate cooking time: 15–20 minutes (about 5 minutes preparation time)

UTENSILS

vegetable knife
measuring cup
teaspoon
medium (10-inch) stainless-
  steel skillet with lid

cooking chopsticks
porcelain or glass serving
  bowl

INGREDIENTS

3 cups very thinly sliced (on the diagonal) green string beans
1 teaspoon dark sesame oil

¼ cup spring or well water
¼ cup slivered almonds
1–2 teaspoons (to taste) tamari soy sauce

PREPARATION

1. Wash the beans and pull the stems off with your fingers.

2. Slice the beans, one at a time, very thin on the diagonal.

3. Place the oil in the skillet and heat for 1 minute over a high flame.

4. Place the sliced beans in the hot skillet and sauté with cooking chopsticks for 2–3 minutes.

5. Add the water to the skillet.

6. Sprinkle the slivered almonds on top of the beans. Do not mix.

7. Place the cover on the skillet, bring the water to a boil, turn the flame to low, and simmer for 7–8 minutes until the beans are tender.

8. Remove the cover and add the tamari soy sauce. Put the cover back on the skillet and simmer for another 1–2 minutes.

9. Remove the lid, mix the beans and almonds with the cooking chopsticks, and sauté, uncovered, until all the liquid is gone.

10. Place in a serving bowl.

BROILED SOLE

Although this recipe uses sole, any low-fat white-meat fish can be substituted. This recipe makes 4 servings.
Approximate cooking time: 5–7 minutes (about 2–3 minutes preparation time)

UTENSILS

medium (2-quart) porcelain
    or glass bowl
colander
stainless-steel baking sheet
teaspoon

vegetable knife
metal spatula
porcelain or glass serving
    platter

INGREDIENTS

4 fresh fillets (about 1
    pound total) of sole or
    other white-meat fish
2 teaspoons tamari soy
    sauce

1 small lemon, washed and
    sliced in half crosswise
4 sprigs of parsley, washed

PREPARATION

1. Place the sole (or other white-meat fish) in a bowl and rinse under cold water. Remove and place in a colander to drain.

2. Place the fish on a dry baking sheet. Preheat the broiler.

3. Sprinkle ½ teaspoon of tamari soy sauce on top of the fillets.

4. Halve the lemon and squeeze the juice from one of the lemon halves on the fillets.

5. Place the fillets under the broiler and broil for about 5–7 minutes, until tender and slightly browned.

6. Take the baking sheet out of the broiler and remove the fillets with the metal spatula. Place them on the serving platter.

7. Slice the other lemon half into 4 lengthwise wedges. Then wash the parsley under a stream of cold water.

8. Garnish the platter with the lemon wedges and parsley sprigs.

GRATED DAIKON

This garnish is eaten like horseradish to help digest the fats and oils in fish and seafood.

Approximate preparation time: 2–3 minutes

UTENSILS

vegetable knife
flat grater
measuring cup

porcelain or glass serving
bowl
tablespoon

INGREDIENTS

¼ cup grated daikon (3- to
  4-inch piece)

PREPARATION

1. Slice a 3- to 4-inch piece off a whole daikon. Wash the daikon and grate it on the flat grater.

2. Place the gratings in a serving bowl.

3. Serve about 1 tablespoon to each person. Place grated daikon on each plate to eat along with the fish.

Preparing for the Following Day: Set aside and refrigerate 1 cup of brown rice with pearl barley for morning porridge, along with the skin peeled from the buttercup squash.

DAY EIGHT

B R E A K F A S T

SOFT RICE WITH PEARL BARLEY (HATO MUGI)
MISO SOUP WITH SQUASH SKINS
BOILED KALE
CONDIMENTS AND BEVERAGE ·
Approximate preparation time: 20 minutes

Putting the Meal Together: The soft grain porridge can be started first. While the porridge is cooking, begin the miso soup, then finish with the boiled kale. Cutting the kale after it is cooked produces an especially delicious serving of greens; when cooked whole, the vegetable retains its sweetness and nutrients, rather than letting them escape into the cooking water. This method can be used several times a week in preparing greens.

SOFT RICE WITH PEARL BARLEY (HATO MUGI)

Leftover brown rice with pearl barley makes a wonderfully creamy breakfast porridge.

Approximate cooking time: 20 minutes (about 5 minutes preparation time)

UTENSILS

measuring cup
small (2-quart) stainless-
   steel saucepan with lid

wood spoon
individual serving bowls

INGREDIENTS

1 cup leftover cooked
   brown rice with pearl
   barley (hato mugi)

3 cups spring or well water

PREPARATION

1. Place the leftover rice with barley in a saucepan and add the water.

2. Cover the pot, turn the flame to high, and bring to a boil. Then lower the flame and simmer for 10–15 minutes, until the grains become soft and creamy.

3. When the grains are ready, spoon into individual serving bowls.

MISO SOUP WITH SQUASH SKINS

The squash skins give the miso soup a naturally sweet flavor. Make sure that the squash is unwaxed.

Approximate cooking time: 15–20 minutes (about 5 minutes preparation time)

UTENSILS

small (1-quart) porcelain or
   glass bowl
vegetable knife
measuring cup
porcelain or glass dinner
   plate

medium (4-quart) stainless-
   steel cooking pot with lid
tablespoon
teaspoon
ladle
individual serving bowls

INGREDIENTS

¼ cup soaked and sliced wakame

½ cup spring or well water for soaking wakame

3–4 cups spring or well water

1 cup unwaxed squash skins, sliced into matchsticks

½ cup diced onion

1½–2 tablespoons (to taste) miso, pureed in ¼ cup spring or well water

2 teaspoons finely chopped scallion

PREPARATION

1. Wash wakame, soak in ½ cup water for 3–5 minutes, slice, and place it on a plate.

2. Place 3–4 cups water (enough to cover the wakame) in the saucepan, cover the pot, turn the flame to high, and bring to a boil.

3. Turn the flame to medium low, add the wakame, and simmer for 1–2 minutes.

4. Slice the squash skins and arrange on a plate. Peel the onion, wash, dice, and arrange on a separate section of the plate.

5. Place the onion in the boiling water, cover the pot, and cook for 1–2 minutes.

6. Add the squash skins, cover, and cook for 3–5 minutes.

7. Place ¼ cup water in a measuring cup. Add the miso and puree.

8. Turn the flame to low and add the pureed miso. Cover the pot and simmer for 2–3 minutes.

9. Wash the scallion and chop fine.

10. Ladle the hot soup into individual serving bowls and garnish each serving with chopped scallion.

BOILED KALE

Approximate cooking time: 5–7 minutes (about 3 minutes preparation time)

UTENSILS

measuring cup
medium (4-quart) stainless-
    steel cooking pot with lid
cooking chopsticks

colander
vegetable knife
porcelain or glass serving
    bowl

INGREDIENTS

3 cups spring or well water   1 small bunch kale, washed

PREPARATION

1. Place the water in the pot and cover. Turn the flame to high and bring to a boil.

2. Wash the kale and leave whole.

3. Place the kale in the boiling water, cover the pot, and boil for 2–3 minutes.

4. Remove the kale with the chopsticks and place it in the colander.

5. Rinse the kale under a stream of cold water and let it sit to drain.

6. Place the kale on the cutting board and slice into 1-inch pieces.

7. Place the sliced kale in a serving bowl.

L   U   N   C   H

VEGETABLE SOUP
FRIED TOFU SANDWICHES
CONDIMENTS AND BEVERAGE
Approximate preparation time: 20 minutes

Putting the Meal Together: Fried tofu sandwiches will appeal especially to newcomers to macrobiotics and can be quickly prepared at any time. Start with the soup and, while it is simmering on the stove, begin making your tofu sandwiches.

VEGETABLE SOUP

Approximate cooking time: 20 minutes (about 7 minutes preparation time)

UTENSILS

measuring cup

medium (4-quart) stainless-steel pot with lid

vegetable knife

2 porcelain or glass dinner plates

porcelain or glass saucer

tablespoon

teaspoon

ladle

individual serving bowls or thermos

INGREDIENTS

3–4 cups spring or well water

1 strip of kombu, 3–4 inches long

½ cup diced onion

⅓ cup diced carrot

½ cup sweet corn kernels (1 ear)

¼ cup diced celery

¼ cup shelled green peas

3 tablespoons kuzu, diluted in 6 tablespoons spring or well water

2–2½ tablespoons (to taste) tamari soy sauce

2 teaspoons finely chopped scallion

PREPARATION

1. Place the water (enough to cover the kombu) and kombu in the cooking pot and cover. Turn the flame to high and bring to a boil.

2. While the water is heating, wash and slice the vegetables (except scallion). Place the sliced vegetables on plates, keeping them separate.

3. When the water starts to boil, remove the kombu and set it aside on a saucer.

4. Place the vegetables in the boiling water, cover the pot, and bring to a boil again. Turn the flame to medium-low and simmer for about 10 minutes.

5. Dilute the kuzu in 6 tablespoons of water. Then add the diluted kuzu to the pot, stirring constantly to prevent lumping.

6. Add the tamari soy sauce, cover the pot, and simmer for another 2–3 minutes.

7. Wash the scallion and chop it fine.

8. Ladle the hot soup into individual bowls or a thermos. Garnish each serving with chopped scallion.

FRIED TOFU SANDWICHES

Fried tofu sandwiches are quick and easy to make. You can enjoy them anytime as a snack or quick light meal. This recipe makes either 3 or 4 sandwiches.

Approximate cooking time: 15 minutes (about 10 minutes preparation time)

UTENSILS

vegetable knife

teaspoon

medium (10-inch) stainless-
  steel skillet

tablespoon

metal spatula

porcelain or glass plate

porcelain or glass serving
  platter or lunch box

INGREDIENTS

1 1-pound cake firm-style
  tofu, cut crosswise into
  6–8 slices

2 teaspoons dark sesame oil

1 tablespoon tamari soy
  sauce

Enough organic whole-
  wheat bread to make 6–8
  slices

3–4 lettuce leaves, washed

3–4 tablespoons sauerkraut

PREPARATION

1. Slice the tofu into 6–8 crosswise slices about ¼–½ inch thick.

2. Place the oil in the skillet and heat for about 1 minute.

3. Place the tofu slices in the skillet and pour several drops of tamari soy sauce on top of each. Fry for 2–3 minutes.

4. Turn the slices over with the spatula and sprinkle several drops of tamari soy sauce on the other side. Fry for 2–3 minutes.

5. Place the fried tofu on a plate.

6. While the tofu is frying, slice the bread and wash the lettuce under a stream of cold water.

7. Place 2 slices of tofu on each of 3 or 4 slices of bread. Then put 1 tablespoon of sauerkraut and a lettuce leaf on top of the tofu.

8. Place the top slice of bread on each sandwich. Slice in half and place on a serving platter or in a lunch box.

GLOSSARY

Agar-agar A white gelatin derived from a species of sea vegetable. Used in making kanten desserts and aspics. It can be purchased in bar or flake form.

Amasake A sweetener or refreshing drink made from fermented rice. It can be made at home or bought in some natural foods stores.

Arame A thin, wiry black sea vegetable similar to hijiki.

Azuki bean A small, dark red bean imported from Japan but also grown in the United States. Used as a staple in macrobiotic and Far Eastern cooking.

Bancha tea Correctly named *kukicha*, bancha consists of the stems and twigs from tea bushes that are at least three years old. It is grown in Japan. Bancha aids digestion, contains no dyes or caffeine, and makes an excellent beverage at any time.

Brown rice vinegar A naturally fermented vinegar made from brown rice.

Burdock A wild, hardy plant that grows throughout most of the United States. The long, dark root is highly valued in macrobiotic cooking for its strengthening qualities. Burdock is used as a staple in Far Eastern cuisines.

Daikon A long, white radish. It makes a delicious side dish, and raw daikon helps in digestion of oily foods or fish and shellfish and, when eaten from time to time, also helps the body dissolve stored deposits of saturated fat.

Daikon, dried   Shredded daikon that has been sun-dried. Used in soups and stews and as a side dish.

Dulse   A reddish-purple sea vegetable harvested in the north Atlantic. Used in soups, salads, and vegetable dishes. Very high in iron.

Food mill   A special hand food mill used to make purees, sauces, dips, baby foods, and other creamy dishes.

Fu   Wheat gluten that is dried into sheets or cakes.

Ginger   A spicy, gold-colored root used in cooking and home health care.

Gluten   The sticky substance that remains after the bran has been kneaded and rinsed from whole-wheat flour. Used to make seitan and fu.

Gomashio   A table condiment made from roasted ground sesame seeds and sea salt. Either white or black seeds may be used in making gomashio. Gomashio can be made at home or bought ready-made.

Goma wakame powder   A powdered condiment that can be prepared at home from roasted ground sesame seeds and baked or roasted wakame.

Hatcho miso   Miso made from soybeans and sea salt and aged for at least two years. Hatcho miso has a rich, strong flavor and can be used to supplement lighter misos.

Hato mugi   A variety of barley known for its properties in dissolving deposits of fats in the body originating from animal-food consumption. It can be used in soups or in combination with brown rice.

Hijiki   A dark brown sea vegetable that turns black when dried. Hijiki has a wiry consistency and is native to Japan. It is especially rich in calcium and other minerals and is used in making side dishes.

Hokkaido pumpkin   A round squash with dark green or orange skin and orange flesh that has a naturally sweet flavor. It is harvested in early fall. Originally from New England, the squash was introduced to Japan in the 19th century. Named after the northern island of Hokkaido.

Jinenjo soba   A variety of buckwheat noodle made from a combination of buckwheat and jinenjo flour.

Kanten   A jelled dessert made from fruit and agar-agar sea vegetable.

Kasha   Whole buckwheat, known as buckwheat groats.

Kelp   A large variety of sea vegetable similar to kombu.

Kinpira   A style of sautéing in which root vegetables are cut in very thin slices or shaved and seasoned with tamari soy sauce. Kinpira can be prepared with or without sesame oil.

Kombu   A wide, thick, dark green sea vegetable that grows in deep oceans. Used in soup stocks, cooked with vegetables and grains, and used in soups, condiments, candy, and other dishes.

Kombu powder   A condiment made by roasting kombu in a skillet and crushing it in a suribachi. Can be used along with gomashio as a regular condiment on grains, soups, and other dishes.

Kukicha   Usually called *bancha*. Older stems, twigs, and leaves of a tea bush grown in Japan and used as a staple beverage in macrobiotic cuisine.

Kuzu   A white starch powder made from the root of the wild kuzu plant. In the southern United States, where the plant is plentiful, it is referred to as *kudzu*. Used in making soups, sauces, gravies, and desserts and in traditional home health care.

Lotus root   The root of a variety of water lily that is brown-skinned with a hollow, chambered, off-white inside. Used for centuries as a part of traditional home health care and as a regular food item.

Lotus root, dried Fresh lotus root that has been sliced and dried.

Lotus seeds Edible seeds of the lotus root plant. They are often cooked along with brown rice and other grains.

Mirin A sweet cooking sake (wine) made from sweet brown rice.

Miso A fermented paste made from soybeans, sea salt, and rice, barley, and other grains. A staple food in macrobiotic cuisine, miso is used in soups, stews, spreads, baking, and as a seasoning.

Mochi A rice cake or dumpling made from cooked pounded sweet rice. Mochi can be bought ready-made or prepared fresh at home.

Mugicha A tea made from roasted unhulled barley. (*Mugi* is the Japanese word for "barley.")

Mugi miso Miso made from barley, soybeans, sea salt, and koji. Barley miso is one of the most commonly used varieties in macrobiotic cooking.

Mu tea A tea made from the balancing of various herbs, some of which have been traditionally known for their healing properties. Mu tea is used as an occasional beverage.

Natto Soybeans that have been cooked and mixed with natural fermenting enzymes. Natto is rich in nutrients and is known for its distinctive flavor.

Nigari Hard, crystallized salt made from the liquid drippings of dampened sea salt. Used in making tofu.

Nishime Long, slow style of boiling vegetables or other foods. Vegetables are cut into large chunks. Often referred to as "waterless cooking" since the vegetables cook mostly in their own juices.

Nori Thin sheets of dried sea vegetable. Black or dark purple when dried. Roasted for a few seconds over a flame before use. Nori is used as a garnish, wrapped around cooked rice to make rice balls or homemade sushi, or used in making condiments.

Pearl barley   A small white variety of barley often called *hato mugi.*

Pearled barley   A polished or partially polished variety of barley.

Rice syrup   A sweetener made from malted brown rice.

Sake   A wine made from fermented rice. Traditionally warmed and served in small cups.

Sea salt   Salt obtained from the ocean as opposed to land salt. It is either sun-baked or kiln-baked. Rich in trace minerals, it contains no chemicals or sugar.

Seitan   Wheat gluten cooked in tamari soy sauce, kombu, and water. It can be made at home or bought ready-made. Seitan is sometimes called *wheat meat* because of its consistency and appearance and its high protein content.

Shiitake   A variety of mushroom that can be used fresh or dried in soups and other dishes. Originally imported from Japan, shiitake are now grown in this country.

Shio kombu   Pieces of kombu cooked for a long time in tamari soy sauce and used in small amounts as a condiment.

Shiso leaves   Leaves from the beefsteak plant that are pickled with umeboshi plums to give them a reddish color. They can also be eaten fresh.

Soba   Noodles made from buckwheat flour or a combination of buckwheat flour and whole-wheat or other flours.

Somen   A very thin whole-wheat noodle.

Suribachi   A grooved earthenware bowl used for grinding and pureeing.

Surikogi   A wood pestle used to grind or puree foods in a suribachi.

Sushi   Rice rolled with vegetables, fish, or pickles, then wrapped in nori and sliced into rounds.

Sushi mat   A mat made from strips of bamboo tied together with string. Used to make rolled sushi.

Sweet rice vinegar   A type of vinegar made from fermented sweet brown rice.

Takuan   Daikon that is pickled in rice bran and sea salt.

Tamari   Name given to traditional, naturally made soy sauce to distinguish it from commercial, chemically processed varieties.

Tekka   Condiment made from hatcho miso, sesame oil, burdock root, lotus root, carrot, and gingerroot. Sautéed over a low flame for several hours.

Tempeh   A traditional Indonesian fermented soybean product. Used in soups, stews, sea vegetable dishes, sandwiches, salads, dips, and a variety of other dishes.

Tempura   Sliced vegetables, fish, or patties made of grains, vegetables, fish, or tofu dipped in batter and deep-fried until golden brown.

Tofu   A cake made from soybeans, nigari, and water.

Tofu, dried   Sliced tofu that has been frozen and dried. It has a spongy texture, light weight, and creamy beige color. It is lower in fat than fresh tofu.

Udon   A thick unbleached white wheat or whole-wheat noodle.

Umeboshi   A salty pickled plum.

Umeboshi vinegar   A traditional vinegar that is produced when making umeboshi plums. It has a salty-sour flavor and can be used in salad dressing and in making pickles.

Wakame   A long, thin, green sea vegetable used in soups, salads, vegetable dishes, and condiments.

MACROBIOTIC RESOURCES

MACROBIOTIC WAY OF LIFE SEMINAR

The *Macrobiotic Way of Life Seminar* is an introductory program offered by the Kushi Institute in Boston. It includes classes in macrobiotic cooking, home health care, kitchen setup, lectures on the philosophy of macrobiotics and the standard diet, and individual way-of-life guidance. It is presented monthly and includes introductory and intermediate-level programs. Information on the *Macrobiotic Way of Life Seminar* is available from:

The Kushi Institute
17 Station St.
Brookline, MA 12146
(617) 738-0045

MACROBIOTIC RESIDENTIAL SEMINAR

The *Macrobiotic Residential Seminar* is an introductory program offered at the Kushi Foundation Berkshires Center in Becket, Massachusetts. It is a one-week live-in program that includes hands-on training in macrobiotic cooking and home health care, lectures on the philosophy and practice of macrobiotics, and meals prepared by a specially trained cooking staff. It is presented monthly and includes introductory and intermediate levels. Information on the *Macrobiotic Residential Seminar* is available from:

Kushi Foundation Berkshires Center
Box 7
Becket, MA 01223
(413) 623-5742

KUSHI INSTITUTE LEADERSHIP STUDIES

For those who wish to study further, the Kushi Institute offers instruction for individuals who wish to become trained and certified macrobiotic teachers. Leadership training programs are also offered at Kushi Institute affiliates in London, Amsterdam, Antwerp, and Florence, as well as in Portugal and Switzerland. Information on Leadership Studies is available from the Kushi Institute in Brookline.

OTHER PROGRAMS

The Kushi Institute offers a variety of public programs, including an annual Summer Conference in western Massachusetts, special weight-loss and natural beauty seminars, and intensive cooking and spiritual development training at the Berkshires Center. Moreover, a variety of introductory and public programs are offered through an international network of over 300 educational centers in the United States, Canada, and throughout the world. The Kushi Foundation publishes a *Worldwide Macrobiotic Directory* every year listing these centers and individuals. Please consult the directory for the nearest macrobiotic center or qualified instructor.

PUBLICATIONS

Michio and Aveline Kushi have authored numerous books on macrobiotic cooking, philosophy, diet, and way of life. These titles are listed in "Recommended Reading" and are available at macrobiotic centers and at natural foods stores and bookstores. Ongoing developments are reported in *Return to Paradise*, a quarterly magazine with an international readership. The magazine features regular articles by Michio and Aveline Kushi and associates and is available at macrobiotic centers, natural foods stores, and by subscription.

RECOMMENDED READING

Aihara, Cornellia. *The Dō of Cooking*. Chico, CA: George Ohsawa Macrobiotic Foundation, 1972.

―――. *Macrobiotic Childcare*. Oroville, CA: George Ohsawa Macrobiotic Foundation, 1971.

Aihara, Herman. *Basic Macrobiotics*. Tokyo and New York: Japan Publications, Inc., 1985.

Benedict, Dirk. *Confessions of a Kamikaze Cowboy*. Van Nuys, CA: Newcastle, 1987.

Brown, Virginia, with Susan Stayman. *Macrobiotic Miracle: How a Vermont Family Overcame Cancer*. Tokyo and New York: Japan Publications, Inc., 1985.

Dietary Goals for the United States. Washington, D.C.: Select Committee on Nutrition and Human Needs, U.S. Senate, 1977.

Diet, Nutrition and Cancer. Washington, D.C.: National Academy of Sciences, 1982.

Dufty, William. *Sugar Blues*. New York: Warner Books, 1975.

Esko, Edward, and Wendy Esko. *Macrobiotic Cooking for Everyone*. Tokyo and New York: Japan Publications, Inc., 1980.

Esko, Wendy. *Aveline Kushi's Introducing Macrobiotic Cooking*. Tokyo and New York: Japan Publications, Inc., 1987.

Fukuoka, Masanobu. *The Natural Way of Farming*. Tokyo and New York: Japan Publications, Inc., 1985.

―――. *The One-Straw Revolution*. Emmaus, PA: Rodale Press, 1978.

Healthy People: The Surgeon General's Report on Health Promotion and Disease Prevention. Washington, D.C.: Government Printing Office, 1979.

Hiedenry, Carolyn. *Making the Transition to a Macrobiotic Diet.* Garden City Park, NY: Avery Publishing Group, 1987.

Hippocrates. *Hippocratic Writings.* Edited by G. E. R. Lloyd. Translated by J. Chadwick and W. N. Mann. New York: Penguin Books, 1978.

I Ching or *Book of Changes.* Translated by Richard Wilhelm and Cary F. Baynes. Princeton, NJ: Bollingen Foundation, 1950.

Ineson, John. *The Way of Life: Macrobiotics and the Spirit of Christianity.* Tokyo and New York: Japan Publications, Inc., 1986.

Jacobs, Leonard, and Barbara Leonard. *Cooking with Seitan.* Tokyo and New York: Japan Publications, Inc., 1986.

Jacobson, Michael. *The Changing American Diet.* Washington, D.C.: Center for Science in the Public Interest, 1978.

Kaibara, Ekiken. *Yojokun: Japanese Secrets of Good Health.* Tokyo: Tokuma Shoten, 1974.

Kohler, Jean, and Mary Alice. *Healing Miracles from Macrobiotics.* West Nyack, NY: Parker, 1979.

Kotsch, Ronald. *Macrobiotics: Yesterday and Today.* Tokyo and New York: Japan Publications, Inc., 1985.

_____. *Macrobiotics Beyond Food.* Tokyo and New York: Japan Publications, Inc., 1988.

Kushi, Aveline. *How to Cook with Miso.* Tokyo and New York: Japan Publications, Inc., 1978.

_____. *Lessons of Night and Day.* Garden City Park, NY: Avery Publishing Group, 1985.

_____. *Macrobiotic Food and Cooking Series: Arthritis; Stress and Hypertension.* Tokyo and New York: Japan Publications, Inc., 1988.

_____. *Macrobiotic Food and Cooking Series: Diabetes and Hypoglycemia; Allergies.* Tokyo and New York: Japan Publications, Inc., 1985.

_____. *Macrobiotic Food and Cooking Series: Obesity, Weight Loss, and Eating Disorders; Infertility and Repro-*

ductive Disorders. Tokyo and New York: Japan Publications, Inc., 1987.

Kushi, Aveline, with Alex Jack. *Aveline Kushi's Complete Guide to Macrobiotic Cooking*. New York: Warner Books, 1985.

Kushi, Aveline, and Michio Kushi. *Macrobiotic Pregnancy and Care of the Newborn*. Edited by Edward and Wendy Esko. Tokyo and New York: Japan Publications, Inc., 1984.

――――. *Macrobiotic Child Care and Family Health*. Tokyo and New York: Japan Publications, Inc., 1986.

Kushi, Aveline, and Wendy Esko. *Aveline Kushi's Wonderful World of Salads*. Tokyo and New York: Japan Publications, Inc., 1989.

――――. *Macrobiotic Family Favorites*. Tokyo and New York: Japan Publications, Inc., 1987.

――――. *The Changing Seasons Macrobiotic Cookbook*. Garden City Park, NY: Avery Publishing Group, 1983.

Kushi, Aveline, with Wendy Esko. *The Macrobiotic Cancer Prevention Cookbook*. Garden City Park, NY: Avery Publishing Group, 1988.

Kushi, Michio. *The Book of Dō-In: Exercise for Physical and Spiritual Development*. Tokyo and New York: Japan Publications, Inc., 1979.

――――. *The Book of Macrobiotics: The Universal Way of Health, Happiness and Peace*. Tokyo and New York: Japan Publications, Inc., 1986 (rev. ed.).

――――. *Cancer and Heart Disease: The Macrobiotic Approach to Degenerative Disorders*. Tokyo and New York: Japan Publications, Inc., 1986 (rev. ed.).

――――. *Crime and Diet: The Macrobiotic Approach*. Tokyo and New York: Japan Publications, Inc., 1987.

――――. *The Era of Humanity*. Brookline, MA: East West Journal, 1980.

――――. *How to See Your Health: The Book of Oriental Diagnosis*. Tokyo and New York: Japan Publications, Inc., 1980.

――――. *Macrobiotic Health Education Series: Arthritis; Stress and Hypertension*. Tokyo and New York: Japan Publications, Inc., 1988.

_____. *Macrobiotic Health Education Series: Diabetes and Hypoglycemia; Allergies.* Tokyo and New York: Japan Publications, Inc., 1985.

_____. *Macrobiotic Health Education Series: Obesity, Weight Loss, and Eating Disorders; Infertility and Reproductive Disorders.* Tokyo and New York: Japan Publications, Inc., 1987.

_____. *Natural Healing through Macrobiotics.* Tokyo and New York: Japan Publications, Inc., 1978.

_____. *On the Greater View: Collected Thoughts on Macrobiotics and Humanity.* Garden City Park, NY: Avery Publishing Group, 1985.

_____. *Your Face Never Lies.* Garden City Park, NY: Avery Publishing Group, 1983.

Kushi, Michio, and Martha Cottrell, M.D. *AIDS: Macrobiotics and Natural Immunity.* Tokyo and New York: Japan Publications, Inc., 1989.

Kushi, Michio, with Alex Jack. *The Cancer Prevention Diet.* New York: St. Martin's Press, 1983.

_____. *Diet for a Strong Heart.* New York: St. Martin's Press, 1984.

_____. *One Peaceful World.* New York: St. Martin's Press, 1987.

Kushi, Michio, and Associates. *Doctors Look at Macrobiotics.* Edited by Edward Esko. Tokyo and New York: Japan Publications, Inc., 1988.

Kushi, Michio, and Aveline Kushi, with Alex Jack. *The Macrobiotic Diet.* Tokyo and New York: Japan Publications, Inc., 1985.

Kushi, Michio, and the East West Foundation. *The Macrobiotic Approach to Cancer.* Garden City Park, NY: Avery Publishing Group, 1982.

Kushi, Michio, with Stephen Blauer. *The Macrobiotic Way.* Garden City Park, NY: Avery Publishing Group, 1985.

Kushi, Michio, with Olivia Oredson Saunders. *Macrobiotic Palm Healing.* Tokyo and New York: Japan Publications, Inc., 1988.

Mendelsohn, Robert S., M.D. *Confessions of a Medical Heretic.* Chicago: Contemporary Books, 1979.

_____. *Male Practice.* Chicago: Contemporary Books, 1980.

Nussbaum, Elaine. *Recovery: From Cancer to Health through Macrobiotics.* Tokyo and New York: Japan Publications, Inc., 1986.

Nutrition and Mental Health. Washington, D.C.: Select Committee on Nutrition and Human Needs, U.S. Senate, 1977, 1980.

Ohsawa, George. *Cancer and the Philosophy of the Far East.* Oroville, CA: George Ohsawa Macrobiotic Foundation, 1971 edition.

_____. *You Are All Sanpaku.* Edited by William Dufty. New York: University Books, 1965.

_____. *Zen Macrobiotics.* Los Angeles: Ohsawa Foundation, 1965.

Price, Western A., D.D.S. *Nutrition and Physical Degeneration.* Santa Monica, CA: Price-Pottenger Nutritional Foundation, 1945.

Sattilaro, Anthony, M.D., with Tom Monte. *Recalled by Life: The Story of My Recovery from Cancer.* Boston: Houghton-Mifflin, 1982.

Scott, Neil E., with Jean Farmer. *Eating with Angels.* Tokyo and New York: Japan Publications, Inc., 1986.

_____. *Macrobiotics and Human Behavior.* Tokyo and New York: Japan Publications, Inc., 1985.

Yamamoto, Shizuko. *Barefoot Shiatsu.* Tokyo and New York: Japan Publications, Inc., 1979.

The Yellow Emperor's Classic of Internal Medicine. Translated by Ilza Veith. Berkeley, CA: University of California Press, 1949.

About the Authors

Aveline Kushi was born in 1923 in a small mountain village in the Izumo area of Japan. At college she was a star gymnast, but her athletic career was cut short by World War II. During the war she taught elementary school in her mountain district and after the war became involved in world peace activities at the Student World Government Association near Tokyo directed by George Ohsawa. In 1951 she came to the United States and married Michio Kushi. Along with her husband, she has devoted her life to spreading macrobiotics. As co-founder of Erewhon, the *East West Journal*, the East West Foundation, the Kushi Institute, and the Kushi Foundation, she has taken an active role in macrobiotic education and development.

During the last 20 years in the Boston area, many thousands of young people have visited and studied at her home in order to give their way of life a more natural direction. She has given countless seminars on macrobiotic cooking, pregnancy and child care, and medicinal cooking for cancer, heart disease, and AIDS patients. She has been instrumental in arranging visits to the United States by teachers and performers of such traditional arts as the Tea Ceremony, Noh Drama, and Buddhist meditation.

Aveline has written and illustrated several books, including *Aveline Kushi's Complete Guide to Macrobiotic Cooking* (Warner Books, 1985), *The Changing Seasons Macrobiotic Cookbook* (Avery Publishing Group, 1985), *Macrobiotic Diet* (Japan Publications, 1985), *Macrobiotic Child Care and Family Health* (Japan Publications, 1986), and *The Macrobiotic*

Cancer Prevention Cookbook (Avery Publishing Group, 1988). The mother of five children and the grandmother of five, she resides in Brookline and Becket, Massachusetts, and, with her husband, spends about half the year teaching abroad. Her autobiography, *Aveline: the Life and Dream of the Woman Behind Macrobiotics Today*, was published in 1988 by Japan Publications.

Wendy Esko was born in upstate New York in 1949. She began macrobiotic studies in Boston in 1973 and, with her husband, Edward, pioneered macrobiotic educational programs in the 1970s, including summer study programs at Amherst College in Massachusetts and annual conferences on the macrobiotic approach to cancer. She has taught macrobiotic cooking for more than 12 years and is the former director of the Kushi Institute School of Cooking in Brookline, Massachusetts. She has coauthored several popular books, including *Macrobiotic Cooking for Everyone* (Japan Publications, 1980), and, with Aveline, *The Changing Seasons Macrobiotic Cookbook, Introducing Macrobiotic Cooking* (Japan Publications, 1987), and *The Macrobiotic Cancer Prevention Cookbook* (Avery Publishing Group, 1988). Wendy lives with her husband and seven children in western Massachusetts and teaches at the Kushi Institute in Becket.

INDEX

Activity, level of, 3
Additives, 3
Agar-agar, 80
Age, 3
Alcoholic beverages, 99–100
Amasake, 31, 93
  Amasake Pudding, 220–21
  as a sweetener, 51
  storing, 116
American Association for the
  Advancement of Science,
  11
American Diabetes
  Association, 11
American Heart Association,
  10, 11, 74
*American Journal of
  Epidemiology*, 18–19
*American Medical Association
  Family Medical Guide*, 21
American Society for Clinical
  Nutrition, The, 11
American diet, the, how it's
  changed, 15
Ammonia, 24
Animal food, 29
  ratio to plant food, 24
  vs plant foods, 42–44
Animal protein, 28
Antagonistic aspects, 36
Antigravity, 39
Apple Kanten, 264
Arame, 80
  cutting, 143
  with Snow Peas and Sesame
    Seeds, 216–17
Arame with Snow Peas and
  Sesame Seeds, 216–17

Arrowroot flour, diluting, 137
Artificial food colors, 15
Atherosclerosis, 10, 96
Autumn, 70
  selection of food, 32–33
Azuki Bean Soup, 259–60
Azuki Beans
Azuki Bean Soup, 259–60
  with Kombu and Squash,
    247–48
Azuki Beans with Kombu and
  Squash, 247–48

B vitamins, and fish, 83
Bacteria, 24
Baking, 29
Baking food, vs frying food,
  21
Balance, in food, 47
Bancha Tea, 157–58
Barley, 29
Brown Rice with Barley,
  214–15
  Brown Rice with Pearl
    Barley, 265–66
  Rice, Barley and Squash
    Soup, 228–29
  Soft Rice with Pearl Barley,
    274
  storing, 116
Barley malt, 93–94
  as a sweetener, 51
Baths, 53
Bean products, 78–79
Beans, 44–45, 78–80
  soaking, 136
Beta-carotene, 74, 78
Beverages, 97–100

Grain Coffee, 192
high-quality, 98–100
recipes, 157–59
Blanched Salad, 218–19, 237
Blanched Watercress, 172–73
Blood alkalinity, 96
Blood lipid levels, 20
Blood pressure, 18–19
Blood sugar, 51
Body scrubbing, 53, 55–56
Boiled Broccoli, 257
Boiled Collard Greens, 212
Boiled Kale, 191, 276
Boiled Tempeh with Scallions, 256–57
Boiled Turnip Greens, 206
Boiled Watercress, 262
Brine Pickles, 162–63
Broccoli
  Boiled, 257
  Steamed, 178
Broiled Sole, 270–71
Broths, 32
Brown Rice
  with Barley, 214–15
  with Chestnuts, 230–31
  with Pearl Barley, 265–66
  Pressure-cooked Brown Rice, 248–49
  with Wheat Berries and Chick-Peas, 200–2
  varieties of, 28
  vinegar, 93
  as your principle grain, 70–71
Buckwheat, 28
Burdock and Carrot Kinpira, 251–52
Burdock root, 40

Cabbage
  how to slice, 141
  Miso Soup with Chinese Cabbage, 242
  Miso Soup with Soft Cabbage, 242
  Steamed Cabbage, 245
Cancer, 10, 19, 97
  decline in rate of, 16
  lowest rates in the world, 17

Cardiovascular Disease, prevention of, 18
Carrots
  Burdock and Carrot Kinpira, 251–52
  Kombu Carrot Rolls, 266–67
  Water-Sauteed Carrots, 171–72
Cast-iron skillets
  cleaning, 126
  seasoning, 126
Cauliflower
  Cauliflower Miso Soup, 209–10
  Millet with Cauliflower, 186
  Pureed Cauliflower Soup, 204–5
  Soft Millet with Cauliflower, 194
Centrifugal force, 38–39
Ceramic crocks, 122
Chewing, 54
Chinese Cabbage Rolls, 196–97
Cholesterol, 10, 19
  consumption of, 13
Circulation, 53
Cleaning your kitchen, 118–19
Clear Broth Soup, 236–37
Climates, 27, 49, 66
  and sea vegetables, 81–83
  and use of certain grains, 29, 69–70
Clothing, synthetic, 53
Colanders, 122
Collins, Karen, 9
Complementary aspects, 36
Complex carbohydrates, 7, 13, 68, 74
Complex sugars, 68
Condiments, 89–91
  high-quality, 91
  preparing beforehand, 153
  recipes, 154–57
Containers, 122
Convenience, 8
Cooking
  as an unnecessary chore, 4
  classes in, 52
  methods of, 27–28, 31
  space needed for, 7

time needed for, 4
variety in, 150
Cookware, 125–26
Corn, 28
Corn Grits, 255–56
Corn oil, storing, 116
Coronary heart disease, 10
Cosmetics, natural, 53
Cucumbers
  Leftover Cucumbers and
    Wakame, 212–13
  Pressed Cucumbers and
    Wakame, 202–3
Cutting, 137–43
  boards used for, 125
Cysts, 96

Daikon
  Daikon Greens and Kombu,
    249–50
  Dried Daikon with Kombu,
    203–4
  Grated Daikon, 271
  how to cut, 143
  soaking, 134–35
  storing, 116
Daikon root, 39
Dairy products, 44, 51
Degeneration, 97
Degenerative disease, 26
Depression, 57
Desserts, 95–97
  Amasake Pudding, 220–21
  Apple Kanten, 264
  Oatmeal-Raisin Cookies, 187
  Oatmeal with Raisins, 208
  Whole-Wheat Crepes with
    Peach-Raisin Sauce,
    224–26
Dextrose, 95
Diabetes, 10, 19
Diastolic pressure, 19
Diet
  balanced, 12
  and cancer, 16
  high fiber and low fat, 12
  naturally balanced, 3
  and personal needs, 50–52
  relationship to health, 7
Diet for a New America, 30

Diet, Nutrition and Cancer, 11,
  16–17, 74
*Dietary Goals for the United
  States*, 11, 12–14, 21
Digestive system, 23–24
Dill Pickles, 199
Diluting, 136–37
Disaccharides, 96
Double sugars, 96
Dressing, Ume-Parsley
  Dressing, 238
Dried chestnuts, soaking,
  135–36
Dried Daikon with Kombu,
  203–4
Dried fruit, soaking, 136
Dried fu, soaking, 135
Drying foods, 120
Dulse, 82, 90
  how to cut, 143

East West Foundation, 18
Eating habits, 54
Ecological eating, 27–30
Educational programs, 52
Electric skillets, 127
Energy
  contracting, 44
  natural source for, 119–21
Environment, 27
Equipment, 121–29
Eskimos, the, 27
Estella, Mary, 121
Exercise, 59–60

Fabrics, natural, 52
Fat, 28
  and heart disease, 10
Fatigue, 56–58
Fibrous plant foods, 65
Fire, 119
Fish, 83–84
  Broiled Sole, 270–71
Fish-eyes, 79
Flame deflector, 127
Food and Agricultural
  Organization, 17
Food and Healing, 121
Food processing, methods of,
  27–28

Food preparation, 131–43
Food spectrum, and yin and
    yang, 40–47
Food storage, 115–16
Food systems, inefficiency of,
    30
Foods
    combining of, 68
    ideal, 24
    indigenous, 15
    role of, 3
    shopping for, 7
Four food groups, the, 65, 67
Framingham Heart Study, 18
Fresh Garden Salad with Ume-
    Tahini Dressing, 183
Fresh produce, shopping for,
    109
Fried Rice with Wheat Berries
    and Chick-Peas, 210–11
Fried Soba with Vegetables,
    243–45
Fried Tofu Sandwiches,
    278–79
Fried Tofu with Kuzu Sauce,
    189–90
Fructose, 85
Fruit juice, 99
    storing, 116
    Fruit, 85–86
    and concentrated energy, 46
    high-quality, 86
    how to cut, 143
    storing, 116
    and suitable climates, 86
Fu, how to cut, 143

Garnishes, 95
Ginger body scrub, 59
Glucose, 96
Glycogen, 96
Goma-Wakame (Sesame-
    Wakame) Powder, 156–57
Gomashio, 90, 154–55. See also
    Sesame salt
Gomashio powders, 151
Grain Coffee, 192
Grains
    and energy, 44
    high quality, 71–73

Grated Daikon, 271
Graters, 123
Gravity, 39
Great American Life Diet, 50
Green Beans Amandine,
    269–70
Grobstein, Dr. Clifford, 16

Hand food mill, 123–24
Harvard Medical School, 18
Hatcho miso, 73
Headaches, food-related, 51
Health, and your diet, 9–33
Health foods, vs natural foods,
    11
Healthy living, suggestions for,
    52–54
Healthy People: Health
    Promotion and Disease
    Prevention, 11
Heart disease, 10
Hijiki, 80
    cutting, 143
Hijiki with Onions, 232–33
Homemade Grain Teas, 159
Homemade Sushi, 260–61
Human needs, balancing of,
    23–24
Hunza, the, 26
Hypoglycemia, 57

Illness, chronic, 7
Insulin, 96
Iodine, 81

Journal of the American
    Dietetic Association, 17
Juices
    fruit, 99
    vegetable, 99

Kale, 193–94
    Boiled Kale, 191, 276
Kanten, 32, 80
Kass, Dr. Edward, 18
Kelp, 82
Kelp powders, 90
Kitchen, 117–29
    setting up, 7
Kombu Powder, 155

Knives
  caring for, 123
  how to sharpen, 137
Kombu, 80
  Azuki Beans with Kombu
    and Squash, 247–48
  Carrot Rolls, 266–67
  Daikon, Daikon Greens and
    Kombu, 249–50
  Dried Daikon with Kombu,
    203–4
Kombu Carrot Rolls, 266–67
Kombu matchsticks, 142
Kombu rectangles, 142
Kombu sea vegetable, as a
  seasoning, 78
Kombu squares, 142
Kukicha tea, 99
Kushi, Aveline, 66
Kushi, Michio, 12, 18
Kushi Foundation, the, 52, 72,
  101
Kushi Institute, the, 287
Kuzu, diluting, 137
Kuzu sauce, 189–90

Leaf, Dr. Alexander, 26
Leftover Pressed Cucumbers
  and Wakame, 212–13
Leftover Turnip Greens, 208
Lentil Soup, 180
Lentils, 167
  Soup, 180
  and Vegetables, 167–68
Life extension, 26
Liver disease, 19
Lotus root, 90
Lotus seeds, soaking, 135

*Macrobiotic Child Care and
  Family Health*, 66
Macrobiotic diet, vs lacto-ovo-
  vegetarian diet, 20–21
Macrobiotic Dietary
  Recommendations, 14
Macrobiotic kitchen, the,
  63–143
Macrobiotic lifestyle, adoption
  of, 49–60
Macrobiotic principles, 23–33

Macrobiotic resources, 287–88
*Macrobiotic Way of Life
  Seminar, The*, 52, 287
Macrobiotics
  as climatically based, 30
  definition of, 10
Mail order shopping, 101
Materials, natural, 52
Meal planning, 6
Meditation, 56
Michio, 66
Microwave, 8
Millet, 29
  with Cauliflower, 186
  Soft Millet with Cauliflower,
    194
Millet with Cauliflower, 186
Mirin, 93
Miso, 4–5, 67, 72
  Cauliflower Miso Soup,
    209–10
  diluting, 136
  high quality, 73
  Miso Soup with Mochi,
    176–77
  as a seasoning, 78
Miso soup, 73
  with Chinese Cabbage, 242
  with Daikon and Shiitake,
    169–71
  with Mochi, 176–77
  Quick Miso Soup with Udon,
    195
  with Squash Skins, 274–75
  with Wakame and Onions,
    223–24
Mochi, 32, 89
Mottern, Nicholas, 12
MSG, 21
Mugi miso, 73

National Academy of Sciences,
  17, 74
National Cancer Institute, 11
National Geographic, 26
Natto, 31
Natural foods, vs health foods,
  11
*Natural Foods Cookbook:
  Vegetarian Dairy-Free*

Cuisine, 121
*New England Journal of
    Medicine,* 19
Nigari, 80
Nishime-Style Vegetables,
    234–35
Noodles, 31
Nori, 80, 82, 90
Nourishment, ideal pattern of,
    23
Nutrients, found in beans, 78
Nutrition, 4
    and cancer, 16
Nuts, 87–88
    in temperate climates, 88

Oatmeal-Raisin Cookies, 187
Oatmeal with Raisins, 208
Onion Soup, 215–16
Onions
    Hijiki with Onions, 232–33
    Miso Soup with Wakame and
        Onions, 223–24
    Onion Soup, 215–16
Overweight, 13

Paddy rice, 71
Parsley, as a garnish, 150
Personal needs, balancing of,
    50–52
Pickle press, 124
Pickles, 86–87
    Dill Pickles, 199
    high-quality, 87
    recipes, 160–63
    storing, 116
Pickling foods, 120
Plant foods, vs animal foods,
    24, 42–44
"Plasma Lipids and
    Lipoproteins in
    Vegetarians and Controls,"
    19–20
Polysaccharides, 68
Polyunsaturated oils, 21
Potatoes, and climate, 74
Power meals, 10
Preparation of food, speed of,
    4–5
Preroasted Barley Malt Tea

(Mugicha), 158
Preservatives, 3
Pressed Cucumbers and
    Wakame, 202–3
Pressed Salad, 185, 250–51
Pressure-Cooked Brown Rice,
    166, 248–49
Pressure cooker, 124
Protease inhibitors, 88
Pureed Cauliflower Soup,
    204–5
Pureed Squash Soup, 268–69

Quality of food, 4–5
Quick cooking, 8
Quick Miso Soup with Udon,
    195
Quick Red Radish Pickles,
    168–69

Radishes, Quick Red Radish
    Pickles, 168–69
Recommended Dietary
    Allowances (RDA), 17
Refined sugar, 46, 68
Rice
    Barley and Squash Soup,
        228–29
    brown vs. short-grain, 44
    Brown Rice with Barley,
        214–15
    Brown Rice with Pearl
        Barley, 265
    Fried Rice with Wheat
        Berries and Chick-Peas,
        210–11
    paddy, 71
    Sesame-coated Rice Balls,
        182
    Soft Rice with Chestnuts,
        240
    Soft Rice with Pearl Barley,
        274
Rice balls, 89
Rice cakes, storing, 116
Rice syrup, as a sweetener, 51
Roasted brown rice tea, 99
Roasted Pumpkin Seeds, 229
Roasted Sunflower Seeds, 258
Robbins, John, 30

Root vegetables, and
 concentrated energy, 46
Rye, 28, 29

Sacks, Dr. Frank, 18
Salads
 Blanched Salad, 218–19, 237
 Pressed Salad, 185, 250–51
Saliva, 68
Salt, 21, 28
Sandwiches
 Fried Tofu Sandwiches,
  278–79
 Tempeh Sandwiches, 227–28
Saturated disease, 10
Saturated fat, 10
 consumption of, 13
Sauerkraut, storing, 116
Scallions
 Boiled Tempeh with
  Scallions, 256–57
 preparing as a garnish, 150
Scrambled Tofu with
  Vegetables, 240–41
Sea salt, 72, 89, 94–95
 as a seasoning, 78
Sea vegetable powders, 90, 151
Sea vegetables, 32, 67, 80–83
 and concentrated energy, 46
 how to cut, 142–44
 soaking, 134
Seafood
 and climate, 84
 high-quality, 85
Seasonal fruits, 31
Seasonings, 78, 91–95
 high-quality, 92
 recommended, 92–95
Seasons and food, 30–33,
  40–47
Seeds, 87–88
 Roasted Sunflower Seeds,
  258
 in temperate climates, 88
 washing, 134
Seitan, 31, 50
 how to cut, 143
 storing, 116
Seitan Sandwiches, 198
Serving bowls, 128

Sesame-coated Rice Balls, 182
Sesame oil, storing, 116
Sesame salt, 90–91
Sesasme Seeds, Arame with
 Snow Peas and Sesame
 Seeds, 216–17
Sex, 3
Shampoos, natural, 53
Sharpening stone, 123
Shellfish, 83–84
Shiitake mushrooms
 soaking, 135
 storing, 116
Shio kombu, 90
Shopping for natural foods,
 101–16
Shopping list, 103–8, 110–14
Shopping schedule, 103
Shopping tips, 109
Showers, 53
Side dishes, 66
Simple carbohydrates, 68
Simple sugars, 96
Singing, 60
Snacks, 88–89
 high-quality, 89
 Roasted Pumpkin Seeds, 229
 storing, 116
Snow Peas, Arame with Snow
 Peas and Sesame Seeds,
 216–17
Soaking, 134–36
Soaps, natural, 53
Soba, 83
 Fried Soba with Vegetables,
  243–45
Sodium, 13
Soft Millet with Cauliflower,
 194
Soft Rice Porridge with
 Umeboshi, 176
Soft Rice with Chestnuts, 240
Soft Rice with Pearl Barley,
 274
Sole, Broiled Sole, 270–71
Somen, 32
Soups, 32, 72–73
 Azuki Bean Soup, 259–60
 Cauliflower Miso Soup,
  209–10

Clear Broth Soup, 236–37
Lentil Soup, 180
Miso Soup with Chinese Cabbage, 242
Miso Soup with Squash Skins, 274–75
Miso Soup with Wakame and Onions, 223–24
Onion Soup, 215–16
Pureed Cauliflower Soup, 204–5
Pureed Squash Soup, 268–69
Rice, Barley and Squash Soup, 228–29
Udon in Broth, 188–89
Vegetable Soup, 277–78
Watercress, 252–53
Soy foods, vs dairy products, 51
Soy milk, 51
Soy sauce. See Tamari
Soy yogurt, 51
Soybean miso, storing, 116
Spring, and the selection of foods, 30–31
Squash
  Azuki Beans with Kombu and Squash, 247–48
  how to cut, 140–41
  Miso Soup with Squash Skins, 274–75
  Pureed Squash Soup, 268–69
  Rice, Barley and Squash Soup, 228–29
Standard Macrobiotic Lifestyle, the, 49–60
Standard macrobiotic Diet, the, 65–100
Staples, preparing beforehand, 153–63
Steamed Broccoli, 178
Steamed Cabbage, 245
Steamer basket, 128
Strainers, 122
Stress, 55–56
Stroke, 10
Sugars
  naturally occurring, 13
  processed, 13
  refined, 3, 13

Summer, 70
  and the selection of foods, 31–32
Summer foods, 31
"Surgeon's General Report on Nutrition and Health," 10, 11, 21–22
Suribachi, 124
Sushi, 89
  Homemade Sushi, 31, 260–61
Sushi mats, 125
Sweet rice vinegar, 93
Sweet Vegetable Drink, 57–58
Sweeteners, 68
  artificial, 46–47
  concentrated, 46–47
  grain-based, 89
  natural, 50–51, 94
Sweets, 97
  craving for, 57
Systolic pressure, 19

Table salt, 95
Tahini, Fresh Garden Salad with Ume-Tahini Dressing, 183
Tamari, 95
Tamari dispenser, 122
Tamari soy sauce, 72, 89, 116
Tamari Soy Sauce Pickles, 161–62
Taste, 4
Tea strainer, 129
Teapot, glass, 128
Teeth
  and the digestive system, 22–24
  brushing, 53
  structure of, 65–66
Tekka, 91
Tempeh, 50, 67, 68
  Boiled Tempeh with Scallions, 256–57
  how to cut, 143
  storing, 116
Tempeh Sandwiches, 227–28
Tempura, 33
Tofu, 67, 68, 78
  Fried Tofu Sandwiches, 278–79

Fried Tofu with Kuzu Sauce, 189–90
how to cut, 143
Scrambled Tofu with Vegetables, 240–41
soaking, 135
storing, 116, 116
Tofu Dressing, 219–20
types of, 80
Tofu cheese, 51
Tofu cheesecake, 51
Tofu dishes, 32
Tofu Dressing, 219–20
Tumors, 96
Turnips
Boiled Turnip Greens, 206
Leftover Turnip Greens, 208

Udon, 32
Quick Miso Soup with Udon, 195
Udon in Broth, 188–89
Ume-Parsley Dressing, 238
Ume-Sho-Kuzu, 58
Umeboshi, Soft Rice Porridge with Umeboshi, 176
Umeboshi Pickles, 160–61
Umeboshi plums, 31, 67, 72, 90, 91
U.S. Department of Agriculture, 11
Utensils, 52, 121–29
wooden, 127

Vegetable brushes, 122
Vegetable juice, 99
Vegetable knives, 122–23
Vegetable Soup, 277–78
Vegetables, 73–76
and concentrated energy, 46
for use in temperate climates, 75–76
high-quality, 76
how to cut, 138–42
nutrients found in, 74–75
Scrambled Tofu with Vegetables, 240–41
storing, 116
Vilebamba, the, 26
Vinegar

brown rice, 93
sweet rice, 93

Waard, Dr. F. de, 16
Wakame, 80, 142
Leftover Cucumbers and Wakame, 212–13
Miso Soup with Wakame and Onions, 223–24
Pressed Cucumbers and Wakame, 202–3
Walking, 59
Washing bean products, 132
Washing fruits, 133
Washing grains, 131–34
Washing sea vegetables, 133–34
Washing vegetables, 132–33
Water, 119
Water-Sauteed Carrots, 171–72
Watercress
Blanched Watercress, 172–73
Boiled Watercress, 262
Watercress Nori Roll, 181
Watercress Nori Roll, 181
Watercress Soup, 252–53
Weight, 17–18
Wheat, 29
Whole cereal grains, 68–72
Whole foods, vs canned and frozen, 5
Whole grains
soaking, 136
within climates, 69–70
Whole-Wheat Crepes with Peach-Raisin Sauce, 224–26
Winter, selection of food for, 33
Winter barley, 31
Winter wheat, 28
Wood utensils, 127
World Health Organization, 17
Worldwide Macrobiotic Directory, 52, 102

Yang, definition of, 35
Yang foods, 45
Yin and yang, 21, 33–47

Yin foods, 45
Yin, definition of, 35